FISHING MINNESOTA

A book devoted to the Minnesota Fisherman: A book specifically about fishing Minnesota's lakes, rivers, and streams by professionals who have spent years unraveling the mysteries of successfully fishing Minnesota's waters.

Author's Note: As the title suggests, "Fishing Minnesota" was written for the Minnesota fisherman. But it has an even more specific audience in mind: The advanced beginner through the expert level fisherman. Moreover, its pages are not filled with diagrams on how to use downriggers, pictures of how to rig plastic worms, or cross-sectional drawings and photographs of the various lake cover possibilities for fish and lake bottom configurations, etc. since that basic level of fishing information has been well covered in most other books on fishing that have preceded this one.

This book was edited with those considerations in mind and moves quickly from topic to topic.

FISHING MINNESOTA

FISHING MINNESOTA includes eleven exciting and informative chapters featuring:

Gary Roach on Walleyes
Dan D. Gapen, Sr. on Rivers
Ted Capra on Largemouth Bass
Mark Windels on Muskies
Kevin Koep on Northerns
Captain Dave Cooley on Lake Superior
Gary Korsgaden on Crappies
Grant Hughes on Smallmouth Bass
Laun "E" Anderson on Sunfish
Paul Hedlund on Streams
    and a
Dedication to Clarence Luther—
Minnesota's Foremost Guide

BOB BERG

FIRST EDITION
Book by Bob Berg
Marilyn Grinols—proofreader
Cover Art and Layout by Nelson Graphic Design, Brainerd, Minnesota
Copyright © 1985 by Bob Berg
All rights reserved
Published by Berg Publishing Company
P.O. Box 359
Shakopee, Minnesota 55379
Printed in the United States of America
ISBN-0-932861-00-8

First Printing 1985
Library of Congress
Catalog Card Number
85-70955
ISBN-0-932861-00-8
Library of Congress
Cataloging in
Publication Data
Berg, Bob
  Fishing Minnesota
Shakopee, Minnesota:
Berg Publishing Co. 253p.

ACKNOWLEDGMENTS

No book is the product of any one individual's efforts, especially this one. Therefore, I must acknowledge those who gave so much to make "Fishing Minnesota" possible.

First, the major contributors:
Gary Roach, Dan D. Gapen, Sr., Ted Capra, Mark Windels, Kevin Koep, Gary Korsgaden, Grant Hughes, Laun "E" Anderson, Captain Dave Cooley, Paul Hedlund, Clarence Luther.

Second, those who gave advice and support:
Jerry & Karen Mathwig, Jim Berg, Joel Hafermann, Trudy Eidsness, Poncho Henderson, Mike Furtman, Arlan Berg, Janet Williams, Gale Fink, Bob Pritchard, Dave Conn, Ray Hennes, Mike Theis, John Daily, Ed Livingston, Art Ollrich, Eileen & Bob Lee, Chuck Nelson & the staff at Nelson Graphic Design, and Gail, Eric, & Ryan Berg.

TABLE OF CONTENTS

Page

INTRODUCTION

Dear Minnesota Fisherman,

"Fishing Minnesota" has been published especially for you!

This book was written in conversational-style English which allows each professional fisherman to speak to you in his own words rather than the words of a ghost writer. Also, in using the conversational-style approach in writing this book we discovered that there was a valuable by-product we hadn't foreseen; we were able to address many technical aspects of fishing without using technical jargon. I am confident that you will enjoy listening to these professionals weave their way through the mysteries of successful fishing in Minnesota.

Each chapter includes *highlights* from many hours of recorded conversations on the most important aspects of fishing: Location, presentation, fish behavior, weather and biological factors affecting fish, equipment and tackle, and a miscellaneous section which includes information that did not neatly fit into the other sections.

These sectional divisions in each chapter are not mutually exclusive; that is, it would be impossible to discuss only one aspect of fishing without mentioning other aspects of fishing. The nature of conversation doesn't allow for that much specificity. For example, in discussing location we often overlapped into presentation, fish behavior, etc. But in the editing process I attempted to edit out information that had already been covered previously in each chapter. Further, if Gary Roach, for instance, discussed lure size (which is technically a presentation aspect) in the location section, I edited out that information in the presentation section to avoid any redundancies. So to fully appreciate the fishing wisdom of these pros, I would suggest that you read an entire chapter in one sitting.

I am very grateful to the professional fishermen who contributed to "Fishing Minnesota". It was their knowledge, time, and patience that made this book possible, and I am also very proud and pleased to have been associated with them in the production of this book.

Good Fishin'

Bob Berg

DEDICATION

When I began to work on "Fishing Minnesota," I had not seriously thought about dedicating it to any one individual. But then, at Gary Roach's suggestion, I met with Clarence Luther: A fisherman's fisherman. A man who had been a professional fishing guide since 1920 which is the year my father entered elementary school, and my father has been retired for more than a decade now.

To say Clarence Luther is a die-hard fisherman would be like saying Carl Lewis is a pretty fast runner.

Moreover, Clarence's perspective of fishing in Minnesota is a perspective that no other human being shares. With over sixty years of professional guiding experience, including many years of market fishing, Clarence Luther has carved out his place in Minnesota's fishing history. The breadth and depth of his fishing knowledge is inspiring if not overwhelming; therefore, "Fishing Minnesota" is respectfully dedicated to Clarence Luther—Minnesota's Foremost Fishing Guide.

Chapter 1

LUTHER'S LEGACY

Where does a writer begin a profile on a fisherman who started his professional guiding career in 1920? Think about it: Woodrow Wilson or a young Babe Ruth could have been his customers. If my memory serves me, that was the year the Eighteenth and Nineteenth Amendments were enacted outlawing the manufacture and sale of alcoholic beverages and giving women the right to vote, respectively.

Indeed a long time ago, but, nonetheless, this pre-graphite, pre-depth finder, pre-water temperature gauge, pre-tournament fishing era remains as clear in Clarence's mind as do today's fishing techniques and methods.

In 1920, at the age of fourteen, Clarence took out his first fishing party. In those days, prior to gasoline-operated outboard motors, guides did all of the rowing which is probably how Clarence earned the nickname of "Popeye".

Although Clarence had hoped someday to become a guide, he hadn't planned on starting quite so young.

What happened was that a party of fishermen arrived at the Luther home and asked if someone could take them out and get some fish, since they had heard in Nisswa that the Luthers were good fishermen. Young Clarence obliged by saying, "That's right down my alley," and he added, "they weren't disappointed; they all went home with a mess of fish." The fourteen-year-old Clarence wasn't exaggerating; it was right down his alley since he had fished for market (caught fish and sold them to fish markets which in turn sold them to grocery stores) with his parents from the time he was seven years old.

These days Clarence's boat is no longer for hire since he has recently (1982) given up guiding to younger men. But in the Brainerd/Nisswa area his reputation will, no doubt, live on for years to come.

"Clarence is still the man," said Gary Roach, "who can put you on the best sunfish in the state."

Now I'll let Clarence speak for himself:

How many years did you make your living as a full-time guide?

Luther: I was a full-time guide from 1920 to 1978 and part-time until 1982. For twelve of those years my wife and I went to Florida and worked at odds and ends during the winter months. But other than those winters in Florida, my wife and I have made our living guiding.

Your wife also guided?

Luther: Yeah! And she's a real good guide, too.

How did you promote your guiding business?

Luther: It was all by word of mouth. In fact, I usually had more business than I could handle. I was so loaded up with fishermen that I was out seven days a week.

In the early days what kinds of lures did you use?

Luther: You could throw any, and I mean any, kind of a plug in the water and catch bass. In the 1920's the guiding business was all plug fishing for bass.

What were some of the plugs that you used in those days?

Luther: Basserenos, Surferenos, and Heddons. The Heddon 200 was probably the best of those. It was a surface plug with a tin collar with three sets of treble hooks on it. They used a lot of hooks in those days; in fact, I've got one old plug with five sets of hooks on it.

So the largemouth bass was the main game fish in the 20's?

Luther: For guides, at that time in Minnesota, it was all bass. Most of the people who hired guides were from Illinois and other southern states, and they loved to fish bass. Of course I did have some customers from the Minneapolis and Saint Paul area, too.

What were the main species of fish that you and your parents caught for market?

Luther: Crappies and sunfish were the main market fish at that time (1913-1920). Market fishing for walleyes and bass had already been closed by 1913 when I started market fishing. Crappies were the main fish we fished for market, and there was no limit on them.

What kind of equipment did you use to catch them?

Luther: We weren't allowed to use nets. We caught all of them by hook and line, and you could use all the hooks and lines you wanted to use. We used six a piece.

We'd cut willow branches for poles and tied a cotton line on them. Three on each side of the boat. I can very well remember many evenings when I would catch as many as seventy crappies, and I was a very young kid using very crude equipment. Those crappies would run from a pound to a pound and three-quarters. They were real slabs.

Did your family make a living at market fishing?

Luther: They didn't try to. They'd go out when they needed some money for groceries. There were six or seven families around here who did the same thing. When they needed a little cash, they'd go out and catch a barrel of fish.

How did you ship them to market?

Luther: There were about six or seven commission houses in the cities, and they would send us a price list every month. They would also send us a bunch of empty barrels. We'd pack a layer of ice and then a layer of fish and then another layer of ice and then another layer of fish until the barrel was full, and then we'd nail a burlap sack over the top of it.

How big were those barrels?

Luther: They were fifty gallon barrels which held about a hundred pounds of fish.

When the trains stopped at the stations, there'd be fishermen waiting to load their fish. The trains would start picking up fish at Bemidji, and by the time they got to Nisswa they would have fish all over them.

How much money did you get for a hundred pounds of fish?

Luther: I can tell you pretty close: sunfish ran from nine to fifteen cents a pound. Fifteen cents a pound for the big ones. But crappies were always the highest priced fish; they went from sixteen to twenty cents a pound.

How much did northerns bring?

Luther: They sold for about nine to eleven cents a pound no matter what size they were.

Comment on fishing in the 20's.

Luther: It was all bass fishing. Most people didn't seem to care about fishing for walleyes or northerns then. There were plenty of walleyes and northerns to be caught, but the fishermen who hired guides were mainly after bass.

Then in the 30's everybody went wild for walleye fishing.

Why?

Luther: I don't know. Just all of a sudden all of the guiding business was for people who wanted to catch walleyes. I guess it's like any other trend. And in the 20's and 30's very few people wanted to fish for crappies, and the crappies were big, so I never understood that either.

What was the limit of walleyes in those days?

Luther: You could have fifteen in possession.

There were no limits on crappies or sunnies at all?

Luther: They had limits on them. It was in the days that we fished for market that there weren't any limits on panfish, but about the time I started guiding (1920) there were limits on panfish, too.

It seems to me the limits were a little different for northerns, sunfish, bass, walleyes, and crappies, but it was about fifteen each in possession. Maybe a few more for panfish.

How did you feel about the lowering of the limits on fish which occurred in about 1941?

Luther: At first I didn't think it was necessary, but now I know it was. Very necessary! There were more and more people coming up here and fishing was thinning out.

So fishing is not anywhere near as good as it was years ago?

Luther: No. Oh no!

Do you have any idea why it's worse?

Luther: The pressure. Fishing pressure.

You mentioned that the fishing season was shorter in the early days of your guiding career.

Luther: The fishing season used to open on the twenty-first of June for bass, walleyes, crappies, and sunfish. That was that way for years. You can't imagine what kind of a season a guide had in those days. The twenty-first of June to Labor Day. The season didn't end on Labor Day, but that's when everybody went home and didn't come back until the following summer.

You couldn't convince them that the best fishing was in the fall. They figured it was all over by Labor Day. I tried so hard to lengthen my guiding season and convince my customers that the best fishing was in the fall, but they just wouldn't come back in the fall.

Well Clarence, you're in good company. Most experts agree that the best fishing is in the fall. Do you have any idea why?

Luther: No. No idea at all, but it's always been that way.

And after everybody left in early September, I would take my shotgun and some frogs and go hunting and fishing. That was my vacation. Many times in the fall I would come home with fifteen mallards, which was the limit at that time, and a stringer of fish that I could hardly carry.

How did you locate fish in the 1920's?

Luther: There were no depth finders of course. We used our experience and instincts, and there wasn't any deep water fishing at that time either.

When walleye fishing became popular (1930's), was that limited to shallow water fishing, too?

Luther: No. In the 30's we knew about fishing deep water. We used a piece of lead attached to a string to determine how deep we were fishing. You'd hold the string attached to the lead in your hand as you rowed the boat. Then when you felt you were in a good spot, you would stop and check the depth.

What were the 40's like?

Luther: The 40's were good walleye fishing. But in the late 40's and early 50's was when fishing pressure started to get real heavy, and that's when you could start to see how all that pressure hurt fishing. Since the late 50's fishing has continued to slide.

What were your prices for guiding?

Luther: Up until 1964 we only charged twelve dollars for a half a day.

But when I started back in the 20's, I'd have to fish from the time you could see in the morning until noon for two dollars and a half. And that was all rowing.

What species of fish have you guided for throughout the years?

Luther: During the 20's it was almost all bass. And then during the 30's up through the 40's most of my guiding was for walleyes. In the early 50's when walleye fishing started to decline, I started what I call "Diversified Fishing." When I took a party out fishing, using this diversified method, they were liable to catch walleyes, northerns, bass, sunfish, or crappies.

Why was that?

Luther: Because we used jigs exclusively and also because of where we fished. In the last five years I guided, I didn't have six parties come off of the lake without a good mess of fish. And besides that, I realized that most people really enjoyed catching a variety of fish.

When did you first use outboard motors?

Luther: I had my first new motor in 1942. Prior to that I had used, used motors for seven or eight years. Actually, it was in the mid-thirties before I ever had a motor.

How many different lakes did you guide on?

Luther: When I was into it, I fished on thirty-nine different lakes, and I knew all thirty-nine of them like I know my back yard.

What makes a good fisherman?

Luther: Taking an interest in fishing. Watching what goes on under all conditions, and that's what made a fisherman out of me. Knowing how to catch fish under different conditions is what separates the good fishermen from the poorer ones.

Other than a means of making a living, what has fishing meant to you?

Luther: It's been the best life that I know of; I just love being out in the open.

Earlier you said that your fishing has slowed way down in the last couple of years?

Luther: I have slowed way down. I had to hit the brakes since I have a bad leg, but I still get out some.

Is there anything that you would like to add about fishing?

Luther: It's something that I still enjoy. It's something that I'll never tire of.

Chapter 2

GARY ROACH ON WALLEYES

I will long remember the day that I announced to my wife that Gary Roach had agreed to do this book. (Until that time this book was in its tentative stage.) "Which chapter is he going to do?" she asked. "Anyone he wants to," I replied since Gary may well be the best multi-species angler in the country today. But, I must admit, for selfish reasons I had hoped he would do the walleye chapter; because with his reputation for catching walleyes, the book would very likely sell quite well. But most of all, Gary's willingness to contribute to this book gave me the confidence to proceed from the "I think it's a good idea" stage of writing a book to the "Let's do it and find out" stage.

Further, Gary Roach's reputation goes far beyond the Minnesota State Line. In the Washington and Oregon area he is known for his ability to catch lunker walleyes from the Columbia River. He performs the same feats equally as well on large reservoirs like Greers Ferry in the South. Here in the Midwest, and particularly in Minnesota, fishermen recognize Gary as one of the two or three best walleye fishermen around. Those in the inner-circle of professional fishing know that Gary is also an expert bass, northern, and panfish fisherman.

Recently, Dan Nelson, who is a respected Midwest outdoor sports writer, said of Gary, "If there's a better walleye fisherman alive, I'd sure like to share a boat with him." And only a few months later when Gary and

Dan were on a walleye expedition on the Columbia River in Oregon, Dan landed a fifteen pound two-ounce walleye which established a new state record in Oregon. On that same trip Gary caught two walleyes over thirteen pounds and several in the twelve-plus range.

Gary was born and grew up on the shores of Upper Mission Lake in northern Minnesota. Life there was uncomplicated and the Roach family did without luxuries. "It was a good time and place to grow up," Gary said, "and I didn't even mind the days before we had electricity." The Roach family lived in a cabin on forty acres of land that Gary's father had purchased for five hundred dollars. It was there that he began fishing and hunting. According to his mother, Gary was fishing before he was old enough to be on the dock alone. When Gary was ten years old, he would catch and sell frogs for twenty-five cents a dozen to the Missouri bass fishermen who vacationed in Minnesota, and by the ripe old age of twelve, he was earning spending money by guiding for crappie fishermen.

After a tour of duty in the Navy, Gary purchased a service station and business was good, but his love for fishing would distract him from repairing cars and pumping gasoline. "I'd look up in the sky and know the walleyes were biting on Lake Pelican," Gary said. "Then I'd say, Jake would you mind watching the station for a while, I'm going to take a little trip. Then I'd sneak off to Lake Pelican and pop a few walleyes."

When he left the service station business, he became a full-time multi-species guide and was one of the original members of the Nisswa Guide's League. During the wintertime he would go on the road promoting the Lindy Rig and the Dingo Jig for Al and Ron Lindner. After Gary won the first national bass tournament held on Lake Minnetonka, which perhaps was the first bass tournament held in Minnesota, he went to work for the Lindners on a full-time basis. As time went on, Gary gained more and more recognition for his ability and success as a fisherman. This recognition, combined with his enthusiasm for promoting fishing products helped shape the career he would then pursue as a seminar speaker, an author of numerous magazine articles, and a rod, lure, and boat designer.

Moreover, Gary excels in fishing because of his experience and his willingness to experiment. He particularly enjoys figuring out fishing patterns on the days when the fish seem to have "lockjaw" "To be a constantly good fisherman," Gary observed, "you must be a versatile fisherman willing to try different things." He is also successful as a fishing educator because when he writes or speaks, it's a mixed bag of Roach-style humor, fishing savvy, and Gary's genuine love for the sport of fishing.

Do you ever get skunked? That is one of the questions Gary is most frequently asked. And he replies, "There are some days when you don't catch fish; I don't care who you are. Some days the fish just don't go. And with more and more fishing pressure, the more that's going to happen. Bob Wilson, a Canadian fishing guide, once said, 'The difference between a good guide and a bad guide is one day.' That comment has stuck with me for a long time."

Nowadays, when Gary isn't on the water, which isn't often, you can find him speaking at seminars and clinics for his new company called Fishing Pro-Mo's. He and his long-time friend and fishing partner, Randy Amenrud recently teamed-up to form Fishing Pro-Mo's which is a company that conducts seminars and clinics for outdoor sporting goods stores and marine dealers.

Finally, one of the ironies of Gary's life is that he may well become better known for "Shore Lunch" than he is for his fishing prowess—the Colonel Sanders of fish batter, so to speak. "Shore Lunch" is a breading mix used in frying fish which took Gary years to perfect.

The original "Shore Lunch" had its beginnings when Gary was a guide and his wife would pack a lunch for him and his customers. A pan full of potatoes and onions, etc., and he would mix up a little batter to fry the day's catch in. As time went on, Gary was continually refining his batter until it pleased almost everyone that tried it. Then an Ohio fishing buddy, Big John Christenson, said, "Gee Roach, you ought to sell this stuff, it's great!" That idea stuck with Gary and one day he found himself frying walleye fillets coated with "Shore Lunch" for executives at the Pillsbury Company. They loved Gary's batter, and the subsequent market research that Pillsbury did on "Shore Lunch" was overwhelmingly favorable. So as things go these days, the "old guide's secret batter" is now available throughout the country in sporting goods and grocery stores.

WALLEYE BEHAVIOR

What are the most important factors that determine walleye behavior?

Roach: Walleyes relate to water temperature, wind, moon phases, barometric pressure, calendar periods, and other variables which will determine where they will be located on a given body of water or what they will be doing at a given point in time. And don't forget instinct.

In the spring of the year, they are most concerned with spawning. Other times of the year, they probably are most concerned with feeding or just finding someplace in the lake that meets their comfort needs.

You have to work hard to learn about each species of fish, and each lake is somewhat different than all of the other lakes that you might have fished before.

What are the major differences in lakes?

Roach: Enough to write a whole book on. But the basic differences are what each lake has to offer the walleye. Its structure, bottom content, size, cover, weed growth, depth, water clarity, available spawning area, forage, etc. These basic considerations apply to most lakes.

Do walleyes school by size?

Roach: Walleyes are very much a schooling fish, and they do school by size. The smaller ones (a pound to a pound and a quarter) school together. Then the one and a half pounders to approximately three pounders will school together. When they are mature spawners, it seems, is when they start separating from the smaller fish. A mature female, in most lakes, is about three pounds. Then the next break is the six to twelve pounders which will school together, and walleyes bigger than that are often loners.

What does this schooling by size information mean to the fisherman?

Roach: The location of a school of small walleyes can sometimes help you locate larger ones. I have found that sometimes when the bigger fish are up shallow, they will force the smaller fish out deeper and vice versa.

Many fishermen will stay on a school of small fish hoping to catch a larger one. Well, that doesn't happen very often. If you are catching small walleyes, move. Don't spend the day killing a school of small fish.

Comment on active, neutral, and negative fish.

Roach: An active walleye is a hungry walleye. He is aggressively searching for food and will be much easier to catch when he's in this mood. And when a walleye is in a neutral mood, he can be enticed into striking, but fishing will be somewhat more difficult. And, of course, when a walleye is in a negative mood, he isn't interested in eating or probably even moving at all, and fishing will be very, very difficult.

But fishing for negative fish is what separates the men from the boys.

Of course, these moods apply to all species of fish, and remember, when fishing, you are not very often going to be fishing truly active fish. Usually they will be somewhere between neutral and negative.

Do all walleyes have similar preferences as to location, for example?

Roach: In general they probably do, but some walleyes will prefer to stay in the cabbage weeds while others will prefer to stay in the rocks, for instance.

My feeling is, whatever food source they are after will determine their habits to a large extent. That is, other than during the spawning season.

On Ten Mile Lake near Hackensack, Minnesota the walleyes love to eat the dwarfed tullibees. I'm told, it's the only lake in the world with dwarfed tullibees in it, and they are a major food source for walleyes there. Therefore, where the dwarfed tullibees are often determines where the walleyes will be located on that lake.

What is a dwarfed tullibee?

Roach: It's a stunted tullibee that only grows to be about four to six inches because of the limited amount of food that is available for them.

Do walleyes remember? In terms of lures, for example.

Roach: Yeah. I think they get educated. If they've been caught on a certain lure, they might get spooky and not strike that lure again. But a change in your presentation can sometimes help.

Is that why certain lures run a course of popularity with fishermen?

Roach: That and fishermen are always looking for a new magic lure. It's both. Also, lure manufacturers have something to do with it, too. And many fishermen don't adapt their fishing to the seasonal movements of walleyes which change the walleye's food source.

Comment on walleye movements and migrations.

Roach: Many walleye fishermen term the movement of walleyes to spawning areas in the spring as a migration. Then they use the term "movement" to describe the walleyes moving from feeding place to feeding place, for example.

Now I could be wrong, but, I feel the term "migration" doesn't really apply to the walleye's behavior. It's a term better used when describing the behavior of a migratory fish such as the salmon. The distinction between movement and migration certainly isn't anything a walleye fisherman in Minnesota has to be concerned about. Well, maybe, the term "migration" can apply to walleyes in a river system.

How does walleye behavior vary from a clear water lake to a dingy colored lake?

Roach: In darker, dingy water they will be more aggressive. And, conversely, in the clearer water lakes they will be less aggressive and more easily spooked by the angler or his presentation. And that applies to all species of fish.

What are some other variables in catching walleyes that are not often spoken of or written about?

Roach: Well, there is the mayfly hatch that can be a factor. This hatch varies between a light to a heavy hatch. The years when it's a light hatch, the walleye fishing will be much better since the walleyes are not filling up on mayfly larva.

There are times when I've caught walleyes whose stomachs were full of mayfly larva. They go through larva almost as whales feed on plankton—just swim through a bunch of them and fill their mouths. This phenomenon is a big factor on Lake Mille Lacs, for instance.

Often fishermen talk about a lake that is fished out. But what probably happened is that the fish started feeding on a different food source, and the fishermen did not compensate for that change. Since the fishermen are not catching fish, they say the lake is fished out.

Are you saying that given a choice of mayflies or minnows to eat, the walleye would opt for mayflies?

Roach: Yes. That's just like comparing raisin pudding to mashed potatoes. Mashed potatoes are great, but raisin pudding with a little cream on it is better. So when raisin pudding is available, you must compensate for that.

To what extent does the walleye's food preferences affect fishing?

Roach: It can be a big factor. Once on Mission Lake, where I lived, I used some small tullibee minnows for bait and had some great fishing. Then I switched to fathead minnows for bait, and I couldn't even get a strike. So, I feel, fish *definitely* have food preferences. (Underline definitely!) There are times when a night crawler will be better than a leech and vice versa. But remember, a fish's food preference depends on what is available in a given lake.

A couple of years ago Al Lindner and I were fishing with a group of friends. Al and I noticed that the walleyes we were catching were spitting up little perch. So I tied on a Lindy perch colored crank bait and caught seven walleyes in as many casts. Other members of our party were using a shiner colored lure and weren't doing nearly as well. That indicates to me that fish do indeed have bait preferences.

LOCATING WALLEYES

Comment on the locational aspect of fishing for walleyes.

Roach: Location is the most important aspect of fishing. You could use dynamite, but if you don't know where the fish are, you won't get any.

Location is also the most misunderstood aspect of fishing. Once you've determined the location, you have to determine what depth they are at. The best way to do that is to start shallow working out deeper at varying intervals.

Let's go through a typical season from early spring to ice-over with location in mind.

Roach: Early spring and spring are the times of the year when most of the walleyes caught, are caught in shallow water.

The spring of the year in Minnesota is spawning or post-spawn time. The walleyes will locate themselves in shallow water on rock piles, sandbars, near the mouths of rivers, in rivers, and around bridge embankments where there are a lot of rocks. They definitely prefer a rocky, hard bottom in the spring of the year.

And don't just fish the shore in the spring. Many lakes have humps which top at one to five feet, and if these humps have rocks or just a rock pile, for that matter, they may very well hold spring walleyes.

How about later in the spring as summer is nearing?

Roach: This is the post-spawn time of the year. The walleyes have left the spawning beds or are leaving real soon. They will look for deeper water and areas where the weed growth is just starting. Of course, if you remember where the weeds grew last year, you're one step ahead of the location game.

Also, the first break in a lake's structure is as deep as you should have to fish at this time of the year. But this is not written in stone.

Now that it's summer where should I look for walleyes?

Roach: The most important thing to know about summer fishing is the importance weeds play in walleye location.

In some lakes the summer walleyes use the weeds very heavily because of oxygen problems in other parts of the lake. Weeds produce a lot of oxygen during the summer. And let's not forget there are a lot of bait fish in the weeds during this time of the year, so walleyes, like other predator fish, will use the weeds as an area to feed. In fact, even in the spring, you can take walleyes in early weed growth cabbage if the bait fish are there.

Comment on cabbage type weeds.

Roach: In some clear water lakes cabbage will grow in fifteen feet of water, but in stained water lakes it will only grow in four to six feet of water. And depending on the food source, the walleyes may be feeding on the inside of the cabbage or on the outside of the cabbage. That is, the inside or outside weedline. Although the cabbage type weeds are the most important weed to a walleye, as it is with many other species of fish, they will use other types of weeds, too.

You're smiling. Do you have a trick you're not telling me about?

Roach: Well, what I do in the summertime as soon as I have launched my boat, I take a swing out to deeper water. Then I watch my locator to see where the blips are. It's the easiest way to tell what depth the fish are going to relate to. I've never before said this to anybody, never, ever, in my life. I just take off across the lake to see how far down the bait fish go. Most of the time it's seventeen to twenty feet. I figure if the bait run at that depth all the way across the lake, when the walleyes feed, that's the depth they will be feeding at. So I'm going to start fishing at that depth on the breakline or the weedline.

You should go wide-open, zigzagging out from the weedline to find the biggest concentration of bait fish, so the bait fish don't have time to get away from you. Also, the dirtier the lake is, the closer the bait fish will be to the surface. In dirty water lakes, for example, you will usually find them at the ten to twelve foot depth.

For example, when you see bait fish at eighteen feet, that has to be tullibees (if they are in that body of water) since they will stay as close to that cooler water as they can. But the minnows and fry will stay up higher because tullibees will feed on them.

What I'm watching for on my locator is their primary bait and their secondary bait which is bigger bait fish. And if there are any big blips below, it will probably be walleyes, northerns, bass, or crappies.

That's the best way to find out what depth the bait fish are at in a given lake on a given day. Usually they will stack up like a Christmas tree with the little ones on the top and the bigger ones on the bottom.

As long as you're in the mood to spill the beans, maybe there are some more locational tricks that you are willing to share?

Roach: Why not. I also watch the live well to see what the walleyes might be spitting up. If they are spitting up tullibees, you can bet the walleyes are deep since tullibees are almost always in deep water. If they are spitting up perch, you might want to fish in shallower water since the small perch usually don't go as deep as tullibees will. Now this applies to daytime fishing because at night walleyes will move up and feed on other kinds of bait fish.

Also if you are fishing a point, start where the wind is blowing onto that point. That will be the main spot. Then farther back, are your secondary spots.

And sometimes when you are fishing a point, there will be an undertow coming back from shore because the wind is so strong. That is, as the point rises from thirty feet of water to fifteen feet, for instance, an undertow can be created by a strong wind. The water on top is going the opposite direction as the water on the bottom is going. It's like putting a garden hose in a wash tub. You can spray it in, but it has to come back somewhere.

Once Dave Csanda and I were fishing, and we found the walleyes on the shore side of a hump which was the side away from the surface current. They were facing the undercurrent coming back from the shore instead of the surface current. So if we were fishing where we were supposed to be fishing, we wouldn't have caught any fish.

Is there anything that you would like to add regarding summer location of walleyes?

Roach: Sometimes summer fishing for walleyes is best in deep water, say twenty-five feet or so. My favorite summer spots are sunken islands with deep water surrounding them.

Also when fishing cabbage beds, fish the inside as well as the outside. Fish the outside first and then gradually fish it out deeper if it is a long tapering point. Walleyes like the fastest access to deep water that they can find. Sometimes though, if the wind is blowing into the weedline, it will move the fish to the inside of the weeds and even closer to the shoreline. If there are scattered rocks on the shore side of the weeds, fish that area also. This is especially true during early morning hours, late evenings, and at night. Casting or long line trolling with shallow running minnow imitations work well in this situation.

Let's move on to locating walleyes in the fall.

Roach: Fall walleye fishing can be very good or very bad. Picking the right lake is very important.

Your best bet in the fall can be a large lake since they cool off slower. When the large lakes begin to turnover, go back to a small lake which will have completed its fall turnover and the fish have started their fall feeding surge. Then go back to the larger lakes when they've completed turnover.

Is there any easy way of telling if fall turnover is completed?

Roach: When the water surface temperature is forty-eight to fifty degrees, the turnover is usually over.

Comment on location in a lake that has stained water.

Roach: In a stained water lake the weedline will be shallower, and stained water lakes will warm up faster and stay warm longer than clear water lakes.

Do you depend on topographical maps when you are fishing new water?

Roach: They are a great help on a new lake. Use your tools and use your head, and a topo map is a very important tool. But remember no map is totally accurate.

PRESENTATION FOR WALLEYES

Let's go through that same typical season that we did regarding location, but this time with presentation in mind.

Roach: In early spring we're back to catching most of our walleyes in shallow water, probably not deeper than seven to eight feet. This is a colder water period, and a slow presentation should be used. Fish move slower in colder water since they are cold-blooded creatures, so a slower lure retrieve or a slower trolling speed is required.

What are the most productive lures to use in the spring?

Roach: I prefer a small jig and Lindy Rigs with light weights on them. Unless it's rather windy, I will use an eighth ounce jig tipped with a minnow. And on a Lindy Rig I also use an eighth ounce weight since I'm fishing fairly slow at this time of the year. Remember, in the spring of the year, fish can be really spooky even in dingy colored water.

During pre-summer when the water temperature is in the high fifties to low sixties, trolling or casting with a crank bait over the weeds can be a good way to catch walleyes. You need to use a real slow presentation at this time of the year, too.

Then during the summer when the walleyes are in the weeds and on the edge of the thermocline or on sunken islands, live bait rigs with leeches will work well and on Lake Mille Lacs you can use slip bobber rigs off of the mud flats.

In clearer water you can use minnow imitation lures in the perch color, for example. If you're fishing a dirty water lake, a fluorescent orange or shiner colored lure might work better. But every lake can be different: In a real weedy lake like Round Lake, you can catch walleyes in thirty to thirty-five feet of water. In Cass Lake during the summer you can catch walleyes in thirty to thirty-five feet of water way off of the breaks and in the evening they'll move up into twenty to twenty-two feet of water.

How about fall presentation?

Roach: Now we are back to the colder water and once again a slower presentation is needed. Also fish tend to shorten up their feeding time in the fall; they feed once or twice a day. Then as fall progresses, they will feed once a day and that will be during the warmest time of the day.

In the fall the schools of walleyes you find are the most active during the warmest part of the day. If you are on a school, it doesn't matter if they are in ten feet of water or in forty feet of water, they will be the most active during the warmest part of the day. That's important to know.

Why are some schools of fish active in a given lake when other schools in that same lake are not active?

Roach: Food, water temperature, and bottom content can vary in different parts of a lake. If they are in a muddy bottom part of a lake, the walleyes are probably feeding on tullibees. Then in another part of the lake the walleyes located on a rock pile might be feeding on perch, for example.

So possibly both schools are active at the same time, but you are only catching fish from one school since you did not change your presentation from the school of walleyes feeding on perch to the school feeding on tullibees?

Roach: Right. But it is also possible that one of those schools isn't active. I have found three to four different patterns on the same lake on a given day. Sometimes thirty feet of water might be where to catch them in one part of the lake, but not in another part of the lake. They could be on a mudline in one part of the lake and on a breakline in another part of the lake. And it might take a different presentation to take fish from each school.

What is a mudline?

Roach: It's where the silt meets the hard bottom of a rock pile or a drop-off. Walleyes will lay right along the edge of a mudline.

Are there any general rules about lure size?

Roach: Usually I use pretty small lures except when the water is very warm in the summer months. During cold water periods use the smallest lure you can get by with.

Randy Amenrud and I have fished on the river in thirty-three degree water temperature and used very small jigs tipped with small crappie minnows and caught a lot of walleyes when other fishermen were using regular sized walleye minnows and not catching much at all.

Comment on the importance of color in presentation.

Roach: I feel color is very important. If walleyes are hitting pink and white jigs in the morning, sometimes you will do a lot better in the middle of the day with a chartreuse-yellow or chartreuse-green or maybe even a brown and orange. So don't be afraid to switch to a different color jig, especially if the fishing slows down. During the nighttime if you're not having any luck on black, go to yellow with red dots, for instance. I've used a blue back shadling with pearl sides at night and it's worked very, very well.

I hear so many guys say color doesn't make any difference. Well, they're wrong. There is always one color that will out-produce all other colors at a given point in time. And this predominate color might change throughout the day. For example, in the brighter part of the day pink and white or chartreuse and yellow might be the best color combinations, and in the evening fluorescent colors might be the best choice. Believe me, I have seen it happen many, many times where one color would out-produce all other colors. Color really makes a difference.

How do lures attract fish; or why do they attract fish?

Roach: I suppose they imitate bait fish. Probably a forage fish in distress. A flutter action lure is supposed to look like an injured bait fish falling down out of a school of bait fish.

How does your presentation vary in clear water?

Roach: First of all, use light, clear line. In super clear water, where you can seen the bottom in ten to twelve feet of water, you will probably have to fish deeper than you would in a dirty water lake and use an electric trolling motor to minimize noise. Also, in clear water you will have to use longer snells to keep the sinker away from your bait so there will be less noise near your bait. For these situations I like a floating jig head in fluorescent, white, or yellow. If you're using a minnow, try a white floater.

Dark days on a clear water lake will also make a difference. On a dark day in a clear water lake, like Lake Pelican, you can use a fluorescent-red flicker snell which is a little bitty blade. It helps get the fish's attention. A Lindy Red Devil has a long three foot snell, and sometimes I tie on a four to a four and a half foot snell instead. It's my favorite for fishing finicky fish. It works especially well when you can see walleyes suspended off of the bottom on your locator. And don't forget to slow down your presentation when fishing suspended fish.

Do you use fish attracting scents?

Roach: Walleyes feed by scent, and there are products that will help you catch more fish. I had the opportunity to use the various fish attracting scents that Whizkers produces before they even had a name for them. It works on crank baits as well as jigs. Now there are a lot of scents out there that are nothing more than cod liver oil and anise, and all they do is cover up the human scent. The Whizkers brand is the real scent of a crawler or a leech, for example.

How do they get the real scent of those critters mixed in with the oil?

Roach: They use a fresh, freeze-dried product ground up into a dust form which they mix with a special oil. This oil sinks in the water, so it goes to the bottom where it is supposed to go, and it doesn't rise to the top like most of the other products do.

Does the texture of an artificial lure make a difference?

Roach: Texture is the toughness or the tenderness of a lure, and it is very important. Fish will hold a soft textured lure much longer than a hard textured lure which will give you more time to set the hook after you detect a strike. Actually, texture is the last step in presentation.

How do you know when it's time to set the hook, with Lindy Rigs and those types of lures, that is?

Roach: If you are fishing with a Lindy Rig, for instance, and your rig comes back with half a night crawler on it, you only gave him half enough time. If you reel it in and the night crawler is whole, with a few teeth marks in it, you didn't give the fish enough time. And if your lure comes back with the bait gone, you were probably holding your line too tight, and the fish jerked it off of your hook. But if you come back with a walleye on, you did it just right.

When walleyes are biting very lightly, you have to wait about thirty to thirty-five seconds before you set the hook; that is, with live bait rigs.

What is the best method of trolling?

Roach: Backtrolling is usually preferred over trolling forward since you can present your bait slower. You can also follow the contours of the lake bottom better when backtrolling since it's an easier way of controlling your boat.

But an electric trolling motor is a must when fishing shallow water or clear water since being very quiet is important so you don't spook the fish.

Comment on drifting as a method of presentation.

Roach: A controlled drift can be an excellent method of trolling. The wind pushes you along and you use your motor only to correct your position by shifting the motor into gear when necessary. Once you've corrected your position, shift your motor back into neutral and continue drifting.

Also when trolling, don't let yards and yards of line out. This will only decrease your chances of detecting a strike and increase your chances of getting your lure hung up.

Comment on trolling speed.

Roach: Vary your trolling speed until you find the speed that will work best. Actually, for walleye fishing, you don't even want to talk about speed. You want to talk about slow. How slow can I troll!

Of course there are times when you will want to troll a little faster. In the summertime when you are fishing over weeds, you should go a little faster which will eliminate many of the perch and sunfish bites. But always start out slow and then go a little faster when it's necessary.

Any last comments on presentation?

Roach: Yes. Mostly regarding lure size. I sometimes fish with an eighth ounce jig in thirty feet of water with six pound test line. But that's when I've really got my location put together because it's very slow fishing waiting for that light jig to get down to the fish in thirty feet of water.

And when you are fishing in thirty feet of water with an eighth ounce jig, you are not fishing a whole sunken island, for example. You are fishing the area of that island that is holding fish. You have pinpointed the fish, and then you fine tune your presentation. In fact, I've used as small as a one-sixteenth ounce jig for walleyes.

It's like the old saying, "There's never enough time to do things right, but there's always time to do them over." So when you are fishing, do it right the first time.

WEATHER AND BIOLOGICAL FACTORS AFFECTING WALLEYES

How important is the pH level of water to walleyes?

Roach: Everybody has their own opinion about it, but it does seem to have a lot to do with catching walleyes in the summer months. That is probably because during the summertime there is much more stress on fish than during other times of the year, especially when it's a very hot summer. But I have had good fishing when the pH wasn't in the desirable range. Actually, I feel, at this point in time, only a few people really know that much about it.

How does wind direction affect fishing?

Roach: Wind direction is important. I don't like north winds since they usually mean a cold front is here. A northeast wind isn't too bad, but a northwest wind in the summertime can also mean a cold front is approaching. A southwest wind is usually the best. And a south wind isn't too bad unless it is accompanied by a high glare day. We all know a high glare day can mean bad fishing because sun penetration, especially in clear water lakes, will force fish to deeper water or to heavier cover which makes them harder to catch.

How about the barometric pressure?

Roach: When a weather front moves in and the barometric pressure goes down, the fish tend to turn off. I have seen fish roll on the surface when the barometric pressure changes. You are crazy to fish during a lightning storm, but I have been out there, and the fish really turn on during a lightning storm.

The day after a storm has hit when you have bluebird skies, the fish are reluctant to feed. It will take until at least the middle of the afternoon before the fish even start to turn on again.

Why?

Roach: Because a cold front condition turns fish off. If you have another front following the first storm, it really can get tough to catch fish. During these weather conditions you should fish a lake with darker colored water or a river system.

Why a darker water lake?

Roach: Darker lakes warm up faster since they absorb the warmth from the sun faster. Also, a shallow water lake will warm up faster than a deep water lake.

How does rising and falling water affect fishing?

Roach: Rising water will usually turn fish on, and falling water will usually turn them off.

Are certain moon phases better for catching fish than other moon phases?

Roach: These days everybody is studying that, and everybody has their own theory. I really don't have any concrete evidence yet; anything I would say would be just speculation.

Do walleyes relate to the thermocline in any certain way?

Roach: When a lake is thermoclined, that is the time of the year when it's easier to fish because the thermocline eliminates a lot of water. Sure walleyes can go below the thermocline, but they prefer not to. Some fish are right on the thermocline or right above it, but most of the fish, game fish in particular, are in the weeds at this time of the year.

But I should mention that although the thermocline does eliminate a lot of water that you don't have to fish, it can be tough fishing since the walleyes have so much bait to choose from right in the weeds for most of the thermocline period. They're not desperately striking anything they see.

Generally, what time of the year do lakes thermocline?

Roach: It depends on water temperature and water clarity. Gull Lake, for example, thermoclines in about twenty-eight feet of water, and on Pelican Lake the thermocline is in about forty feet of water. But to answer your question: lakes that thermocline usually start to thermocline from mid-June to late June. And then about Labor Day they will turnover. Shallow, windswept lakes might not thermocline at all.

How do you know when a lake has turned over?

Roach: The most accurate way is to drop a temperature probe down into the water. If the surface temperature is the same as the bottom temperature, the lake has turned over. The reason fish can be anywhere after the turnover is because turnover distributes oxygen to the lower level of the water.

EQUIPMENT AND TACKLE FOR WALLEYE FISHING

What type of rods do you prefer for walleye fishing?

Roach: Graphite or boron. Boron rods are much stiffer. The ideal rod is light, strong, and sensitive.

The rods I have designed for rod companies were all fast taper rods with "forgiving" tips. That is, the last twelve to fourteen inches is real flexible, and the rest of the rod is stiff. You need a "forgiving" tip because the fish feels you long before you feel them; so if you pull too hard, they will spit out your lure or bait.

What kind of spinning reels do you prefer?

Roach: Get one with a big spool. Even in an ultralight, get one with the biggest spool you can find. Small spool reels cause too much memory (line coil) in your line. I know the small spool reels looks good, but they aren't worth a damn. It's also harder to cast with a small spool reel.

What type of line do you use?

Roach: In the spring I use six and eight pound test Berkley Trilene in the clear color. And then when it warms up, I use XT. I've always used Trilene, even long before I rep'd for them.

What's the best way to put line on a reel?

Roach: Always wrap it on tight. If you put it on loose, when you catch a fish, the top line will bury into the bottom line of your spool. In fact, many fishermen think it's the reel's drag that's sticking when they have problems, but often it's actually their line. Also when the line sticks, the next fish that strikes will feel the resistance and drop your lure before you can hook him.

How about outboards? Any favorites?

Roach: I should point out that most of the products that I use are products that I get paid to promote. But I certainly wouldn't promote or use a product that didn't work well. You wouldn't see a race car driver promoting and using a motor he didn't think he could win with. Would you?

As for outboards, I use a fifty horse power Mariner. The fifty Mercury or Mariner, which is basically the same engine, are the best all-around fishing motors on the market today. That four cylinder will give you plenty of power and troll just like a ten horse motor will.

What do you look for in an electric trolling motor?

Roach: Get one with lots of power that is quiet because fish can hear very well. When you see walleyes on a graph two to three feet off of the bottom and they hear a motor, they will go right to the bottom, and then, of course, they will be harder to catch.

I've used Mercury, Mariner, Minn Kota, and Eagle trolling motors and they all have done a good job for me. Of course, the gear driven trolling motors, no matter who makes them, are noisier than the smaller nongear driven motors. But if you are fishing for walleyes in big, windy lakes with big boats, you have to have an electric motor with lots of power.

I assume since you promote for Lund, you use their boats?

Roach: Yes I do. I use the fourteen, sixteen, and eighteen foot Lund Pro Angler and the new deep-vee. I've also had some input on the design of some of their fishing boats. Seriously, they make a good boat that can withstand one hell-of-a-beating. And there is no other boat on the market that has a high a resale value either.

Comment on flashers and graphs.

Roach: Learn to use a flasher before you buy a graph. Besides, a graph is not a must for walleye fishing like it is for salmon fishing. In fact, I usually don't use my graph for walleye fishing; I use my flasher. You are going to see it on a flasher before a graph can print it anyway.

But a graph can help you better determine what the blips are on your flasher. Use your flasher until you need to know exactly what's going on down there. Then turn on your graph. That way you won't go through very many rolls of graph paper. In fact, last year, with all the fishing I do, I only used four rolls of graph paper.

But all the equipment in the world isn't going to catch fish for you. The equipment only helps. It's what's between your ears that catches you fish.

Do you use swivels or do you tie your lures directly to the line?

Roach: I use swivels a lot. Especially if I'm using the type of lure that twists my line.

If you are using a bait that is not supposed to tangle your line, and it does tangle it, the bait is probably out of tune. But if I'm using a crank bait, I tie directly to the O-ring because the action of the crank bait is better without a swivel.

Comment on snells.

Roach: A shorter snell will travel lower in the water, and a longer snell will travel higher in the water. This, of course, depends on your boat speed, too. The faster you are going the lower the lure will travel on a snell.

Do you modify lures before using them?

Roach: A little. I make sure they are tuned properly. Even if they are tuned from the factory, they can get out of tune. I tune spinners, crank baits, and jigs. With spinners and cranks I tune them so they will run straight in the water. With jigs, sometimes, I will turn the hook out and up a little so they will hook fish better.

What is the best knot to tie?

Roach: Many fishermen tie the improved clinch knot, but it is not the strongest knot. I prefer the palomar or the Trilene knot; those two knots seem to be the best. But whatever knot you tie, test it. Give it a pop and see if it breaks. And retie every so often and cut off a couple feet of line each time you retie. That last couple feet of line is where most of the breaks occur since that portion of the line gets the most abuse.

Is there anything that you want to add regarding equipment or tackle?

Roach: Match your tackle with your rod and reel. Most good tackle dealers should be able to match your equipment for you if you're not able to.

MISCELLANEOUS INFORMATION ABOUT WALLEYE FISHING

What is your favorite lake in Minnesota?

Roach: I like Pelican Lake since so few fishermen fish it properly. It's a tough lake to fish. Somedays the walleyes are on the thirty foot weedline, and on other days they might be suspended or in the weeds. Pelican Lake is a challenging lake to fish.

Gull Lake is also a very good lake, and Lake of the Woods is good, too. But I really don't have a favorite lake. I just like to go to different lakes to find new rocks and bars.

Do you have any idea why fishing isn't as good as it used to be?

Roach: Yeah! Overbagging and filling freezers is what is killing our fishing. I'm glad they are checking car trunks. Make sportsmen realize who the heck is taking the fish. Many people blame it on the Indians, but the Indians don't net all that many fish. I remember the days on Lake Mille Lacs when the walleye population was unreal — you'd think nothing of catching fifty or more walleyes in a day on the reefs. But what killed it was overbagging. Of course, we now have more fishermen and they are much better educated, too.

Do you think the D.N.R. should lower the limits on fish?

Roach: I wouldn't care if they had a limit of three or four walleyes, just enough for a meal, that's all we need anyway.

What is your favorite time of the year to fish for walleyes in Minnesota?

Roach: Anytime I can get on the water.

I should have known better than to have asked that question. What are your favorite conditions?

Roach: It depends. On a clear water lake, I prefer a cloudy, overcast day with some wind—a good walleye chop. Just so the waves hit the back of the boat not getting you wet, but they slow you down.

Why are you a successful fisherman?

Roach: I never give up. I've got a good attitude, too. Even if I only catch one fish, it's been a beautiful day.

Also, don't sit on one spot too long either. Fish spots where other fishermen don't fish. Fish inside corners or straight shorelines. You'll be surprised; you'll pick up some stragglers when all the school fish are out in deeper water. There are many scattered fish living in that weedline that never move. They don't look like good spots to fish, but they can be.

Have you ever had any bad experiences with people that you've fished with?

Roach: Only one time out of all the people I've fished with did I have a problem. I was guiding this guy who had fished the lake we were on before. He kept wanting to fish where he'd caught fish last year on this lake.

Well, they weren't biting on the inside, but he kept insisting on fishing there. He had caught them on that pattern in June of the previous year and this was September.

I said, well sir the fish have moved down, and I tried to explain why they had moved. We had already caught three fish on the outside, but he still wanted to fish the inside of the weeds. The water was clear and you could see there weren't any fish in there. Not even any bait fish.

We went back to the outside and caught two more, but again he insisted on fishing the inside. So after the third unsuccessful try at fishing his pattern, I told him to reel his line in and he said, "What for?" Then I informed him we were going back to the bait shop since I couldn't get him any fish where he insisted on fishing. I told him that if he came back next summer and fished that very same spot, he'd probably have some good fishing there. He was madder than hell. I didn't charge him anything.

He was the only person I ever had any trouble with in all those years of guiding and taking tackle buyers out and just plain fun fishing. Of course, he never hired me again, but I never would have booked him anyway.

One other time I had a customer who hooked a twelve or so pound northern, and we lost it because my landing net was bad. I felt like a fool. And to make things worse, it was the biggest fish he had ever had on, and he had fought that fish beautifully with ultralight equipment.

He didn't say anything, but he picked up some twine and started repairing my landing net which made me feel two inches high. Needless to say, I now have a new net every year.

What are your thoughts on live bait -vs- artificial lures?

Roach: Live bait in walleye fishing does the trick—leeches, night crawlers, and minnows. Artificials are a lot of fun, but when fishing is tough, that's when the live bait rig will out-produce anything else.

Are there any times of the year or situations when artificials are more productive than live bait?

Roach: Yeah. In the spring of the year when walleyes are in shallow water or on the weedline. When it's hot, they will come up early in the morning or late in the evening and artificials will work better in this situation.

And walleyes prefer a minnow type artificial lure, but you can catch them on bass type crank baits, too. One of my favorites is a perch color crank bait when I'm fishing a weedline. It can be fantastic!

What do you do on those cold front days when fishing is tough?

Roach: You can save yourself by going to a sixteenth or an eighth ounce jig tipped with a minnow, crawler, or leech. For post frontal conditions, that's probably the best presentation.

What is your best catch of walleyes in Minnesota?

Roach: Surprisingly, I've done very well in the middle of the summer in the middle of the day when it's hot and still, and the walleyes come up on rock piles chasing perch.

My best walleye catch in Minnesota was on Gull Lake near Brainerd. One morning I was fishing with tackle buyers, and I caught seven walleyes and the smallest one was ten pounds and two ounces and the largest two were just under twelve pounds. We were using Lindy Floating Rigs tipped with jumbo leeches.

Is that one of the lures you designed for Lindy?

Roach: Yeah. And we got that catch on film, too. But my biggest single walleye in Minnesota was thirteen and a quarter pounds. But in the Columbia River in Oregon walleyes of this size are quite common.

What are the chances of a new state record walleye being caught in Minnesota?

Roach: I don't know what the chances are, but I think there are some twenty-plus-pound walleyes swimming around in a few of these lakes. The D.N.R. has reported netting some on the Pine River that were close to twenty-one pounds. That's the Pine River that runs into Whitefish Lake.

What are some of the most common mistakes fishermen make?

Roach: Many times people will catch one fish and they don't relate it to the schooling fish. Bass, for example, are a schooling fish. They catch one and just keep moving and there are probably three or four more there that are catchable, using the same presentation. Then they could change lures and catch two or three more, but many fishermen are too hung up on one method of fishing or one lure or one color to make the most of a situation.

They say, "I'm a jig fisherman or a rig fisherman," etc. I hear that so much. Or "I don't use nothing but a spinner bait because that's all you need." Well, that's B.S.

In a tournament I once caught three fish with a crank bait and then all of a sudden they got spooky. Then I put on a bottom cruiser with a Little Joe spinner with a gold blade and went through again and bam, bam I got two more walleyes. Then I put on a Fuzz-E-Grub and reeled as if I was drifting back downstream and got a couple more.

I go right back where I've caught fish and try a different method, and many times I will take two to three more fish than I would have if I hadn't changed my methods of presentation.

A walleye is an elusive fish, but when they start to feed, they really feed. They won't hit a lure out of anger like a bass will; a walleye usually tastes the bait.

How do you know when a walleye has taken your offering?

Roach: I don't care if a walleye is nine inches or nine pounds, they all bite the same, especially on live bait. But they will hit an artificial lure pretty hard.

How much of successful fishing is luck?

Roach: That two percent always helps. Sometimes it's ten percent.

Comment on the walleye's ability to smell.

Roach: I think their ability to smell is really important to the fisherman. If you get into a school of two hundred fish that are feeding, it probably doesn't make any difference. But with spooky fish on a hard fished lake, it probably makes a big difference.

If walleyes aren't active, what then?

Roach: The important thing is to fish more spots since the main school is not active. You are trying to catch the stragglers that may be active.

What is the best time of the year to go hawg hunting?

Roach: First of all, you should be fishing a lake that produces big walleyes and also has a good population of fish. The best seasons of the year would probably be pre-summer and fall. Actually, night fishing in the fall with live bait would probably be a good way to catch a lunker walleye. Although you can catch big fish during the pre-summer period, they won't be lunkers at that time of the year. They will tend to be very skinny then because they've been off of feed for some time since they were more concerned with spawning than eating. If you caught an eleven pounder right after the spawning season, that fish would probably have weighed thirteen pounds in the fall.

Comment on night fishing.

Roach: If you have the time, do it. Most people who fish walleyes at night, bobber fish which takes little skill. You find the right side of the reef and wait for the school to move in. Another good place to night fish for walleyes is where there is a stream or current running into the lake, and the walleyes will come right up into two or three feet of water. Or you can use crank baits on the sandy area right inside of the weedbeds. For this type of fishing use crank baits, but be sure to work them slow even in warm water since fish really can't chase a lure at night like they can during the daylight hours. Also, trolling spinners with crawlers and leeches works well at night.

Do you have any thoughts on the future of walleye fishing in Minnesota?

Roach: I'd like to see the walleye made a game fish only. That way it could not be sold in restaurants. I'd like to see fishermen catch their own walleyes. Muskies and bass are not sold in grocery stores or restaurants, so why is the walleye? Also, by outlawing the commercial sale of walleyes, you would stop most of the bootlegging of walleyes since there wouldn't be commercial customers for them.

We as sportsmen put the walleyes into the lakes, and the commercial fishermen harvest them. It isn't right! I'm not saying put the commercial fishermen out of business. Buy them out like they've done in other states.

We'd better handle our fisheries better than we handled our pheasant population. Also, spawning areas on lakes should be off limits to fishing pressure during the spawning season. At least, they have stopped people from completely destroying the lake shore which destroys fish habitat.

It's just like years ago when people threw beer and pop cans in the ditches—they're becoming more aware of our environment and our resources, including the walleye.

What's special about Minnesota fishing?

Roach: There are so many different lakes and different types of water.

You can fish four or five lakes in a couple of days. And almost every lake is good for one species or another. If you get tired of fishing for bass, you can go to another lake and fish for northerns, and so on.

I'd love to fish every lake in Minnesota, but I will never live long enough; so I'll fish as many as I have time to.

Chapter 3

KEVIN KOEP ON NORTHERNS

In many sports, like swimming or gymnastics, we have come to expect that those in the winner's circle will be youngsters—fourteen to twenty years of age being the norm. But in the sport of fishing where knowledge, experience, versatility, and concentration are the hallmarks of the successful, the youngsters tend to be in their early thirties.

However, by the time Kevin Koep was sixteen he had already developed the qualities necessary to be successful at the sport of fishing, and he had learned the secrets of locating and consistently catching fish. At this time, he was already a member of the Nisswa Guide's League, and by the time he was eighteen he had competed very successfully in fishing money tournaments against some of the very best anglers in the country.

Moreover, Kevin's second place finish in the first Northerns, Inc. tournament, which was held on Gull Lake and consisted of over two hundred contestants many of which were full-time guides and other professionals, established this youngster as a serious contender. In addition, Kevin has been featured in fishing movies, the subject of outdoor spots segments on television news programs, and recognized by the "In-Fisherman" magazine and other outdoor sports publications before he reached his nineteenth birthday. And this recognition wasn't qualified recognition; that is, hey this kid is really quite good for his age. It was recognition for achievement in the sport of fishing, and his age was only incidental.

Initially, Kevin's apprenticeship began in the dungeon of his father's store, Marv Koep's Bait and Tackle Store which is located just south of Nisswa, Minnesota. The dungeon, as it is affectionately called, is the back room of the store where Kevin would pack leeches for sale to customers. "It was fun," Kevin stated, "and a good way for an eight year old to make money. And I always gave a good count—at least thirteen or fourteen in a one dozen package."

At the age of nine, under the watchful eye of his father, Kevin began fishing from a row boat. "My dad would watch me through binoculars to make sure I was all right."

Then Kevin was promoted to fish cleaner for the customers of the guides that worked out of his father's store. And guides like Al Lindner and Gary Roach kept Kevin very busy. He would clean everything from crappies to northerns for ten cents a piece. In fact, he had it down to where he could fillet and skin a crappie in eight seconds, and at eleven years of age, he thought he might well be the fastest fish cleaner in the world. Perhaps he was.

After Kevin, at the age of twelve, had convinced his father that he could safely handle a motorized boat, he took his first customer out fishing. On that first trip his customer, a New York defense attorney, caught a three pound walleye and Kevin caught a seven pounder. But when it came time to pose for a picture, the attorney held Kevin's seven pounder and Kevin held the three pounder. The fee for the trip was a hunting knife, and Kevin considered that good pay.

His fishing education continued with the help of guides like Gary Roach, Al Lindner, Rob Romin, and Bobby Collette who he fished with when the guiding business was slow. These professionals along with his father taught Kevin that hard work and versatility will pay off. But, most importantly, they taught him sportsmanship and showed him how to appreciate and love the out-of-doors.

Gradually his father worked Kevin into professional guiding, and at sixteen he was getting booked regularly and began to establish his own clientele. "So I thought to heck with dishing out minnows in the store," Kevin said, "I might as well guide full-time in the summers and be on the lake all day."

Currently, Kevin is attending Saint John's University at Collegeville, Minnesota where he is majoring in business and keeps in shape by wrestling on the college team. For the present, he plans to continue guiding during the summer months for a few more years and staying very close to fishing. In the future, he hopes to conduct seminars to help people learn more about fishing, but he enjoys the sport too much to continue guiding for too many more years since he feels it could get tiring and ruin his enjoyment for the sport of fishing.

NORTHERN BEHAVIOR

What comes to mind when you think of the northern pike's behavior patterns?

Koep: The northern pike is a weedline predator that likes to wander out in-to deep, cool water and chase big schools of ciscoes and tullibees, etc. Then at certain times of the year, northerns will move up to the edge and into the weedline and forage for other bait fish like sunfish, perch, and suckers.

Also, the northern is a ferocious fish that is fun to catch. Walleyes are fun, but there is no more excitement in fishing than you can get from cat-ching a northern. They're a show fish. The action is there, and they are the ones that make good stories.

When you were the fish cleaner in your father's bait store, you must have noticed what northerns were usually feeding on.

Koep: In many of the northerns that I have cleaned early in the season, I just didn't seem to find bait fish in their stomachs. They just don't seem to be feeding a lot at that time of the year. During mid-summer they will have a lot of perch in their stomachs. And later on in the season, I have cleaned many northerns with big tullibees in their stomachs. In fact, I have caught three to four pound northerns that had six to twelve inch tullibees in their stomachs.

How frequently do big fish eat?

Koep: Big northerns need a lot of food to maintain their weight. To satisfy their hunger, they eat big meals. I also feel they spend a lot of time over or in the deepest water in the lake. Thus the problem. How do you get the pro-per presentation with a very, very large lure or large bait in very deep water.

Actually, if there is a new state record northern pike caught, he will probably be caught in shallow water since a fish that size would be im-possible to catch in deep water.

Since we are discussing big fish eating big meals, comment on lure size.

Koep: Generally, big fish will look for a bigger lure. If I were hawg hunting, I would use thirty-six pound test dacron line with an eighteen inch steel leader. I prefer the leader material by Trilene that you can cut to the length that you need and then melt the plastic coating to secure the ends. Lures eight to twelve inches long or longer are your best bet for attracting big northerns.

However, you can catch big fish with smaller baits, too. When I'm guiding, I will use a four to six inch minnow with a quarter ounce jig with the Trilene leader material. And I will often use lighter line (twelve pound test) without a leader because leaders sometimes deter strikes. But I've probably broken off the really big ones that have hit because of this.

Do northerns follow schools of bait fish?

Koep: Oh yes! Especially in deep water they will follow schools of tullibees and ciscoes, etc. Almost every time I have caught northerns, there will be some type of bait fish nearby.

Do northerns school?

Koep: I think they congregate because of food or water temperature. It's not really a school like walleyes or bass. I've caught three to four northerns in an area, and then nothing will strike. Then you can return later, and there will be three or four more in that same area. With walleyes you can catch your limit in a given spot, and there will still be more there. Schools of three or more northerns in a given spot are hard to find unless they are schooled for the spawning run.

How well developed is a northern's memory?

Koep: I don't think they are able to remember lures or anything like that. In fact, when I was young, I put some northerns in our pond and then caught them on a jig and released them and later recaught them on the same jig. If they are active, they will hit the same lure time and time again.

Of course, they have the ability to remember where weedbeds are and where spawning beds are, etc., but, other than that, they don't seem to have a very highly developed ability to remember, even for a fish.

But if your presentation doesn't look natural, they probably won't hit your lure.

How does a northern's ability to smell or taste affect your ability to catch them?

Koep: Sometimes smell and taste are important factors in fishing, and other times they aren't important at all. If the fish are really biting, it doesn't seem to make any difference. If fishing is tough, I would make sure I didn't drop my lure in gasoline, for example.

There are days when you can catch northerns on any lure regardless of smell or taste. That's the fish. That's fishing.

Do northerns have the ability to communicate with each other?

Koep: Yes I feel they are able to communicate with each other. When bass are schooled or congregated, if you turn one on, it will cause the others to turn on also. Sometimes one active northern will turn on another northern nearby.

Once I hooked a five pound northern that was thrashing around a lot, and then suddenly he stopped thrashing. I looked into the water, and I saw that a larger northern had him in his mouth. I feel, this thrashing caused excitement in the other fish which caused this larger fish to grab the fish I had hooked. This larger northern was about twelve to fourteen pounds, and there was no way he could have swallowed the fish I had on, but he got so excited he attacked him anyway. Also, I have had northerns take bass away from me or take a swipe at them when I was reeling the bass in. A northern is one aggressive critter.

The ones that get to a real large size are the ones that eat their brothers and sisters. The real cannibals are the ones that you want to catch since they are going to be the bigger ones.

How much do northerns move?

Koep: Northerns move around quite a bit and quite freely because northerns and muskies are the major predators in most Minnesota lakes. They use a wider variety of structure than any other game fish in Minnesota, too.

What are some of the locational habits of the northern?

Koep: Northerns will school up near creeks in the springtime. They will stay shallower where there is warmer water early in the year. Perhaps five to eight feet of water.

As the season progresses, they will move deeper. In most Minnesota lakes you can catch northerns from weedline down to forty feet or so of water.

What are northerns relating to in forty feet of water?

Koep: Perhaps it's an oxygen or temperature preference. Or else they could be feeding on schools of tullibees or ciscoes. I've seen people on Gull Lake fishing for northerns with jigs in ninety feet of water and once in awhile catching a huge one. I suppose those northerns are roaming about feeding on schools of ciscoes.

And when you are jigging in very deep water, it is necessary to use a spoon that does not have much resistance so you can get it down deep fast. It is not a method that I have a lot of confidence in, but if you stick it out, you have a chance of catching a big fish.

During the wintertime northerns will frequently move to the deepest part of the lake.

Does fish behavior vary from lake to lake?

Koep: Yes, on a given day it will. But during the period of a season, I would say their behavior will not vary much from lake to lake in Minnesota.

The reason their behavior can vary on a daily basis is because their particular eco-system might be in a different stage on a given day or week. For example, a deeper lake will warm more slowly than a shallower lake; so since spawning is triggered by water temperature the fish in a shallower lake will spawn before the fish in a deeper lake will, etc.

Why do big fish sometimes suddenly turn on?

Koep: It has to do with the change in season or a change in the fish's life pattern. Anytime in the year when there is a change in the fish's life pattern, they are more vulnerable. Every seasonal change that causes a change in the fish's life pattern will suddenly trigger better fishing, and then it will taper off until the next seasonal change. As the summer period begins, for instance, the fishing will be great and then taper off until the fall period begins and so on.

Through fishing the many different types of lakes in the Brainerd area, I have found that if the northerns in one type of lake are turned on, another lake that is quite similar in depth, size, and eco-system will also have active northerns. Knowing when and why northerns suddenly turn on is the biggest challenge to the fisherman.

LOCATING NORTHERNS

I'd like to begin the location section by asking you about the significance of weeds.

Koep: The best weed is red-top cabbage. Although some lakes do not have red-top cabbage, they will have some type of cabbage.

I also look for northerns in coontail, but not the really thick coontail. There is also a weed that looks like a small lily pad that will hold northerns. It grows in four to five feet of water, and the northerns will use it for shade and protection.

In the Brainerd area lakes the northerns tend to prefer the cabbage type weeds, but they will also use coontail frequently. My best spots contain a good mixture of different types of weeds.

It is important to note that in the fall if you stay in shallower water and cast into deeper water, you will do much better. I know that's the opposite of what most fishermen do, but it does work better in the fall.

Are you saying that you should position your boat in shallow water and cast toward the deeper water?

Koep: Yes. The northerns are coming up out of deeper water and cruising at eight feet or so in fifty feet of water, and when they move into shallower water, there is less chance of spooking them if you are casting out toward the deeper water. I have found that in the fall if you cast from deep water to shallow water, you will get a lot of hits, but you won't catch as many fish.

Of course, in the summertime it is almost always better to do the opposite—stay on the deeper edges of the weeds and cast to shallow water.

What time of the year do northerns relate to rocks?

Koep: Northerns will relate to rocks in the fall, especially in deeper water (twenty to thirty feet). The best way to take these fish is with a jig and a minnow combination or a live bait rig with a big shiner on it.

What is the best way to fish a point for northerns?

Koep: Look for anything irregular. For instance, deep water off of one side of a point or a deep break or where you have weeds on one side of a point are areas of a point you should really fish hard.

When I first approach a bar, I will stay in about fifteen feet of water, and I will cast up into the weeds working my lure down off the break right underneath my boat, and then pop it up underneath the boat a few times, and then bring it up and cast it out again. And always remember to keep a tight line.

If nothing happens, move a little deeper and vertical jig your lure. Use a short cast—if you are in fifteen feet of water, cast your lure so it lands ten to twelve feet from your boat. Remember you might be casting it out twenty feet but by the time it hits bottom, it is only ten feet or so from the boat. Keeping your line tight will cause it to pendulum toward the boat.

Also, the edge of a food shelf is a good spot especially where there might be a sharp break on it. There will always be northerns there. A gradual break will not hold them as well.

How important are clam beds in locating northerns?

Koep: Very important on many lakes. A good sand bottom with a lot of clams will hold many northerns. Even if you are fishing in water that is too dirty to see clams, you can tell if clams are there since sometimes they will clamp onto your line. And be sure to make a mental note of these clam bed areas because they are an important locational factor for northerns.

How important is oxygen content for locating northerns?

Koep: It is tremendously important. Northerns will follow schools of tullibees and ciscoes which seek out areas of cool water combined with good oxygen content. And if you have a real hot summer, the tullibees and ciscoes will go really deep to find cool water. In fact, sometimes they will go so deep in their search for cool water that they will run out of oxygen and die.

In the summer of 1983 I saw tullibees stacked up dead on Lake Mille Lacs. It was a hot summer which forced the tullibees into deeper water where it was cooler which eventually killed them because of the lack of oxygen. The same thing happened to many walleyes on Gull Lake at that time. They went deep to find cool water and ran out of oxygen. Then when they ascended to the top too quickly for oxygen, they got the bends and died.

So it may not be a question of how important oxygen content is to the northern, but how important is oxygen content to the prey fish that the northern forages for.

Comment on water temperature.

Koep: I've caught a lot of northerns while I was fishing for walleyes, and I assume it is because they both prefer about the same water temperature. But I am not so sure of how important a locational factor that might be. Of course water temperature is a much more important locational factor in the spring and the fall than it is in the summer. In the spring and fall fish seek out warmer water.

Some of the best northern fishing is in the summertime, but that's for small to medium size northerns. The large northerns tend to be real active only during the cooler water periods.

How important is wind, or more specifically wind direction, in locating northerns?

Koep: I almost always use the wind to my advantage. I like to fish a bar where the wind is blowing onto it since it gives me an edge. It's not only because I feel the fish are more active in these areas; I can control my boat much better by backing into the wind or drifting along the edge of the bar with the wind which makes presentation easier and much more accurate.

Why do you feel fish are more active on the windy side of the lake?

Koep: Wave action blows plankton and bait fish into these areas, and then the smaller fish will be there feeding which will make them available for the larger fish. Even when fishing is slow, there seems to be some fish active on the windswept side of the lake. Of course, if northerns are really active, you will be able to catch them almost anywhere on the lake.

Comment on location from a seasonal standpoint; that is, the season opener on thru ice-over.

Koep: About mid-May the active fish will be in warmer water—usually the five to eight foot depth. Although this can be a tougher time of the year to catch northerns, it can be done with some regularity.

Look for an area with sand and sparse weeds and use lighter line—about ten pound test should work well. Lighter line will enable the jig to fall much better giving it better action.

What would the approximate water temperature be at this time of the year?

Koep: About fifty-four to fifty-five degrees. Also it helps to find an area where the wind is blowing into a big flat; that is where the warmest water will be. And many times this will be the north end of the lake because of the warming southerly winds. Again look for areas of sand and sparse weeds; the weeds will be sparse because they haven't had time to develop at this time of the year. This pattern should hold through the third week in June or so.

Then in the end of June to early July the northerns will move to fifteen to twenty-five feet of water. And later in July they will go to depths of twenty-five to forty feet.

In August they will start coming back up into the shallow water. It is the lack of oxygen that forces them to the shallows at this time of the year.

Then in mid-September or so the fall turnover begins. The lakes are again well oxygenated with the water temperature being the same from the top of the lake to the bottom, so northerns can be found in any depth of water. I believe most lakes go through this cycle, but each lake will vary in the time it takes to complete its cycle.

Can bait fish be a clue as to where northerns might be located?

Koep: Yes. If you are fishing a spot where there aren't any bait fish, the northerns that might be in that area won't be active.

Since the northern is the major predator in most Minnesota lakes do you think they pick certain locations to feel secure?

Koep: Fish like to relate to a location where they feel secure, where they can find food, where the water temperature is right, and where they can find the right oxygen level. And, I feel, when the shallower water is too warm and the deeper water lacks sufficient oxygen, the northern can't find what he really needs so he will become somewhat dormant. Then, if possible, go to a deeper water lake to fish.

Elaborate on when it's time to change lakes.

Koep: If you are a capable fisherman, and you've tried working the deeper weedlines and breaks with spin rigs and jigs, and you've tried crank baits on the flats and you're still not catching anything, then I would switch to a different lake. That is, a clear water lake to a stained water lake or a shallow water lake to a deep water lake. Don't just switch to another lake that is basically the same as the lake you aren't having any luck on.

In my first year of guiding when I didn't have many trips, a friend of mine and I would go lake hopping to learn more lakes and to learn more about fishing. Some days we'd hit as many as thirteen different lakes. We would size up a new lake for depth, what we could expect to catch, where the major bars were, and the best time of the year we should come back to fish it.

We really hit some honey holes, and even today it seems that when I go to a new lake, I work harder and I am more intense and I seem to catch more and bigger fish. The first time I'm on a new lake I seem to read it better. I guess when I fish the same lake frequently, I do what so many of us do—stop being versatile. I should be as versatile as the first time I was on that lake and stay away from being redundant, especially in my presentation.

One of the most exciting things in fishing is checking out a new lake. I guess it's the anticipation.

What's the first thing you should do when fishing a new lake?

Koep: First of all, I just go out and run the lake to find out how deep it is. I like to find the deepest part of the lake and circle it to find out if there are any sharp breaks or flats related to that deepest part. If I find a good food shelf that is fairly shallow breaking into deep water, I will fish along that shelf about twelve to twenty feet deep making short casts or vertical jigging.

If the lake is really shallow (twenty feet deep or less), I will stay in twelve to fourteen feet of water and cast up into six to eight feet of water. Usually shallow lakes have dirty water; therefore, the weedline will be in shallower water than it would be in a clearer water lake. Just stay close to that weedline, and if you find a point, work it hard.

Are topographical maps an aid when fishing a new lake?

Koep: The problem with using a topographical map is that if there is a good spot on that map, everyone else is fishing it, too. All of my best spots never seem to be on the topo maps.

When I work in my dad's bait shop, I show customers spots that aren't on topo maps.

Is there anything that you want to add regarding the locational aspect of fishing for northerns?

Koep: Yes. Ninety-five percent of my fishing for northerns is in between ten and fifteen feet of water.

PRESENTATION FOR NORTHERNS

I'd like to begin this section by asking you about the seasonal differences in presentation for northerns.

Koep: In the spring I prefer a slower presentation. Live bait seems to work best at this time of the year; I like minnows and shiners. Also, a live bait rig will work better with a little jigging action which will get their attention.

And be particularly alert for the strike because even northerns won't hit a lure very hard in the spring. Spinner baits worked really slow also can be productive in the spring.

Another good presentaiton you can use at this time of year is bouncing a small spin rig real slowly on the bottom; whereas, bigger spin rigs are better for jigging in the summertime.

Let's go on to the summer presentational patterns.

Koep: In the summertime northerns pretty much stay out of shallow water and prefer to locate in the cooler, deeper water between fifteen to twenty-five feet. This time of the year, late June and through most of July, is when you should be using jigs and heavy spin rigs, and sometimes crank baits when the northerns are really active and they have moved up shallower and are suspending off of the weedbeds. That is, sometimes they suspend in six to eight feet of water over fifteen feet of water. This is when a crank bait works really well.

Incidentally, those are the three main lures I use for northern fishing: crank baits, spin rigs, and jigs.

When is the next seasonal change?

Koep: The next change is about mid-August. This is the time of the year that jig fishermen have a hard time catching northerns. Also, this is the time of the year when you should be making longer casts and working your lure faster, not letting the jig hit the bottom. Keep it out of the weeds, and work it off of the bottom when the jig is close to the boat.

And don't hesitate to use the really big baits since during this period the bigger northerns will often be in shallower water.

What is the next seasonal change we should be concerned with?

Koep: After the lake has turned over. During this fall period the fish could be anywhere since the water temperature is the same at all depths in the lake. Ideally, you should look for a feeding flat where the wind has been blowing onto it for maybe a few days. Fish the top first and then the edge of it.

You can use the same methods of presentation that you would use in the spring.

I'd like your comments on presentation regarding specific pieces of structure. Let's start with rocks.

Koep: I like to fish rocks just off of the bottom so I don't get hung up too often. Generally, when I fish rocky areas, I fish deep rocks and use a vertical method of presentation.

If I'm casting and the lure hits bottom, I immediately give it a good snap to keep it from getting hung up in the rocks.

Let's go on to points.

Koep: Be sure to fish all sides of a point since northerns aren't as particular as bass or walleyes are as to where they will locate on a point. Northerns will roam more.

Start out by fishing points shallow with a crank bait and if nothing is happening, go back over the point with a jig and minnow or even a spinner bait.

How about breaks?

Koep: When fishing breaks, look for something different. An irregularity that will give northerns an advantage in ambushing forage fish is where they will tend to be located. Corners or pockets can be the best spots on breaks.

Comment on presentation when fishing a flat.

Koep: I really like to fish big flats. I like to use a crank bait on big flats, but if there is a definite weed edge, I will use a jig or a spin rig.

What's special about flats?

Koep: Big feeding flats are where you are most likely to find big northerns. Stay in twelve feet of water and cast up onto the flat.

How about timber?

Koep: If you find a tree laying in the water, chances are you will find a northern laying by it if it is a lake with little weed growth. A spinner bait would be my first choice to catch that fish.

But most Minnesota lakes have enough weed growth so you won't find northerns relating to timber very often. And if there are northerns relating to timber in a Minnesota lake, they are probably small ones.

In most Minnesota lakes northerns relate to reeds, breakline weeds, or feeding flats.

Does your presentation change when fishing clear water -vs- stained water lakes?

Koep: My presentation doesn't change much, but I do like to use a darker lure in darker water and vice versa. Yellow is a good color in clear water lakes. But I still use both dark and light in clear and stained water, and they will both take fish.

On a clear water lake if the fish aren't too active, I will use lighter line. If northerns are active on a clear water lake, your line size isn't too important. But when they are finicky, you might have to use light line and live bait.

Some people feel it's important to make longer casts when fishing in clear water. I don't. As far as I'm concerned, that is not important. The length of your cast should be determined by how sharp of a break you are fishing; that is, how far do I have to cast to stay away from the weedline to fish it effectively.

Do you feel that bigger lures attract bigger fish?

Koep: Yes. But I do not always use a big lure. If I'm fishing for big northerns, I like to use a big Suick—a ten incher. I have had some real good luck fishing for big northerns on Leech Lake and Lake Winnibigoshish using big Suicks.

Also a big sucker minnow (an eight to ten incher), especially in the winter, will work well for catching big northerns. They might look big as far as bait goes, but even a three or four pound northern can handle a sucker minnow that size. Actually, an eight to ten inch sucker minnow wouldn't even be a snack for a state record northern.

Comment on cold water/small lure theory.

Koep: That smaller lure in colder water theory doesn't really apply to northerns. Other fish yes.

The main thing to change in your presentation for northerns in cold water is to work your lure slower and switch to live bait.

Comment on lures as to color and size.

Koep: Generally, for quantity of fish people use lures that are too large. Smaller lures will hook more northerns. Not necessarily big northerns, just more of them. And larger lures are harder to present in a natural manner.

The color I prefer in jigs is yellow or black. And I usually do not use a weed guard on a jig because it can cause problems in setting the hook.

How does your lure choice vary with the seasons?

Koep: The lure you can get down in front of a northern is the one they are going to bite. You've got to follow the northern down into deeper water as the season progresses and then back up into shallower water later in the season.

Base your choice of lures on the time of the year or, more specifically, the period of the year that the lake is in. That's your gauge. Pick the lure that you can most efficiently present at the depth you want to fish. And to be a consistently successful fisherman, you must be a versatile fisherman. When the fish want something different, give it to them.

We haven't really discussed bobber fishing for northerns.

Koep: If you've got the time, bobber fishing is great. It isn't that much work, and it can be really productive. You have to have good boat control so you can have good control of where your bait is. Then mainly it's a game of patience.

Where's the best place to bobber fish?

Koep: Bobber fish right off of the weedline in ten to fifteen feet of water perhaps using a sucker minnow six to eight feet down. Keeping your sucker minnow or shiner four feet off of the bottom seems to work best. Also in bobber fishing, the bigger your sucker minnow or shiner is, the better.

Is there anyway to know for sure when you should set the hook when you're bobber fishing with live bait?

Koep: It depends on how big the fish is. A big northern can suck down a big sucker minnow very quickly.

A northern will hit a sucker minnow sideways, and swim with it for awhile before he releases his bite to turn it around which enables him to swallow it. They will hold it until the minnow is numb before they maneuver it around in their mouth so they can swallow it head first. If you are using dead bait, they will swallow it sooner; so you can set the hook sooner. Usually when using live bait, the longer you hold off on the hook set, the better.

When I'm using twelve pound test line with a leader, if the fish isn't too close to me, I'll set the hook as hard as I can. If I'm not using a leader, I tend to set the hook real lightly. And if the fish hits really close to the boat, I don't even set the hook at all. I just hold the line tight and pull back, and the northern will set the hook himself.

How do you land a big fish?

Koep: Many people seem to want to land the fish too soon, and they reel it right up to the tip of their rod. I tell my customers to keep their rod tip high with the line tight and do not try to force the fish in.

And if the northern is over eight or ten pounds, I will club him instead of netting him, and then grab him by the eyes and lift him into the boat. Of course, I wouldn't club a fish I didn't intend to keep.

Can you pattern fish for northerns?

Koep: Yes you can but with northerns depth is not always a major variable like it is with many species of fish. If I find northerns on rocks in shallow water, I also can find them on rocks in deep water. If you find them on rocks in eight feet of water, usually you will find them on rocks in twenty feet of water, for example.

A pattern that works well on many lakes is to use a jig and minnow or a spin rig and minnow while keeping your boat in fifteen feet of water letting it drift in or backtroll against the wind up along the edge of a bar. Real slowly. Slowly enough so that you can lift the jig off of the bottom, and it will hit bottom again. And the more you pop your jigs the better they will work. Of course, this pattern doesn't work on all lakes.

And when fishing dirty water lakes, noise becomes a factor in a pattern. With crank baits, use the kind with rattles in them.

Can a fisherman turn on inactive fish?

Koep: Yes. In fact, when I started fishing, I would use a jig and minnow combination and if that didn't work, I would put on a Bomber crank bait and troll through the same area and many times that would produce fish.

That is, sometimes they wouldn't touch a jig and minnow, but they would really turn on with a different presentation. What we're talking about here is what we touched on earlier—versatility in presentation. It's very important.

I think this is an important aspect of fishing (fishing inactive fish). I'd like to hear more about it.

Koep: First of all, there are always fish biting somewhere. If they are not biting on the lake I'm on and I've worked several different locational and presentational patterns, I will move to another lake. I try to figure out which lake will be productive based on the time of the year it is or, that is, what stage a given lake is in.

I will try a lake in a different stage—a smaller lake if I've had bad luck on a large lake like Gull Lake. The fish in a lake in a different stage will be in a different mood. They go on feeding sprees at different times of the year because of the different ecological systems that they live in.

The key can be to find the right lake at the right time. For instance, every lake in the Brainerd area has good fish in it; the trick is to go to the right lake at the right time and use the right presentation.

What you have to remember is, just because it is June twenty-first (the first day of summer) doesn't mean it's the first day of summer on a given lake. That lake could be well into its summer season, or it might be a couple of weeks before its summer season begins. The main determinate in determining what season a lake is in is water temperature. A shallow, dirty water lake will begin its summer period well before a deep, clear water lake will because it warms up faster.

Do you feel lures imitate natural bait?

Koep: I'm not sure. But the short erratic jerks you make with your lure can really turn fish on. On the way down give it a twitch, and sometimes I will give it six or seven twitches as the lure is sinking. Or you can pop the jig so it dances across the bottom which really works well with power-head jigs. Then the northerns will come along and scoop it up off of the bottom. I've seen them do that in shallow water.

Northerns are so quick and they turn their heads the moment they strike and with their razor sharp teeth many times your jig is gone.

When you troll, what method of presentation do you prefer?

Koep: I prefer to backtroll very, very slowly, and when trolling, never cast your lure out while the boat is moving. Stop the boat, drop your lure, and start trolling when the lure is on the bottom. Keep the lure close to the boat not letting the lure hit or drag on the bottom. You'll know if you are jigging right, if when your rod is at its lowest point, the lure is coming in contact with the bottom. And one of the biggest mistakes many people make is letting out too much line. If you are doing it properly, your lure should almost be right underneath the boat. In fact, the lure of the person who is in the front of the boat should be right underneath the person sitting in the back of the boat. That's when you are forward trolling.

What are the best lures or rigs for trolling?

Koep: I like spin rigs and jigs. The best color in jigs is yellow, and in spin rigs I like a white and red combination or a solid green color. As for size, you will probably need at least a three-eighths ounce jig.

What is the best presentation to catch a lunker northern?

Koep: Well, first of all, you need to fish big waters like Leech Lake and Lake Winnibigoshish, etc. I use all big bucktails and big Suicks. And even in smaller lakes, I would use a very big lure if I were after lunker northerns.

Fish for a big northern the way you would fish for a big muskie. Eddy baits will also produce big northerns. But the average fisherman isn't going to have the patience or the endurance necessary to throw those big baits all day.

A lot of fishermen don't believe it, but it's harder to catch a big northern than it is to catch a big muskie. A trophy northern is the hardest fish to catch since there just aren't very many northerns over twenty-five pounds. In fact, there are probably more muskies over thirty pounds in Minnesota than there are twenty pound northerns.

Comment on lure retrieve.

Koep: With a spin rig you should jerk it off of the bottom and then let it flutter down. When it's on the bottom, give the lure a good hard jerk. Remember when using spin rigs or jigs, ninety percent of the hits you get will be when the lure is dropping. And prolong your drop by using the smallest jig you can get by with so that the jig is in the northern's sight range as long as possible. Otherwise it will shoot by him into the weeds and he won't have a very good chance to grab it.

I prefer a quarter ounce jig with a good sized minnow on it because it will just float down slowly, and the fish will have time to get a good look at it. It's really important not to use too heavy of a jig. Of course, the heavier jigs have their place too; you usually need those when you are jigging in windy weather.

With crank baits and spinner baits, I start out with a slow retrieve in the spring and speed up my retrieve throughout the summer. Then as fall approaches, I slow my retrieve down again.

When I use jigs, I use a slow retrieve all year long. With crank baits I use a long cast in the summer and crank it as fast as I can. And if you are fishing a sharp break, you will need a diving crank bait. Sometimes it is preferable to cast a crank bait parallel to the break working the lure along the edge. And you can troll the edges with a crank bait, too. But with that method you will probably get more bass than northerns.

What is the most common mistake fishermen make with regards to presentation for northerns?

Koep: Fishing too fast which is a result of poor boat control. Usually they are trolling in a forward gear rather than backtrolling. There is no easy way you can stay on a bar trolling forward. The best way to troll is with an electric motor or backtrolling with your gas motor.

If you are drift fishing and you find you are drifting too fast, shift your motor in and out of reverse since this will slow down your drift. And you can of course use an electric trolling motor to aid you in drift fishing. Remember you must fish slowly enough so that you can watch your locator and fish at the same time.

Comment on boat control in the wind.

Koep: The easiest way for a beginner to control his boat is to fish the bars where the wind is blowing along the edge. Fish as far down as you can and then back your boat into the wind. Work up against the wind along the edge of the bar. You try to keep the boat pretty much stationary while casting or vertical jigging. Even in the summer months when your presentation changes, you still want to maintain that slow rate of movement with your boat. Sometimes, of course, you'll need to speed troll for them. That's the toughest thing to do in fishing—speed troll and stay on structure. In fact, you almost have to have someone else running the boat while the others are fishing. Speed trolling and staying on structure is enough to do without trying to fish at the same time. But don't limit yourself too much since there are ways to overcome wind problems.

If you are fishing with four people in your boat, you are probably better off drifting with the wind otherwise you will spend a lot of time untangling your lines.

WEATHER AND BIOLOGICAL FACTORS AFFECTING NORTHERNS

How does hot weather affect fishing for northerns?

Koep: Fishing for northerns is the best when it's hot, still, and clear as a bell which is contrary to what most fishermen believe. Also, you don't always have to fish a dark colored lake when the sky is clear either. Sometimes northerns are active on a given lake no matter what the conditions are.

Comment on sky conditions.

Koep: Usually during a clear sky condition I do try to fish lakes with dark colored water and a shallow lake, if possible. But if you are fishing a lake with clear water during clear sky conditions, you have to fish deeper using a spin rig method or vertical jigging techniques.

If I'm fishing a dirty water lake during clear sky conditions, I like to throw crank baits. And when you notice that northerns are following your lure but not striking it, use muskie techniques to catch them—figure eight-ing, etc. Many people don't realize that northerns will follow their lure the way a muskie will since they aren't watching for that behavior.

How about overcast skies?

Koep: Then the opposite is true. Generally, I like to fish a clear water lake during overcast skies, and I use a Mepps spinner, for example, especially if a cold front is coming in. When a cold front is approaching, the big fish move up shallow to feed before they are driven deep by the storm. This is when I switch to big baits because this is my best opportunity to catch a big northern. With jigs, for instance, I would use at least a half ouncer.

Does rain turn northerns on?

Koep: It doesn't seem to affect them much at all. I've had good luck before, after, and during a rain.

Do you like to fish in the fog?

Koep: Super! I love to fish in the fog. I fish shallow water with crank baits and spinner baits, and the northerns really seem to get active when it's foggy.

How does your presentation change during a cold front?

Koep: I tend to use lighter line, go to live bait, and use a much slower retrieve. During cold fronts it is more important to fish thoroughly than it is to try to cover a lot of water. Then if you find one active fish, you will usually find more that are active in that same area.

Work the points real thoroughly and if the northerns are biting really slow, I would suggest that you try fishing for another species of fish because cold fronts can spoil a day's fishing, even for the best fishermen.

How do warm fronts affect fishing for northerns?

Koep: That's the best fishing. Also that is the best time to work on your versatility in presentation. Try everything.

How does a lightning storm affect northerns?

Koep: Northerns are turned on just before and during a lightning storm. After it's over, they seem to be turned off. Of course, I try not to fish during a lightning storm; it is just too dangerous. But I must admit I hate to leave a lake when a lightning storm is approaching since it is during this condition that I have had some of my best fishing.

When I was about fifteen years old, I was making a run from Nisswa Lake to Grassy Point on Gull Lake where my dad had located a good school of walleyes. There were only two or three other boats on the lake. My friend and I started fishing Grassy Point, and soon we caught one walleye and then they started biting better and better.

By the time we had four or five we noticed that a huge, dark cloud bank was coming toward us. The fish must be biting because of the approaching storm we thought. As the storm got closer and closer, the walleyes were biting better and better.

Soon we had eight or nine. They would bite as soon as we could get our lines back in the water. By this time the storm was approaching very, very rapidly. Of course, we didn't want to leave until we had caught our limit, but the storm was right on us.

All of a sudden the wind switched directions while my friend had another bite, and it almost blew my boat over.

Later we found out it was a tornado that had come through the area. After almost being capsized, we headed for shore and it started hailing.

Well, by this time my dad was very worried since he knew we were out there fishing. He was phoning all over and driving around the lake looking for us. We had gone to another friend's house for shelter. When my dad found us, we were eating cookies and drinking milk.

Needless to say, since I hadn't contacted my dad to let him know we were all right, he wasn't in any mood to compliment us on our fine catch of walleyes. Actually, he was very angry with me for not coming off of the lake sooner.

That night at supper he asked if I had learned anything today about fishing. Of course, he expected me to say that I had learned that I should get off of the lake sooner when a storm is approaching.

But, I said, fish sure bite good before a storm hits. Although my answer didn't please him, I did notice a little smile on his face.

What are your thoughts about acid rain?

Koep: I certainly hope they stop it before it does any more damage. I was up in the Duluth area recently, and we checked the pH level in some of the lakes and it was very, very poor. The lakes looked dead and even smelled funny.

Do you use a pH meter to locate fish?

Koep: No I don't. In the spring I use a temperature gauge, but I don't even use that the rest of the year.

How does the barometric pressure affect fishing?

Koep: I like fishing a rising barometer. That seems to do the thing. It gets me excited anyway. All of the guides I know get excited when the barometer is rising, and they like to get out fishing before it starts to drop.

Do you think moon phases affect fishing?

Koep: It seems like within a day or two of the full moon we always had the big walleyes brought into my dad's store. That is, three days before and three days after a full moon.

I think you could follow the moon phase theory for successful walleye fishing, but not as much for northern fishing. Although it may well work for northerns as well, I personally haven't been able to document it.

How about the major and minor periods on the solunar tables that we see published in sporting magazines and newspapers?

Koep: Sometimes it seems to coincide and other times it doesn't. I certainly wouldn't go or not go fishing because of what those tables said.

How does the thermocline affect northerns?

Koep: I never fish below the thermocline, and it's tough fishing when northerns suspend on the thermocline. But much of the time most of the big northerns are suspended right at the thermocline which means there is a lot of deep water to cover.

What method of presentation would you use for fishing those big northerns that are suspended on the thermocline?

Koep: We've tried using many methods including using downriggers, but, as of yet, we haven't had much luck. The guy that figures out how to fish those lunkers suspended on the thermocline will catch many trophy fish.

Comment on fall turnover period.

Koep: That's when the colder water moves to the top of the lake, and the warmer water which is on top goes down. The water mixes creating the same water temperature from the surface to the bottom of the lake.

Turnover is also the time of the year when the dead weeds float up to the surface and the tullibees die.

After the fall turnover, the fish could be anywhere and you should fish old spots over again with anything from a crank bait, a jig and a minnow, to a Mepps spinner since northerns could be at any depth in the lake.

EQUIPMENT AND TACKLE FOR NORTHERN FISHING

What are your favorite lures for northern fishing?

Koep: Although I'm mainly a jig or a spin rig fisherman, my favorite lure is a Lindy rig. I also use a lot of crank baits, and I prefer the Bill Norman Little N or the Fat Raps by Rapala.

We haven't covered color and size of crank baits.

Koep: My favorite colors for crank baits are chartreuse, crawdad, and the baby bass color, and I prefer to use the medium size in both of those crank baits.

Do you ever topwater fish for northerns?

Koep: A spinner bait is the closest I come to topwater fishing for northerns.

Do you modify your lures?

Koep: Some I do. Crank baits you have to tune, of course. If you have the time, you should sharpen your hooks with a hand file to get a good sharp point all the way back to the barb.

What type of rods do you prefer for fishing for northerns?

Koep: Generally I use a five and a half foot bait caster with a stiff action. When I fish an ultralight, I use a Fenwick graphite spinning rod.

What type of reels do you use?

Koep: I like Ambassadeur bait casting reels, and lately I've been using Shimanos because they are so smooth. I use what works best since I have my choice; that is, I don't rep for any companies.

How tightly do you set the drag on your reels?

Koep: You must set it differently for each rod since each rod is different. Have someone hold the line or tie it to something and simulate setting the hook. The drag should give a litte, but not too much.

And when you are putting line on your reel, put it on tight.

Do you use swivels?

Koep: The more equipment you put on, the less chance you have of getting a strike. Most of the time I don't even use leaders when I'm fishing for northerns.

Do you have any preference in locators?

Koep: I use the Lowrance 2230 since it's a super model, and I like the thirty foot scale because it's easier to read. The graph I use is the Lowrance X-15.

The depth finder is the most important tool you will use in fishing. If you don't have one or yours is not working, you can cast a heavy jig to find the right depth. If you are getting too many weeds, you are fishing too shallow. If you aren't getting any weeds on the jig, you are fishing too deep. Also keep track of how much time it takes for your jig to hit bottom.

What kind of boat do you use?

Koep: Currently I'm using an Alumacraft Backtroller which I like very much. But this year Crestliner has a new boat out that I'm interested in.

What type of motor do you prefer?

Koep: I use a fifty horsepower Mercury. Actually, that's about the only motor that the guides are using these days or the fifty Mariner which is the same motor.

How about your trolling motor?

Koep: I use a Minn Kota.

MISCELLANEOUS INFORMATION ABOUT NORTHERN FISHING

I understand that you have guided for some national celebrities.

Koep: Mac Davis, the singer and movie star, would probably be the most famous person that I have ever guided. When he's up, we fish for northerns because he likes the action and the fight. I take him to backwoods lakes because he likes to relax and he likes the seclusion. He usually comes in the middle of July which is a super time for northern fishing. And when he's been here, we've always had good fishing.

Last year we fished on Bass Lake, and the first year he was here we caught over seventy northerns and twenty bass. The next year we did the same thing. The third year he came around the fourth of July and there were thousands of people on the lakes so we didn't do as well, but he did

get a nine pound northern, and I caught a five pound six ounce bass. It was just a little too early for good northern activity.

Is Mac Davis a good fisherman?

Koep: Yes he is. And he's a very persistent fisherman who likes to cast and set the hook hard so northern fishing is a good choice for him. He loves fishing; he's a very good fisherman.

Is night fishing for northerns productive?

Koep: It's usually not too good since northerns aren't often active at night. Generally, it's believed that the northern, unlike some other game fish, is not very active at night.

What is the best type of lake to fish for northerns?

Koep: I like a smaller lake with clear water and a lot of weed growth with a defined weed edge. Now many of these lakes aren't hot for northerns more than a couple of weeks a year, but when they are on, there's guaranteed good fishing.

In some of those lakes you can catch fifty to sixty good sized northerns in a half a day.

How big is good sized?

Koep: From three to five pounds.

Do you practice and encourage "catch and release"?

Koep: It is very important that I encourage all of my customers to practice "catch and release". If you are not going to eat them, release them. Unless it's a fish you want to mount.

I think "catch and release" is especially important with bass. I'm not sure it is as important with walleyes since the D.N.R. stocks thousands and thousands of them every year even in the shallow lakes that freeze out every couple of years or so. They wouldn't be stocking them in those shallow lakes if they didn't have plenty of fry.

But if you are going to keep and eat walleyes, I would suggest that you don't keep any under thirteen inches and with bass don't keep any under fourteen inches.

Let me tell you a story that is sort of a "catch and release" story.

A few years ago a friend of mine and I went to Kego Lake up in the Fifty Lakes area to fish for bass. We fished for about an hour driving around the whole lake. The lake is quite small. It was shallow, and I couldn't find any good weedbeds, and the ones that I did find were really scummy. We said, to heck with this lake and started to leave. On our way in I hit something with my motor. Since I wasn't watching my locator I didn't know how deep the water was. So I turned around and went back, only to realize we had just gone over a six foot deep sunken island.

So I positioned the boat and cast a crank bait up onto that sunken island. About half way back to the boat the crank bait stopped, and then my line broke. Then I tied on the same kind of crank bait, and in twelve consecutive casts I caught twelve bass in the three to five pound range. Actually, I still think I had hit a bass with my motor.

The guy that I was fishing with was using the same crank bait in a different color and he couldn't boat a fish. When he went to live bait, he started catching them. I was using a Bill Norman's Little N in the baby bass color, and he tried the same lure in several other colors, but they just wouldn't hit 'em.

The mistake I made was telling people about the lake who weren't "catch and release" fishermen. If I hadn't told those people or if I had only told "catch and release" fishermen, that lake today would still be a great bass lake to fish. That was one of the best bass catches I had ever had, and today the bass on that lake are far and few between.

Do you think there will ever be a new state record northern caught?

Koep: Well, I've never seen the monsters that others have reported seeing. I can't understand how they keep breaking that heavy line. This summer, for example, I landed a fourteen pound six ounce northern on a fly rod with six pound test line.

There are probably a few monsters swimming around, but I don't think people who are going after these lunkers are using large enough bait. I mean a state record northern is probably eating a five pound sucker for lunch. It's going to take a lot of luck to boat a fish that size, too.

How much does it cost to hire you or one of the other guides that work out of your father's bait store? (Marv Koep's Bait and Tackle Store, Nisswa, Minnesota.)

Koep: The price for two people for a half a day is seventy dollars and that includes everything: rods, reels, bait, rain gear, etc. And for a full day's fishing it's one hundred and forty dollars. If there are three people in a party, it's ninety dollars for a half a day and one hundred eighty dollars for a full day.

How much luck is involved in fishing?

Koep: Luck plays a large part, but it's not all luck. The guy who knows where to fish and how to fish, of course, is going to have a lot better chance of catching fish, but not necessarily the biggest fish. On a given day luck can be everything, but over a period of time, knowledge will win out easily.

What is the biggest northern that you've ever caught in Minnesota?

Koep: A fourteen pound six ouncer that I caught on Dolney Lake near Brainerd. It is a lake with a past reputation for many four to eight pound northerns.

I was using a fly rod with a spinning reel with six pound test line and a quarter ounce sinker and a four inch chub with a twenty inch leader and a small hook. It was a walleye rig.

Lake Dolney is really weedy so I had to keep the bait off of the bottom. We got to a corner with a good drop on it and suddenly my lure stopped. I thought I had a little one. Finally I set the hook and after fighting him for five minutes or so, the fish took off. Luckily I had the reel set on back reel so I could quickly give him line when he ran. He ran about sixty yards into five feet of water.

My reel was just spinning off line. Then he swam around in five feet of water for a long time. I couldn't bring him back to the boat so I drove the boat to him. Then he took off again, so I had to follow him.

Finally he was in deep water again and then suddenly he was up next to the boat and he didn't move. I couldn't believe the size of that fish.

One of the people I was guiding at the time lifted it into the boat for me. He was just barely hooked. As it turned out, it was very close to a line class record.

This fish was caught in the month of August, and it was longer than a nineteen pounder I had compared it to that was brought into my dad's store the same day. It was a long, skinny fish, but it did look healthy.

Lake Dolney is dying off so I suppose he didn't have a good choice of food or he wouldn't have hit that little chub minnow I had on my hook.

The same day that I had caught that fourteen pound six ouncer there was a big celebrity tournament on Gull Lake. No one had done very well in this tournament, and when I was talking to some of the pros that had fished the tournament, I told them that I had caught that fish on Gull Lake which I hadn't, but it was fun to kid them.

What is the best day's fishing for northerns that you've ever had in Minnesota?

Koep: It was the first year Northern's, Inc. held their tournament on Gull Lake. It was a three day tournament, and I was fishing with my dad, and we were using big bucktails. Double blade bucktails about fourteen inches long with three sets of treble hooks. The lures were so big you had to shake the water out of them before you casted otherwise, with all that water in them, they would have been very difficult to cast.

We didn't have to cast very far since it was after fall turnover, and the big northerns were in six to eight feet of water. We were fishing a shallow weedbed which was about eight feet deep with patches of cabbage. We were on the inside in eight feet of water casting to the outer edges into about ten feet of water.

That day I caught two northerns. One weighed eleven pounds twelve ounces, and the other one weighed ten pounds four ounces. And the very next morning I went out and caught one that weighed ten pounds even.

I got second place for the largest stringer of northerns and Gary Roach got first place. First place paid three hundred dollars, and for second place I received nothing.

Gary felt sorry for me so he gave me seventy-five dollars out of his winnings. I really thought that was nice of him.

What is your favorite lake in Minnesota?

Koep: I like Gull Lake because it is an all-around lake. Good bass, good northerns, good walleyes, and good panfish. That's my idea of fun fishing—going to a lake where you can catch many species of fish.

What's special about Minnesota fishing?

Koep: The variety. The best days I've ever had are those days when I've caught several walleyes, several bass, a few northerns, and some sunfish and crappies. And that can happen on many Minnesota lakes frequently. Plus the next day you can go out and fish for muskies. Where else could you do that?

Chapter 4

TED CAPRA
ON LARGEMOUTH BASS

In fishing circles when the discussion turns to tournament fishing, Ted Capra's name, no doubt, will be mentioned frequently since he is the most experienced tournament fisherman in Minnesota and may well have fished as many tournaments as any other angler in the country today. In a typical year Ted might fish as many as twenty-five money tournaments throughout the country, and he has been doing that from the beginning of tournament fishing in Minnesota.

"The best tournament fishermen," according to Ted, "are not the fellows who win a big tournament and then don't even come close for the next three or four years." Consistency is what tournament fishermen respect. The contestant who always brings in a good stringer of fish is the fisherman who commands the most respect among tournament regulars. And it's a rare tournament when Ted Capra doesn't finish high in the standings which can be witnessed by the hundred or more trophies he has earned fishing money tournaments. As one tournament veteran put it, "Even when it's near the end of the weigh-in, and I've got a good lead, I'm never comfortable with that lead until Capra has weighed in."

To begin with, Ted developed a great love for the out-of-doors and fishing in particular by accompanying his father on fishing trips when he was young. From the time Ted was eight years old until he was in his late teens, he and his father would spend many spring and summer weekends walleye fishing on Lake Mille Lacs. In the springtime they would fish the north end of Lake Mille Lacs using shiners, and then during the summer they would go out on launches fishing with spinners tipped with night crawlers.

These weekend trips were the beginning of Ted's long love affair with fishing. But as Ted grew older, his love for fishing became an obsession. "It got so bad," Ted said, "I had to quit my job and get into the fishing industry full-time because I couldn't make a living any other way. All I wanted to do was to go fishing all of the time. And it's still that way; the more I fish, the more I want to fish. I call myself a fish-a-holic."

When Ted left his job, he became a fishing guide and a manufacturer's representative for fishing tackle and equipment companies; these new occupations suited him well. Today he represents Penn reels, Si-Tex depth finders and graphs, B & M boat seats, Culprit plastic worms, Kunnan rods, and Champion bass boats.

Initially, Ted became well known as a muskie fisherman and a muskie guide. Then he discovered the thrills of largemouth bass fishing, and soon he switched his interests to bass fishing and to fishing bass tournaments. The largemouth bass, Ted feels, is a sport fish and not something for the supper table.

Although his son Tony, who is a frequent team tournament partner of Ted's, says his father is "very intense and competitive when fishing tournaments," Ted maintains he enters tournaments more for what he can learn about fishing than he does to compete with other fishermen. "What I'm out there doing," Ted said, "is trying to outsmart the fish. But I do have to admit that it is somewhat of an ego trip that I can outsmart those fish more often than most other fishermen can."

Every so often, in an attempt to avoid fishing burn-out, there are days when he decides that he is not going to go fishing or even talk about fishing or, for that matter, do anything that is fishing related. Then the phone rings. It's a fishing buddy who says the fish are really goin', come on up. Well, like the alcoholic who always has a bottle stashed, Ted's bassin' rig is always nearby and ready—so in a few minutes it's goodbye to a day's solitude, and he's gone fishing again.

LARGEMOUTH BASS BEHAVIOR

What is the most important aspect of the largemouth basses behavior?

Capra: From the fisherman's point of view, you have to realize that the largemouth basses behavior changes from season to season. In the springtime, for instance, their behavior is mostly determined by the spawning cycle. They've got one thing on their mind, and that's spawning.

Also, it is important to remember that the largemouth bass is a predator fish that ambushes its prey. So through most of the year, other than the spawning season, they hide behind or under some form of cover and then dart out and attempt to ambush forage that swims near them.

We know that the largemouth bass is a schooling fish. Do they school by size?

Capra: To a point they school by size. It varies. The half pound to a pound and a quarter size bass definitely school by size. Then when you get into two-plus-pound bass, often there are three and four pounders schooled with the two pounders. And if you are fishing a school of two and a half pounders, you will occasionally catch a five pounder schooled with them. But the largemouth bass that are over five pounds in Minnesota lakes are usually loners and spend most of their time in shallow water. In fact, there are lots of big bass holding in shallow water slop.

What motivates a largemouth bass to strike a lure?

Capra: Hunger, without a doubt, plays the most important part in a fish striking a lure, but, I think, reflex plays a part, too. It's like a dog snapping at someone who has stepped on his tail. He probably didn't really intend to bite you, but out of surprise he did. Well, I think that happens with fish, too.

This striking out of reflex as opposed to striking out of hunger may be especially true when bass hit crank baits, spinner baits, or other fast moving lures—the element of surprise. They're not really hungry, but they hit your lure anyway. It's a reflex action.

The only exception to this may be during the springtime. A bass might strike a lure because of an instinct to protect his young in the nest. In the springtime you can see them pick up a plastic worm, for example, and move it out of their spawning bed. This isn't feeding or reflex. I've thrown live salamanders on their spawning beds, and they will attack it and kill it and then remove it from their nest without eating it.

What do you do when you know you are on a school of bass and they are in a negative mood?

Capra: Well, that can be very difficult. There are times when you locate a school of fifty to a hundred bass, and you might only be able to catch a few.

I've had situations where I know I've located a large school of bass and only been able to take a few, so I will leave and come back later. A half an hour or so later. When you return, you usually can catch a few more, or you may find that they all have become aggressive.

But when you are fishing a school of negative bass, you are lucky to catch a few of them. Truly negative fish are very hard to catch.

You can tell when the fish are really aggressive if when you are reeling one in, two or three more of them are trying to get the lure away from the one you've hooked. This is a situation where you should really be able to capitalize on those fish.

What do you do when they are not aggressive?

Capra: When they are negative, it's time to really work on your presentation. If you get one of them on a plastic worm, then try a jig and a pig, etc., and you may get a few more. Here's where you have to be versatile to catch fish. And don't be lazy; don't say I've caught fish on a particular lure and they aren't hitting on something else. I believe change plays a large part in successful fishing especially if the fish are in a negative mood.

Are you saying that changing lures can be effective even on the same school of fish?

Capra: Yes. What triggers one fish to strike, might not trigger another to strike. Even just changing the color of the worm that you are using can be productive.

In one tournament my partner and I fished an area of the lake very thoroughly with worms and then went back through that same area with a different colored worm and took some more fish. Then we changed to a jig and pig and caught a few more fish. Then we tried crank baits and got one more. Versatility is very, very important.

Why are some fish active and others are not?

Capra: If I knew, I'd be a lot better fisherman than I am. It might be as simple as they just prefer to feed at different times of the day. People are that way; why not fish?

No one has ever really figured out why. That's why trial and error is still the best way to determine what method of fishing will work the best on any given day.

For years and even today many fishermen believe that the walleyes teeth fell out during dog days, etc. Comment on superstitions about fish and fishing.

Capra: Most of those notions have no facts to back them up; therefore, they are myths. The way I look at it is that fish have to eat almost every day, if not every day, especially in the summertime when their metabolism is high.

When you hear that "dog days" are here so the fish aren't biting, it's absolutely ridiculous. Fish eat every day.

Anytime that you are on the water and you are not catching fish, you are doing something wrong because fish are biting everyday somewhere in the lake.

On every lake?

Capra: Yes. Tournaments have proved that. You take two hundred guys in a tournament and sometimes one hundred and seventy-five of them don't figure out how to catch fish, but twenty-five of them will figure it out. So tournaments have shown that some way or by using some method, fish can always be caught. Don't sit around making excuses why the fish aren't biting. Anybody can make excuses why the fish aren't biting; I like to hear why they are biting.

Guys like Gary Roach, Al Lindner, and Larry Bollig will almost always figure out how to catch fish. A cold front can come through and that old story about fish not biting after a cold front is ridiculous. Somebody will figure out how to catch them whether it's with little jigs and small worms or whatever. Just go out and try to figure it out.

Comment on the largemouth basses ability to smell and taste.

Capra: Are you referring to those fish scents on the market that are supposed to help you catch fish?

No. Not now. We'll get to that later.

Capra: Well, I don't think smell and taste are anything a bass fisherman should worry about too much. I feel, largemouth bass feed by sight and sound. And the dirtier the water is, the more important sound becomes in their feeding. Remember the largemouth bass is an ambush fish, and he doesn't have a lot of time to smell and taste his forage. Of course, if a bass hits something that is repulsive to his sense of smell or taste, he probably would spit it out after he struck it.

How highly developed is a basses memory? Specifically, do you think they remember certain lures they've been caught on?

Capra: I think what happens is that you eliminate certain fish that like certain lures, and that's why certain lures will run a course of popularity with fishermen. The only exception in largemouth bass fishing seems to be the plastic worm which, for some reason or another, remains productive year after year.

With crank baits you can eliminate the fish on a given lake that are prone to hit certain types or colors of crank baits. So the next time or, more likely, the next year when you go back to that lake, you may find that, that lure won't catch fish any longer. Then of course you'll have to switch lures. Or possibly just change to a different color lure.

So it's not just a marketing gimmick?

Capra: It is not a gimmick! It's a process of elimination. For example, on Lake Mille Lacs years ago a lure called the River Runt would take walleyes and a three or four inch flat fish type lure tipped with a night crawler would work very well, too. But those lures ran their course. What happened was, the uncaught walleyes were the walleyes who weren't turned on by those lures. But it runs in cycles because, believe it or not, the flat fish lures are again becoming a popular lure to take walleyes on in Lake Mille Lacs.

Do largemouth bass in Minnesota's lakes chase schools of bait fish the way bass chase schools of shad in southern waters?

Capra: If you find the sunfish, you've found the bass. Panfish that is, crappies included. Many times I've seen it happen where first you see little sunfish, and then you see the little bass, and then, all of a sudden, you'll see the big bass. I really believe that if you've found the sunfish, you've found the bass in most instances.

Comment on forage fish.

Capra: Crayfish and sunfish in certain lakes play an important role in the largemouth basses feeding. For the most part, if you are using crank baits without an orange or orangish colored belly in Minnesota lakes, you are using the wrong crank bait. I think that relates to the fact that largemouth bass feed heavily on crayfish and sunfish. These orange bellied crank baits are just much more productive than other colors are.

Are crayfish significant in the largemouth basses diet all year long or is it a seasonal variable?

Capra: The largemouth basses diet varies throughout the year, and crayfish are more of a summer forage for them. In the fall they feed more heavily on sucker minnows and shiners. And in the springtime they eat a little bit of everything including an occasional duckling.

Clarify the terms movement and migration.

Capra: Largemouth bass in Minnesota waters, for the most part, do not migrate. They make seasonal movements from the spawning area to the weedline and not from one end of the lake to the other end of the lake, etc.

Comment on largemouth bass movements during hot weather—"dog days"?

Capra: Hot weather fishing is the time to get into the shallows. Fish shallow water using Super Frogs, buzzer baits, etc. if you are looking for big bass. The hotter it is and the warmer the water is combined with little or no wind, the more active the largemouth bass will be in shallow water areas. If you've had three weeks of real hot weather and little or no wind with eighty-five degree water temperatures in the shallows, go in there with a buzzer bait and you can really tear up some four to five pound bass.

You know most fishermen think the opposite is true believing that during these hot, still conditions that largemouth bass will move to the weedline, but it works in reverse. Most of them will move into the shallow water areas.

Why?

Capra: There is a lack of oxygen out in the deep weed areas, and they move into the shallower weed areas, and we've noticed this happen on Lake Winnibigoshish with walleyes, muskies, and northerns, too. Long, hot days with no movement from the wind will move fish into shallow water because of a lack of oxygen in the deep water.

Also during this type of weather period these shallow areas will produce better later in the morning (10:00 a.m. – 11:00 a.m.) than they will early in the morning because as the day goes on, the oxygen content gets better in the shallows than it is early in the morning. At ten to eleven o'clock in the morning these areas are full of active, catchable bass. Then by six to seven o'clock in the evening the bass have left the shallow water areas.

In fact, in 1955 or so, hundreds of huge muskies were caught in shallow water. It has been called "The Great Muskie Rampage". The reason for this, so called rampage, was the lack of oxygen in the deep water areas of the lakes. They had moved into the shallow water where they were much more catchable. And this also happens with big bass under those conditions. 1955 was a very hot summer with long periods of little wind, but this situation occurs every year to some degree.

LOCATING LARGEMOUTH BASS

You've said that locating fish is the most important aspect of fishing. Let's discuss some of the locational variables beginning with weeds.

Capra: Weeds, to me, are the most important locational factor in a lake for largemouth bass. Weeds are their home. And you must realize that they prefer certain types of weeds. You know everybody talks about how important broadleaf cabbage and other types of cabbage weeds are to largemouth bass, but they aren't as important as most bass fishermen think they are. Take Lake Minnetonka for example, you can find broadleaf cabbage in certain areas of the lake, but you won't find many bass there. Lake Minnetonka bass prefer coontail type weeds. In fact, in Lake Minnetonka, bass, walleyes, and northerns prefer the coontail type weeds more than they do the cabbage type weeds.

So when a bass fisherman makes the general statement that largemouth bass prefer one type of weed to locate in over another type of weed, you can easily prove him wrong.

What I do is fish weedlines, and it is not important what type of weeds they are. It can be cambomba, cabbage, coontail, etc.

Run that by me again.

Capra: The type of weeds that largemouth bass prefer to locate in will vary from lake to lake. To say as many bass fishermen do: "That broadleaf cabbage is the preferred weed of the largemouth bass," is incorrect. It depends on the lake, as I explained in my Lake Minnetonka example.

But weeds in general are very important in bass fishing. And to be specific, it's the inside weedline and the outside weedline, and weedlines are an important locational factor throughout the whole year.

Is the inside weedline as important as the outside weedline?

Capra: Not as important, but important. Many times in July and August I have found bass on the inside weedline where there is clean sand from the inside weedline up to shore. And it is usually during the heat of the day that they will use the inside weedline. It's just completely opposite of what many bass fishermen think is true. People will fish shallow early in the morning, and sure they'll catch some fish early in the morning, but if you've got an inside weedline, coontail in particular, with a clean, sandy bottom near shore, you'll do better in the middle of the day.

Of course there are lakes and areas of lakes where there isn't an inside weedline. The weeds grow all the way up into six inches of water.

How important are bulrushes?

Capra: Bulrushes are really important, and again in the heat of the day the inside (shore side) of the bulrushes are better to fish than the outside. If there is room on the shore side to fish, usually the best bass fishing will be there. And the hotter the day is, the more the bass will locate on the inside of the bulrushes.

Now what I try to do even during a tournament is to fish deep water early in the morning and shallow water in the middle of the day. Also, when the deep weedline bass start slowing up, that's your clue as to when you should move to the inside weedline. Now don't get me wrong—the outside (lake side) of the bulrushes are good, too. Actually, you should fish bulrushes all the way around when you can.

Comment on docks and bridges with regards to locating bass.

Capra: Docks and bridges have produced fish for me all through the whole summer. Bridges are especially good early in the morning, and also channels with steel walls produce well before the boat traffic gets too heavy in those channels. In fact, all the bridges on Lake Minnetonka hold bass, and I've taken a lot of three, four, and five pounders off of those bridges.

Weeds, docks, and bridges are factors throughout the whole year. They have to be fished all the time.

On Lake Minnetonka those channels are a funnel for bait fish, and until the boat traffic gets heavy, the bass will stay there and feed.

Actually, I've probably caught more bass in channels and under bridges than any place else on Lake Minnetonka. Those bridges are almost always one of my early morning spots.

Why do many bass fishermen feel that docks with wooden legs are better when it comes to holding bass than the docks with steel legs are?

Capra: Wood will retain heat longer than steel and usually wooden legs are bigger than steel ones are so there's more for a bass to hide behind. But there are many docks in Minnesota's lakes that have steel legs that have produced many, many good bass. I wouldn't judge a dock by what kind of legs it had at all. Maybe early in the spring the wooden legs on docks with their heat retaining ability might be a small factor. You've probably noticed that in the spring the ice around stumps always melts first because stumps will retain heat.

No one can tell you why one dock is better than another dock. All that is, is trial and error. You can go along and fish twenty docks and not even get a strike, and then, all of a sudden, the twenty-first dock will hold three to four good bass.

How about the notion that the only good docks are the docks that have deep water adjacent to them?

Capra: I totally disagree with that. Pat Jeffers and Curt Johnson are probably the best dock fishermen I know, and they've even designed special rods for dock fishing and have talked me into buying one of those rods.

What do they do differently than the rest of us do?

Capra: They use long, stiff action rods and Penn spinning reels with the capacity to hold fourteen pound test line. With this heavy equipment, they just pull the fish out.

When they cast, they skip the lure way back up under the dock where the rest of us have never fished. You wouldn't be able to skip a lure up under those docks very far with a bait casting reel.

Also, they fish the docks that are not adjacent to deep water. They fish the four foot water docks, real shallow water docks that nobody else fishes, and they do very, very well at it. They can skip a jig fifteen to eighteen feet under a dock.

The other guys are hitting the tip of the docks, but they aren't getting back where there are more fish so they aren't really fishing the docks the way they should be fished. In this situation you're talking about catching fish that have never had a jig thrown to them. And to prove how successful this method is all you have to do is see where Jeffers and Johnson end up in tournaments. Usually very high in the standings if not winning.

Do largemouth bass often relate to rocks?

Capra: Rocks are only important to bass at certain times of the year.

I've got a friend on Lake Minnetonka that catches bass off of rocks in July, but he can't do it consistently. He's a big fish fisherman, and there are times in July and August when some big bass will relate to rocks. He catches a lot of four and five pound bass on rocks in the months of July and early August. Now this isn't a big concentration of bass on the rocks, just a few big fish.

My feeling is that rocks don't play an important role in largemouth bass fishing. In fact, if that friend of mine took the amount of time he spends fishing rocks and devoted that time to fishing weedlines and shallow water, he would catch a lot more fish and as many big ones, too. In general, rocks usually just aren't an important locational factor in locating largemouth bass in Minnesota lakes.

Comment on pH as a locational factor.

Capra: Nobody has figured out whether it's important or not. That's including the people who make and sell pH monitors. Now I do believe that pH is important, but I don't believe anybody has figured out why it is important.

I have a pH monitor on my boat, and I have one hell-of-a-time with it. I mean fish are supposed to die when it's down to four, or there about, and yet I'm catching fish in that water.

You've caught fish in water that registered three to four on your pH monitor?

Capra: Yes! And I've caught fish when the meter is reading ten. Also, I've fished areas where it registered seven to eight which is supposed to be the ideal range, and I haven't been able to catch a fish. There are just too many unanswered questions regarding pH. I've been using a pH monitor in Minnesota for five years, and I don't believe it has ever done me a bit of good.

Now down south the pH concept does seem to work. For example, they have areas of three to four miles long and there are pockets in these areas where the pH is better, and these areas of better pH do seem to produce better fishing.

How about the oxygen level as a locational factor?

Capra: I'm sure it's important to fish. I know it's important to fish, but to sit there with an oxygen meter and say the fish are here and they aren't there is ridiculous.

Sure, as we discussed earlier, we know that during certain times of the year there is a lack of oxygen in deep water which forces fish into shallow water. But, if you sit there playing with all those gauges and meters, you are not going to have enough time to fish. And not only that, you are going to psyche yourself out by reading instruction booklets which tell you that fish can't live in water with pH less than four, for instance. But you go by a spot that reads less than four on your pH monitor and you see people catching fish. Are your eyes lying because the magazine article or the instruction booklet says that there aren't supposed to be fish there? Do you believe the article, or do you believe your eyes?

Furthermore, I don't believe in lunar tables or most of that stuff. I just go fishing. Go fishing when you can and don't worry about all that pH monitor and oxygen meter stuff. I don't even read all those articles because I don't want somebody to tell me today isn't a good day to go fishing.

Comment on water temperature in locating bass.

Capra: As far as I'm concerned, water temperature plays an important role during the spawning season only. It's a springtime factor and a little bit in the fall also.

How does the thermocline affect location?

Capra: In Minnesota lakes the thermocline is just not a significant locational factor for the largemouth bass fisherman to worry about since you are usually fishing from the weedline in toward shore. Or you should be. That is, the thermocline is almost always deeper than the weedline, and there is almost never any reason to fish beyond the weedline.

How about locating bass during and after the fall turnover?

Capra: Fall turnover can be a real tough situation. The fish can be anyplace. A lot of bass fishermen won't agree, but, I feel, the weedline all the way up to ice-over seems to be the most important locational factor even during and after the fall turnover is complete. Those weeds can look dead on the tops, but the bottoms are still green and oxygen producing. Weeds don't just suddenly die; it's a slow process.

What do you do when you can't locate active/catchable fish?

Capra: Keep looking! Keep pounding and pounding that water. And truthfully there has been more than one day that I have been skunked or close to it.

A lot of times when you are fishing for largemouth bass, you'll fish all morning and sometimes into the afternoon before you really get into them, and that makes the whole day worthwhile. And this is especially true in the spring when often it takes the heat of the day to make the fish more active.

What is the best method to eliminate unproductive water in a lake? Especially a lake that is new to you.

Capra: Eliminating unproductive, or dead water as we call it, would be a different process in the spring than it would be in the summer or fall.

In the spring you first look for the warmest bays. This time of the year I don't even bother with the main body of water on a lake. Actually, locating largemouth bass in the spring is relatively easy since you are looking for the spawning areas. Try to locate the warm spawning areas and use plastic worms and spinner baits which will work very well. Also, channels coming into a lake are key areas in the spring.

Of course, spring is the time of the year in Minnesota when the large-mouth bass should be left alone. Not fished. Yet everybody goes out on the lake and catches the females off of the spawning beds, or if they don't catch them, they disturb them. Even if you release a spawning female bass, I think, you will hurt the population of bass because many females will drop their eggs during the fight or when you are handling them. You will disrupt the spawning process. I prefer to leave them alone at this time of the year.

And then during the summer to eliminate dead water I usually start fishing in shallow water and work to deeper water. Sometimes you might find them in real shallow water, and many times you might only have to go to four or five feet of water. Of course, this will depend on the lake that you are fishing. In dirty water the fish won't move out as far as they would in a clear water lake.

But on a lake like Lake Minnetonka, I would start on the weedline and continually work into shallower water until I found active fish. Although there are basics in bass fishing, you must be versatile enough to locate and catch bass under all fishing conditions. If you are not catching fish, you are doing something wrong. That's not to say we don't all have bad days and can't figure out how to catch them.

Ninety percent of the time there is no reason to fish beyond the weedline. Even if it is a dirty water lake, where the weeds don't grow in any deeper water than four to five feet.

Actually, there is no set method of eliminating unproductive water. For the most part it is trial and error—spending time on the water.

Fishing is a never ending learning experience, and in that regard it's no different for Al Lindner, Gary Roach, or me than it is for a beginner. We're constantly trying new things and learning as a result of it. So about the time you think you've got a lake figured out, suddenly the old reliables don't work. You are really confused so try something new and sometimes that will work.

How important are topographical maps?

Capra: I think that they are very important. You can find little points and under water turns on the map, and then you study the map and decide where you are going to fish—today I'm going to hit this bay and those five points. And watch for things that aren't on the map while you are fishing or running from one spot to another.

Set a plan when you go fishing and stick to it. Find those under water points and those inside turns, etc. Figure out what you can fish in a day's time and do it. Then tomorrow fish other areas and check out other patterns. If you are serious about it, you will mark on the map where you intend to fish, and then you will go out and do it. In fact, mark your first spot, then your second spot, and so on.

It sounds like you spend time studying topo maps well before you get to a lake.

Capra: That's right. Take Gull Lake for instance. You put your boat in at the public access, and it's enough to scare you. Where do you start fishing a lake with that much water?

There is so much structure and cover on Gull Lake that it would take you five weeks, if you fished it every day, just to learn the points, so that's why you need a topo map.

You study the map and say I'm going into Wilson Bay today, and I'm going to fish the inside turns and learn what I can about Wilson Bay. And Wilson Bay is one of the smaller parts of Gull Lake, but it's a lake within a lake, and that's how you should look at a large body of water—piece by piece otherwise you can be overwhelmed.

Is there anything else that you would like to say about locating largemouth bass?

Capra: Locating fish, whether it's largemouth bass or any other species, is the whole key in catching them. I believe that anybody can catch fish; the key is to locate them. And some people have the ability to locate fish, and some others don't seem to do it very well.

Location is the hardest thing there is to do in catching fish. Presentation and other factors in fishing are minor when compared to locating fish. And I'm afraid location can't really be explained very well. It's mostly trial and error and being serious about it. Then all of a sudden you will be looking at a topo map and you will know pretty well that the fish should be on that inside turn, for instance. It's a nice sharp drop, it's an inside turn, those fish should be there, and many times you will go there and, by God, there they are.

PRESENTATION FOR LARGEMOUTH BASS

Let's talk about presentation.

Capra: Let's start with springtime presentation when the largemouth bass are in shallow water up against the banks. The male largemouth bass during a typical opener in Minnesota (end of May) are usually still on the spawning beds protecting the hatch. Generally, the females have dropped their eggs by this time of the year.

And presentation at this time of the year becomes a very interesting part of fishing because the largemouth bass are really spooky in the spring. Just the splash of your lure could spook them.

Besides spinner baits are there any other lures you like to use in the springtime?

Capra: Actually, I prefer a plastic worm over any other lure in the spring. And this is when you need to use a one-thirty second ounce or a one-sixteenth ounce slip sinker on a four inch Texas rigged worm since the fish are very finicky because they are protecting their nests and not really on feed that much.

They will be back in bays and in cuts, and a four or six inch worm presented right, without a big splash, is probably more productive than any other presentation at this time of the year.

Do you need to make longer casts in the springtime?

Capra: Yes because the water is clearer even in dirty water lakes. Bass are always spookier in clearer water. The hatch keeps them there; it's not really their first choice of where they'd like to be. Although you will miss a lot of fish since you are making longer casts, you will also get more of them to strike so you should end up catching more of them than you would using a short cast.

How fast do you retrieve a plastic worm in the springtime?

Capra: Real slow. You just barely drag it on the bottom.

How about your retrieve if you are using a spinner bait in the spring?

Capra: Use a steady retrieve cranking it as slow as you can without having it get hung up in the moss. Although you can cover a lot of water with a spinner bait, in the spring you will catch a lot more bass using a plastic worm.

Since we are talking about springtime fishing I will ask you to comment on topwater fishing.

Capra: There are so many different topwater lures, and each one of them is presented a little differently. When you are using the stick bait type of lures like the Rapalas or the Red Fin, it is best to use a spinning rig with eight pound test line.

Cast your stick baits out and let it sit until the water rings created by the lure hitting the water have disappeared and then twitch it a couple of times. That is one good method of presentation, and don't forget to make long casts.

Also there are the stick baits with propeller type blades on them like the Devils Horse which you cast out, let it sit a moment, then give it a couple of twitches, and then reel it in. With these types of stick baits if you haven't had a strike within the first ten feet, you might as well reel it in and start over.

Which type of stick bait is more productive?

Capra: Both types (Rapala type and propeller type) are good, but I prefer the Rapala type.

How about the Jitter Bug type lures?

Capra: There's the Heddon Mouse or the Bassereno types, but again they are not as productive as the Rapala types.

Does color make a difference in topwater lures?

Capra: Yes. A little bit. I prefer the silver colored ones for some reason, but I don't really know why.

Do buzzer baits work in the spring?

Capra: A lot of bass fishermen don't believe they do, but buzzer baits have won many spring tournaments. So believe it; they work in the spring.

When you think that there is a lure that only works during a particular time of the year, you are making a mistake. Although some lures produce better during certain times of the year, all lures can work and work well at any time of the year.

Let's go on to summer presentation.

Capra: Presentation always plays a part as to whether you catch fish or you don't catch fish. Very seldom have I ever seen a situation where you could throw any lure in any manner and catch bass.

If I'm using a crank bait, I will use a snap, not a snap with a swivel on it, just a little snap which allows a crank bait to work the way it was designed to work. If you tie a crank bait directly to your line, the line will retard the action of the crank bait. Using a snap will help maximize the action of a crank bait which means you will catch more fish.

In general, what time of the year are we talking about when we refer to the summer period of fishing?

Capra: In Minnesota we are talking about the end of June through mid-September or so. This will vary somewhat from year to year depending on the weather and how far north you are in Minnesota. The farther north you are in the state, the later the summer period will begin and the earlier the fall period will begin which means lakes in northern Minnesota will have shorter summer periods than lakes in the metro area.

What lure is the most productive lure in the summer?

Capra: The plastic worm. In fact, the plastic worm can be a productive lure all year long. But in the fall the jig and pig becomes more productive than the plastic worm.

How do you rig your plastic worms for summertime fishing?

Capra: I Texas rig them, and also I like to use them on an exposed jig head. And not too heavy of a jig either. You only need one heavy enough to keep your line fairly tight. The jigs I use are a quarter ounce with an exposed hook with a six to an eight inch Culprit worm. The jig and worm is one of the best presentations to take bass on a weedline. I call it the Bollig method because Larry Bollig was the first one to use that presentation up here in Minnesota.

With an exposed hook many times fish will hook themselves. With a Texas rigged worm you will miss at least fifty percent of the fish that have it in their mouth and then spit it out. With an exposed jig hook many times when a bass is blowing it out of his mouth, it will get hooked somewhere in his mouth which gives you more time to really set the hook. Only Texas rig your plastic worm when it's necessary to keep it from getting hung up.

In what types of water can you effectively fish a plastic worm?

Capra: Any type. From six inches of water to the end of the weedline, which is where you'd usually fish anyway.

Are there any tricks in rigging a plastic worm?

Capra: A good rule of thumb is to use the lightest slip sinker that you can get by with.

Is that due to the speed at which the lure falls through the water?

Capra: Yes. The slower your worm falls through the water, the easier it is for fish to locate and strike your lure. I'm sure that they will hit something that drops slowly through the water more often then they will hit something that drops rapidly through the water.

Comment on plastic worm fishing in deep water.

Capra: When you are using a plastic worm in deep water, you will need to use up to a three-eighths ounce slip sinker, and on windy days in deep water you may even need to go to a five-eighths ounce slip sinker.

Let's go back to shallow water fishing for a moment. Actually, in shallow water it's not so much how fast the worm drops; it's the splash that's significant in presentation—not creating a big splash and spooking the fish is very important.

In fact, that's why flipping has become so popular with bass fishermen. You can just lay that lure out there into the strike zone without creating that big splash that you normally get when using conventional casting methods. The velocity of the lure hitting the water creates a big splash that will frequently spook fish especially when they are in shallow water.

Another thing that I have learned, and I don't care if it's worm fishing, jig and pig fishing, or whatever, is that most fishermen, including me, move their lure way too fast. I was just out fishing with Donny Hansen from Rochester (Minnesota), and he was showing me some methods he uses to present lures when largemouth bass are in the lily pads.

I was dropping my lure into an opening in the lily pads and then lifting it out and dropping it into another opening, and I wasn't getting a strike. Then Donny Hansen fished behind me dropping his lure into the same openings and by letting it sit much longer than I had let my lure sit, he was getting strikes and catching the fish I had missed. He would let his lure sit up to thirty seconds or more, and all of a sudden he would catch a bass.

He threw into the lily pads with a plastic worm or a jig and pig and let it sit. Then he would shake it once in awhile without actually moving it from where it was sitting, and he was catching the fish I missed. Now where most guys would fish fast, he's fishing much slower and as a result, on most occasions, he's catching more fish. There's just no doubt about it; a slower presentation is almost always a better presentation, especially when the fish are finicky.

Does this apply all through the year?

Capra: I would say that you are probably better off fishing your lures, especially plastic worms and jig and pig types of lures, slowly all through the year. Learn to be a little more patient, and you will catch more fish.

Do you ever use a flutter down technique with a spinner bait, for example?

Capra: I do a lot. It's a good method of taking bass on the weedline. And weedline spinner baiting is probably not done enough in Minnesota. What I'm talking about is casting to the weedline and letting your spinner bait helicopter down to the bottom. It is important to watch your line as the spinner bait is dropping since most of your strikes (probably ninety percent) will occur when the lure is dropping. If you see a twitch on your line, set the hook. Don't wait until you feel the fish. And the flutter down presentation is a good method of taking fish the year 'round.

Is there anything that you would like to add about summer presentation?

Capra: Let's talk about the long, hot spells in the summertime. A lot of interesting things happen during this time of the year. And when you've had a long, hot spell, contrary to what most fishermen think, largemouth bass do the opposite—they will move into shallow water (I know we've discussed this somewhat before, but it bears repeating). When I'm talking about shallow water, I mean six inches to three feet of water even though the water temperature is seventy to eighty degrees and maybe even hotter. Then those bass will move way back into the junk, and that's when you can really have fun catching big fish.

What lure do you use for this type of fishing?

Capra: Spoons, buzzer baits, Moss Bosses, Super Frogs, Johnson's spoons, Strike Kings—surface type lures.

This is a good time to take big fish. During this time of the year the water is green and slimy and doesn't look good, but those bass are backed right up against the banks, believe it or not. In fact, I'm going to be fishing a tournament this weekend [early August], and I feel it will be won with heavy weight in shallow water. Probably two feet of water or less. This is mainly an August pattern, but it does happen in July, too.

Let's go on to fall presentation.

Capra: Fall is a good time to catch good sized fish and lots of them. A jig and a pig would be your best choice of lures to catch big bass in the fall.

What size jig do you use?

Capra: I usually use a three-eighths ounce jig when I'm fishing the weed-lines in the fall. With a jig and pig that is. Although you can catch bass on almost any lure in the fall, for some reason, you will catch more on a jig and pig than any other lure. Also, the jig and pig is recognized as a big bass lure in the fall.

We've talked about spring fishing, summer fishing, and fall fishing, but the most important thing to keep in mind is that ninety percent of the fish will be between shore and the weedline. You can listen to all those Buck Perry theories, and maybe there are some bass in deep, deep water holding on rocks, etc., but the vast majority of the bass are located from the weedline into shore.

Take Lake Minnetonka for example, you can go in five to six inches of water in the slop in North Arm Bay and catch four to six pounders in the fall, and then go to another part of the lake and do just as well on a weedline.

I concentrate, as most good bass fishermen do, on the weedline into shore. Then it's just a matter of presenting your lure properly.

Are buzzer baits and spinner baits productive in the fall?

Capra: Generally when the water temperature is dropping in the fall, a spinner bait will be more productive than a buzzer bait. But you may find that on a given day on a given lake that buzzer baits will out-produce spinner baits.

Are any particular colors of jigs and pigs better than others?

Capra: Like Henry Ford said of Model T cars, "Any color as long as it's black." Many bass fishermen are into all different colors, but a black jig with a black or dark brown pork chunk is all you really need. I've caught a lot of bass on blue pork chunks, but, day in and day out, black or dark brown are the most consistently producing colors for me.

Is there anything else that you would like to add regarding fall presentation?

Capra: Another aspect of presentation, not just fall presentation, is remembering the basics. I just fished a tournament this past weekend [early September] that I should have won but didn't because I forgot the basics. Since it's fall most bass fishermen feel, as I do, that bass will hit a jig and pig better than other lures, but the bass don't know that. The guy who won this tournament was using crank baits. [Ted finished fourth in this tournament.]

He was cranking the weeds where the fish aren't supposed to be at this time of the year since all the magazines and books tell us that fish leave the weeds when the weeds die.

If the weeds were dead, why do you suppose the bass were still there?

Capra: One reason is that it's the only place for them to live until ice-over.

And those weeds probably weren't completely dead either. Also the bait fish were there.

Sure, fish prefer greener weeds, and if you can find the greener weeds, that is probably where most of the fish will be. But even when the weeds are dead, the fish will still often locate in them all the way up to ice-over.

You said the weeds probably weren't completely dead. Elaborate on that statement.

Capra: Weeds aren't alive one day, and then suddenly dead the next day. It's a slow process. Did you ever notice how a tomato plant, for example, looks dead on the top, but when you look at the bottom of the plant you'll probably find green roots even in late November. So the weeds that appear to be dead—brown and decaying on the tops—may not be completely dead. And if they are not completely dead, they are still producing oxygen during the daytime.

And for the most part, fish really don't have any place else to go except from the weedline into shore. They are going to be there; I'm totally convinced of that. So maybe dying weeds aren't the most desirable place for bass to locate, but if there are minnows or other types of forage in the dying weeds, which I've seen often, that's where the bass will be and the panfish and everything else. You hear all these stories about this and that and every fisherman has his own theories, but I've spent a lot of time out on the water and spent equally as much time discussing fishing with knowledgeable friends like Larry Bollig, etc., and we find that many of the old theories are not right, or, at least, they are not right all of the time.

And remember that every lake presents a different fishing situation. On one lake you can catch bass in six inches of water, and, at the very same time, on another lake you'd have to fish the weedline to take good numbers of bass.

There is no one set method of presentation or location that always works better than another method. You can't go to a lake and say this is how we are going to catch fish. You can't do that because every lake presents different problems, so you need to be versatile.

I'd like to have you comment further on flipping since it's becoming so popular with bass fishermen in Minnesota.

Capra: Most of the time when you are flipping, you are flipping into areas where you can't cast effectively. Take a tree, for instance. You cast up to that tree from a distance and your lure will make such a loud splash when it hits the water that you will probably spook any fish who is holding there. But with flipping, if you lift your rod just before the lure hits the surface of the water, it will enter the water very quietly.

One fisherman can cast up to that same tree several times and never take a fish. The next fisherman comes along and if he's flipping that tree he might be able to take one or more bass from it because of the lure's entry into the water. Also when flipping, you are able to make pinpoint casts. It's the quiet entry into the water and the relative ease at which you can pinpoint your target that makes flipping very effective.

Also there are places where you can't possibly cast to, but you can flip a lure right there without much difficulty.

Do you use a flipping stick for other than flipping?

Capra: Oh yes! I use a flipping stick for a lot of things. I use it for spinner baits, buzzer baits, and crank baits, etc.

I like the versatility of using a flipping stick. If you want your crank bait to run deeper, you can simply stick your flipping stick down into the water and gain another three to four feet which you couldn't do with a casting rod since they are too short.

Flipping sticks are also easier to fight fish with, and in many instances you can cast with them more accurately than you can cast with a spinning or bait casting rod. With a two handed cast, which I use when casting with a flipping stick, I'm much more accurate than I am with a regular rod.

Do you ever troll for largemouth bass?

Capra: Oh yeah! It's a good way to locate schools of bass. I'll take a 7800 series Big O crank bait and get off of the weedline a bit and troll for blocks. I'm looking for one fish on that weedline.

What do you do when that one bass strikes?

Capra: Then I'll throw a marker and go back and work the heck out of that area with worms, crank baits, or flutter down a spinner bait to determine if there's a school of fish down there. If not, I move on.

Why do most bass fishermen look down their noses at fishermen who troll?

Capra: Because of tournaments [Trolling is not allowed during a tournament.] a lot of bass fishermen don't like to troll, but when you've got miles and miles of shoreline to learn on a new lake for tournaments, trolling is a good method of eliminating dead water fast. It's just a good method of find fish in the summertime.

Earlier you talked about fishing plastic worms and jigs and pigs too fast. Are there any situations when you should retrieve a lure fast?

Capra: In the summertime I don't believe you can reel a buzzer bait too fast. And during the summer buzzer baits can be a really effective lure to use, but there isn't a reel made that will allow you to retrieve a buzzer bait as fast as you should.

Comment on boat control and presentation when fishing points.

Capra: Windy, sandy points will usually hold bass. I always put the nose of my boat into the wind for better boat control and work both sides of the point. [Ted uses a front mount electric trolling motor.] When you fish a point, commit yourself to fishing the whole point from one side to the other all the way to where it flattens out because bass can be anywhere on that point. And don't forget the inside turns.

What aspects of presentation are the most important when fishing breaks?

Capra: On breaks you need to use crank baits and plastic worms. Work worms slowly. With crank baits sometimes you'll have to throw into the weeds and rip your crank through them, and be alert because many times when your crank bait rips loose from a weed, you will get a strike. All good crank bait fishermen will tell you that.

What methods of presentation do you use on flats?

Capra: To be honest with you, I've never been able to do that well on flats. I either fish right up next to shore or on the drop. I've just never done that well right up on the flats, but that's not to say there aren't bass there.

Of course, if you are fishing a reservoir down South, it's a different story.

What lures do you use when you are fishing timber for bass?

Capra: Worms, spinner baits, and jigs and pigs. Although we don't have a lot of timber to fish in Minnesota, when I do fish it, I usually use a jig and pig combination.

How do you cast to timber if you are unable to use a flipping method?

Capra: Cast right to it. It takes an accurate cast and then let the lure drop right down on the roots of the tree even if you have to peel line from your reel. This extra line will keep the lure from swinging away from the tree and out of the strike zone. If you don't have enough slack in your line when the lure hits the water, it will pendulum away from your target, and you will have fewer strikes, especially when the bass are not aggressive. Also, when you are casting to timber, you are casting to a specific target, so accuracy is much more important than it is when you are casting to a weedline, for instance.

What is the best method of presentation when you are fishing lily pads?

Capra: Almost the whole arsenal of fishing lures can be used effectively when fishing lily pads, and lily pads are always worth checking because some times of the year you'll catch fish in them. But, I feel, lily pads are highly overrated by many bass fishermen. Usually you don't do that well fishing them.

Do you go along with the notion that one should use smaller lures when fishing in cold water?

Capra: Yes. I generally do.

Does your presentation change when you are fishing during fall turnover?

Capra: I don't really change except I will use a jig and pig more because, I feel, I have a better chance for a big bass with a jig and pig. Also, in the fall, the bigger fish are more active.

Are you strictly an artificial lure fisherman?

Capra: Pretty much. I don't use live baits simply because I prefer to fish with artificial lures. I have fished with Roland Martin in Florida using live shiners, which was fantastic fishing, but I still prefer artificials.

But when things get really tough, you can take a plain quarter ounce jig tipped with a fat head minnow, and sure catch fish. Using live bait is also a good way of locating fish, especially in the spring.

Comment on line weight.

Capra: I will use up to seventeen pound test line and heavy tackle if I'm fishing the junk. But in most situations, like fishing a Texas rig worm on a weedline, I will use twelve pound test line. And if I'm jigging, I will use eight pound test line. I have no trouble with twelve pound test line breaking if I retie my knots every so often. Let me clarify something. If I'm using an eighth ounce jig with an exposed hook, I will use eight pound test line. If I'm fishing a jig and pig, I may even use as heavy as fourteen pound test line.

Would you change your presentation from a lake to a river?

Capra: Presentation is important anywhere you fish, be it a lake or a river, Florida or Minnesota, and usually that means fishing your lure quietly and slowly not letting it drop too fast. This is especially true with plastic worms. Of course on a river you'll have to adjust your presentation to deal with the current.

Is there any area of presentation that we haven't covered thoroughly enough?

Capra: We haven't said enough about crank baits. I think crank baits are a very important lure in the bass fisherman's arsenal, and they are not used enough by most bass fishermen.

Crank baits are an effective lure for taking bass most of the year with the exception of spring when the bass are in real shallow water since it's tough to work a crank bait very effectively in real shallow water.

How do you present a crank bait properly?

Capra: I like an erratic presentation—crank real fast and then pause. Reel and stop, reel and stop is a good method which will often trigger bass to strike. And if you're using a steady retrieve, adjust the speed of your retrieve until you've found the speed that the fish prefer. Again it's trial and error.

How important is the sound that a lure makes?

Capra: Sound plays a factor especially in dirty water since bass feed by sound and sight.

Is there anything that you want to add regarding presentation?

Capra: There are so many variables that you have to consider, and every lake is somewhat different.

In general, the most important aspect of presentation is versatility. That's not to say you have to be an expert at using every lure there is, but you should become proficient at using a few lures from each category of lures: jigs, plastic worms, crank baits, spoons, and spinner baits.

WEATHER AND BIOLOGICAL FACTORS AFFECTING LARGEMOUTH BASS

How does the barometric pressure affect largemouth bass?

Capra: A falling barometer is definitely a plus when you are fishing. It is for muskies and bass anyway. [See the location section of this chapter for more information about the barometer's affect on largemouth bass.]

Earlier you said that you preferred to fish when the sky was overcast. Why?

Capra: An overcast sky is better for fishing. I'm not sure why, but I think the low sun penetration enables fish to be more active and aggressive which, of course, means they are easier to catch.

I suppose that's why a foggy day is also good for fishing?

Capra: Yes. Fog is a plus as far as I'm concerned. It has the same effect as an overcast sky.

How do cold fronts affect largemouth bass?

Capra: Cold front conditions make fishing a little tougher, but they don't completely turn the fish off. During a cold front condition it is important to change your methods of fishing: mainly, use smaller lures and slow down your retrieve.

How small?

Capra: Use little crank baits with big lips so you can still fish the same depths as you would if it weren't a cold front condition. I usually use a half ounce crank bait so during a cold front condition I would go down a size to a three-eighths ounce. With worms I will drop down to a four inch from my usual six or seven inch. And remember when you are fishing a cold front, presentation is twice as important as it is other times. Fish very, very slowly.

In general, how would your locational pattern change when confronted with cold front conditions?

Capra: I believe that cold fronts turn off deep water bass faster than they turn off shallow water bass, so I would concentrate on fishing shallow.

Do largemouth bass significantly change their location when a cold front is approaching or upon us?

Capra: I don't think so. If you've been catching bass in shallow water prior to the front, keep fishing in shallow water during the cold front, but you might have to look for them in the heaviest and thickest cover you can find. I think they will bury themselves in thicker weeds, for example. Of course, this is why presentation is more important here since you need to fish every inch of a brush pile, for instance, rather than just making a few quick

casts and then moving on to the next brush pile because those fish are buried in there somewhere, and they will not be as aggressive as they were before the front moved in.

Now in the fall a cold front doesn't affect bass as much as it does in the middle of summer. In the fall bass seem to be conditioned to the cold water, and, remember, they are doing the same thing that a bear is doing—fattening up for the winter. They don't hibernate in the winter, but they certainly stagnate which is why you don't hear of too many bass being caught by ice fishermen.

So if I'm catching bass today and tonight a cold front moves in, tomorrow I should fish the same spots as I fished yesterday only more carefully and slower?

Capra: That's right. They ain't movin'; they're still there. They just aren't as aggressive.

How about those warm fronts when the heat keeps building and building for days?

Capra: That's when the bass will really get aggressive and attack fast moving lures like buzzer baits. But if you are running a lure fast in cold water, you're running it fast for yourself, not the fish.

How does rain affect bass fishing?

Capra: Usually when the barometer is falling, you've got a weather front coming in. But as for fishing while it's raining, I've done very well and I've done very poorly during a rain and after a rain; so I've never been able to say whether rain is good for fishing or bad for fishing.

A lot of fishermen maintain that when there is a lightning storm nearby, the big fish go on a rampage and hit anything.

Capra: I'm off the lake when it's lightning. As soon as I see a lightning bolt, whether I'm fishing a tournament or not, I'm off of the lake or under a bridge.

Lightning is nothing to monkey with. You can't fool Mother Nature.

What affect do moon phases have on largemouth bass?

Capra: The first of a new moon seems to trigger fish. Big fish. But I really don't feel qualified to talk about it since I've never studied moon phases or followed it in regards to my fishing success or lack of success.

I knew a muskie fisherman who would never go fishing unless the moon and every other variable was just right. This had to be right; that had to be right, and so on. Well, remember, most fishermen are people who can only go fishing on the weekends and not every weekend at that. So why worry about all that stuff since nobody really knows how it affects fishing anyway, especially moon phases and those other exotic variables. Go fishing whenever you can.

In fact, I've caught more muskies than that fellow ever caught. You can't catch them by sitting in the cabin thinking this isn't the right bait, the moon phase is wrong, and some people find more reasons not to go fishing than they can find reasons to go fishing. The only time I don't like to fish is when the wind is blowing forty miles an hour. It takes all the fun out of it.

Now I don't want to leave you with the impression that there isn't something to its affect on fish, but I have yet to see anybody discover what that relationship might be.

We've already discussed turnover quite thoroughly, but I didn't ask you if fall turnover has an affect on the schooling of bass.

Capra: Turnover will usually concentrate bass more. And during turnover if you find a school of fish in deep water, it may very well be a pretty large school of fish.

But after turnover, in the late fall, is the best time of the year to catch good quality fish in numbers. Almost everybody else is duck hunting, bear hunting, and participating in other fall sports, and they are missing out on the best fishing of the year. Some guys will go duck hunting in the morning and go bass fishing in the afternoon which is a great way to spend a day.

Is there anything we haven't already covered on the thermocline's affect on bass fishing?

Capra: No. We covered it. It just isn't much of a factor in my style of fishing.

We covered pH pretty well in the location section, but is there anything that you want to add about it?

Capra: Roland Martin, Basil Bacon, and those other Florida fishermen have pretty much figured it out for southern waters. But in Minnesota no one has yet to find a relationship between pH and how it might affect fishing.

EQUIPMENT AND TACKLE FOR BASS FISHING

Do you have any preferences for certain brands of jigs?

Capra: I prefer jigs with the fiber weed guards over the ones with the Y weed guards since they don't seem to get hung up as much. I use Windels and Stanley jigs, and both of them are real good.

Comment on lure size.

Capra: I throw a lot of different size lures, but I don't use large lures. The biggest spinner bait I use is a three-eighths ounce, and in crank baits an 8000 series Big O would be the largest I use, but generally I use the 7800 series.

Do you modify your lures at all?

Capra: Very little. The only thing I do is sharpen my hooks before I fish a tournament. Of course with crank baits you will need to tune them from time to time, but that's about it.

What's the best knot to tie?

Capra: Everybody has their favorite knot. I just use the improved clinch, and it gets the job done for me.

I don't think I've ever had a knot break on me, but that's probably because I retie my lures frequently. Mostly, I just depend on my reel's drag; that's what drags are made for.

You know everybody seems to get hung up on line strength and all that other stuff. Although I want fine equipment and good line, etc., I concentrate on where I'm fishing much more than all that other stuff.

Many bass fishermen feel white is the only color spinner bait you need.

Capra: Yeah! That's right! Ninety percent of the time that you are using a spinner bait for largemouth bass in Minnesota, white will do the job. The only other color spinner bait you might need is chartreuse.

As far as size goes, I prefer a three-eighths ounce spinner bait, but occasionally I will use a quarter ounce. And I use a lot of tandem spinner baits except when I'm fishing a flutter down technique on a weedline since a single blade helicopters down better than the two bladed spinner baits do.

Do you use the crank baits with rattles in them?

Capra: Yes. Either in clear or dirty water I seem to catch more bass on cranks that have the rattles in them. Some fishermen say that you don't need a rattle in clear water, but it doesn't hurt and it could help, so I use them.

What colors of plastic worms should a bass fisherman have in his tackle box?

Capra: Black, grape, blue, and crawfish. Crawfish has recently become an important color in this area. Also some companies are making multicolored worms. I rep one for Cluprit that has a crawfish bottom and a dark brown top and that color combination works great.

But you really don't need more than about four colors to be in the worm business when fishing for largemouth bass up here.

Comment on the length of worms we should be using.

Capra: Four to seven and a half inches is a good range. I like to throw a six incher when I'm using an exposed jig head.

Why?

Capra: It seems to drop right, and a seven and a half inch worm is a little too big for an exposed jig head, but the seven and a half incher works very well Texas rigged since you are using a bigger hook. In the spring I will use four to six inch worms, and in the summertime I prefer a seven and a half incher.

Comment on spoons.

Capra: Black, silver, chartreuse, and white are the main colors. The important thing to remember when fishing with spoons is to slow down your retrieve. If you reel too fast, you'll lose the action of the spoon. If you retrieve a spoon at the same speed you retrieve a crank bait, the spoon will be skidding on the surface of the water. Retrieve it only fast enough to get that wobbling action on the spoon. Of course there are times when you might want to stop your retrieve and drop the spoon into a pocket in the weeds.

Comment on line weight.

Capra: In clear water you will need to use a lighter line, and if you are fishing in shallow water slop you will need to go as high as twenty pound test.

Comment on reels.

Capra: In bait casting it's pretty hard to beat Garcia or Lew's for bass fishing. Penn has some good bait casting reels with a three to one retrieve which forces you to retrieve slower which is usually better than a fast retrieve.

How about spinning reels?

Capra: Penn makes a good one; probably the best when you get into the inner workings of the reel. Also Lew's makes a good spinning reel for bass fishing.

What types and brands of rods do you use?

Capra: There is no one rod that will work well in every situation. It is important that you have the right rod for the job.

If you are flipping, you need a good stiff action flipping stick. And it is important that your flipping stick has its line guides in the proper place. The first guide should be far enough away from the handle so you can handle your line properly when flipping. The placement of the rest of the guides on a flipping stick aren't nearly so important as that first one.

For jiggin' and piggin' or worming I prefer a heavy action rod. These two types of fishing require a hard hook set, especially if you are fishing a Texas rigged worm.

And when cranking, I believe that a medium action rod with a light tip is best. When you use a stiff rod when you are cranking, it's too easy to lose a fish since there is no "give" with a stiff rod. With a lighter tipped rod you can make a lot of mistakes and the rod will forgive you; that is, there is less chance that you will have slack in your line if you make a mistake.

More fish are lost on crank baits than any other lure, and that's because most bass fishermen are using the wrong type of rod for cranking. You need the stiff backbone to set the hook, but when the hook is set, the light tip will keep the tension in your line much better, especially if you make a mistake. If a fish makes a fast move when you are using a stiff tipped rod and there is momentarily slack in your line, he can very easily spit the hook out of his mouth.

Kunnan is a new line of rods that we are carrying which I'm very excited about since they make a different rod for every type of fishing. They've got the best selection of rods that I've ever seen, and they don't cost a hundred bucks a piece either.

Is a boron rod worth the difference in price?

Capra: It was a drastic change from fiberglass rods to graphite rods, but with the change from graphite to boron no one can even tell the difference when fishing. I can't tell the difference except when I go to pay for a boron rod.

Name some of the better brands of rods.

Capra: Fenwick and Saga make very good rods, but with them you've got a big price tag. Lew's has some good bass fishing rods, too. A twenty-five to thirty dollar rod is all you need anyway. It's marketing—getting big names to promote for a company—that makes a twenty-five dollar rod a sixty dollar rod.

Name some brands of crank baits that are good.

Capra: I like Cordell, Rebel, and Rapala, and also Bombers. Those are the four companies that make the best crank baits on the market today. Bagley is also a good crank bait, but it's too expensive, and they aren't any better than the other four I mentioned.

How about Mann's?

Capra: I don't feel that Mann's makes a good hard bait at all.

Plastic worms?

Capra: I like Productor and Culprit for up in this area. [Minnesota.]

Spoons?

Capra: Johnson's spoons are hard to beat.

How about line?

Capra: I like Stren.

Why?

Capra: It's been a good line for me, and I haven't had any problems with it. I can get all the line I need for nothing, and that's any brand, but I've never had any problems with Stren, so I don't see any reason to switch.

What brand of locator do you use?

Capra: Si-Tex. Because of all of the computer chips in a Si-Tex and the technology behind it. They are the most trouble free unit you can buy.

I noticed that you have a new Champion brand boat.

Capra: Yeah. There are a lot of good boats out there today, but I've switched to Champion. I think, dollar for dollar, it's the best boat on the market. In fact, they're about a thousand dollars less than the big name bass boats.

I assume you are still an Evinrude man?

Capra: It's a good motor, and if you have a problem, you can get it fixed fast anywhere in the state. I don't care where you are in Minnesota, there's an OMC dealer nearby.

What are the best electric trolling motors?

Capra: Byrd and Minn Kota are the best, and Minn Kota is also one of the least expensive on the market, too.

Is there anything that you want to add regarding equipment and tackle?

Capra: Think of your rods, reels, lures, etc. as the tools of your trade, or hobby, and use the right tool for the job.

MISCELLANEOUS INFORMATION ABOUT LARGEMOUTH BASS FISHING

Is the "catch and release" concept important to bass fishing in Minnesota?

Capra: "Catch and release" is a real good thing. Anywhere! But I don't think there is anything wrong with taking some fish home to eat either. Take home the smaller ones and let the larger ones go. Leave those big females in the lake for reproduction so there will be future generations of fish.

There's been such a big deal made about "catch and release" that some people have a guilt complex about keeping a few fish, and that's ridiculous. I keep a few walleyes, but I don't keep bass because I feel they are a sport fish. Bass are so much fun for me to catch that I don't keep any of them.

I know we touched on it earlier, but I'd like you to say a bit more on live bait -vs- artificial lures.

Capra: I fish with mostly artificial lures, but there is a time and place for live bait. If you want to catch fish when conditions are tough, you can take a little jig tipped with a shiner or a fathead minnow and jig the weedlines, and you'll take some good fish.

Nisswa guides are famous for this method. They'll take a customer out on Gull Lake and get on a weedline using this method and they'll catch northerns, bass, and other species of fish.

You should use live bait if you choose to. I prefer artificials, but live bait will out-produce artificials day in and day out on all species of fish except for muskies.

Are you saying that live bait will always out-produce artificial lures?

Capra: I should clarify that. That's when the fish are on the weedlines. In shallow water fishing, artificials will usually out-produce live bait.

Why are artificial lures better in shallow water?

Capra: Because you can use a spinner bait or a buzzer bait much more effectively in shallow water than you can live bait. Also you can cover more water with an artificial lure than you can with live bait, and it follows that if you are covering more water, usually you will increase your chances of catching fish.

For example, if you are fishing shallow water slop, it's pretty hard to use a shiner minnow on a bobber and cover much water. You could probably cover most lakes in Minnesota with an artificial lure in the time it would take you to cover fifty feet with a shiner on a bobber.

Let me say something more about live bait fishing. We push artificial lures a lot, and in tournaments you are only allowed to use artificial lures, but there's no better way to take largemouth bass than on a jig and minnow. Use a quarter to a three-eighths ounce ball head jig tipped with a minnow on the weedline and you will catch bass when you can't catch them any other way.

How about using frogs?

Capra: I did use frogs when I was a young kid, but I don't anymore. I just can't handle drowning a frog. You put the hook in him, and then he looks up at you, I just can't do it.

Last time we got together you said there was more we should discuss about the "Great Muskie Rampage" that occurred on Leech Lake in the mid-fifties?

Capra: People are still trying to figure out why those muskies went nuts on Leech Lake back in 1955. I think it was the lack of oxygen in deep water that caused it.

Once Al Lindner, Marv Koep, and I hit a situation when it had been hot and muggy with little or no wind for a long time and the skies were overcast [in August], and we noticed that whitefish and tullibees were dying and floating on the surface of the water. Now when that happens, I feel, there is a lack of oxygen in the water especially down in the deeper water which forces the fish into shallower water. Then you are fishing fish that would normally never be fished since they would otherwise be too hard to get at.

During long periods of hot weather with little or no wind the thermocline is much shallower, and the fish are forced into shallower water since there is little or no oxygen below the thermocline.

Are you saying that they are in an area of the lake that they would rather not be in, but they are forced to be there because of the lack of oxygen in deeper, cooler water?

Capra: Yes. Anyway getting back to the trip Al, Marv, and I were on, on Lake Winnibigoshish. We caught walleyes that averaged four pounds and seven to eight pound northerns out of the same tiny little weed patch. Then I went back later with my son since I had missed a big muskie there, and he caught that one. [Ted points to a monster muskie hanging on the wall.] It weighed thirty-six pounds and was caught on fifteen pound test line.

Well, I knew he was there because I had lost him. I was throwing a Suick, and my son was throwing a little tiny spinner bait, and that fish hit the spinner bait.

We think what had happened was that the lack of oxygen had forced all those fish into the weeds since weeds give off oxygen during the daytime. Those fish were just stacked in there. You could go around the weed patch with a Lindy Rig and a night crawler and catch the walleyes. Then you could put on a spinner bait and catch the northerns. It was unbelievable.

How big of a patch of weeds are you talking about?

Capra: Actually, there were several patches. These patches were probably no bigger than twenty-five to thirty feet square. All you had to do was to find the patches of weeds that were in four to five feet of water.

Al was the one who figured it out. We had started out fishing in deep water that morning since people had reported catching many fish on the bars for the previous month to month and a half. All of a sudden nobody could catch big fish on these bars. Then we began working into shallower water, and Al found them in four feet of water. In those days I would have never looked for the big fish in four feet of water at that time of the year.

But this situation hasn't changed. Any year, come August, when there's a lack of oxygen, fishermen get a chance to fish big fish. Fish they would otherwise not have the opportunity to fish. This is the time of the year, you'll notice in the newspapers, that many huge muskies are being caught.

Did you ever catch a bass using an unusual method of fishing?

Capra: One time on Gull Lake I was fishing a draw tournament with Roger Janusek who is a real good fisherman. We were fishing a weedline. I had fish located, and I figured we'd go there and both get a limit. And I figured I would get the bigger limit since it was my spot and I knew exactly what to do to catch 'em.

Well, we got there, and we weren't catching anything. Then Roger picked up a crank bait and started throwing it out toward the middle of the lake away from the weedline. You can imagine what I thought. Bass are not supposed to be out away from the weedline according to everybody who has ever said anything about bass fishing.

When Roger caught one that was about two and a half pounds, I thought it was a fluke, and that bass was probably just heading for the weeds anyway. So I just kept fishing the weedline, and he kept fishing away from the weedline, and all of a sudden he catches another one. That didn't bother me too much, but when he landed the third one, that was enough for me. I put my worm down and started throwing a crank bait the way he was. However, we never caught another fish out there away from the weedline.

He ended up beating me that day by a little bit. And I have no idea what those three fish were doing out there, but they were there.

When he started fishing away from the weedline, I thought boy am I going to smoke this guy if he keeps fishing that way. So when you think you've got it all figured out, you don't.

Comment on the largemouth basses ability to smell and taste. (I told you we'd get to this one.)

Capra: As you know there are a lot of scents on the market today, and I can honestly say using them won't help you catch fish at all. Now if anybody wants to believe that stuff makes a difference, whatever brand it is, then go ahead and buy it.

But I've been fishing with others who were using it and I wasn't, and it did not make any difference at all. Now I'm talking about excellent fishermen who are using the same lure that I'm using, and they'd spray that stuff on and we're both catching fish for fish. It doesn't help at all!

Time and time again, I have not used it while fishing with others who were using it, and I've caught as many fish, if not more than they have, without using it [scents].

To me, those scents are a big gimmick! That's the only thing they are. Until somebody proves me wrong, I wouldn't bother using it. If you want to spend eight dollars for a bottle of nothing, go ahead!

Of course, I have friends who are excellent fishermen who firmly believe in using scents.

Let's talk about the future of sport fishing.

Capra: You've got people that are telling young kids don't do this and don't do that. Don't hunt and don't fish, so I don't know exactly where the sport is going, but, I feel, it's declining every year because of teachers in the schools and people like Jacques Costeau saying he can't understand why someone would want to hold a rod and reel in their hand and catch a fish. I don't think we will see a decline in the number of fishermen in our generation, but in the future it will probably decline.

What are your thoughts about the future of fishing in the short term? The next ten years or so.

Capra: If people want a fresh meal of fish, they should take them. But I hope people quit stocking their freezers and bringing limit after limit home to show off to their neighbors or to give them to their buddies to eat.

The knowledge that fishermen have today is so great that, although they can't fish out a lake, they sure can hurt it. That's been proven on Lake Mille Lacs.

"Catch and release" is one of the reasons I'm a proponent of tournament fishing. Tournaments teach people how to release fish. It's easy to release a five pound bass after you've done it a few times. In fact, it makes you feel good. Real good!

Is acid rain as big a threat to our fishing resources as some are saying it is?

Capra: I'm no expert on acid rain, but the whole industry is worried about it. When you start killing off lakes, the fishing is over. And that's not to mention what the other ramifications of acid rain are and will be.

How much of fishing is luck?

Capra: The only thing that luck does is maybe let you catch a five or a six pounder. That's the only part it plays. Knowledge is everything. I believe that fishermen that have knowledge about catching bass can catch them most any day they are on the water. For instance, you get on a weedline and start fishing. That's not luck; you had to know how to find that weedline to begin with.

As far as I'm concerned, luck doesn't mean anything. And when somebody wishes me good luck when I'm going fishing, that doesn't mean anything to me. You are going out there and use your head, and it's because of your knowledge that you are going to catch fish. The guy who says he had a lucky day is wrong. He was doing something he had learned to catch those fish.

Luck is maybe catching the largest bass in a bass tournament. But coming in with your limit of nice bass is because of knowledge, you did something right. You can call it luck, but it isn't.

Comment on boat control.

Capra: Boat control may be almost as important as location and presentation. I don't care if you are walleye fishing, bass fishing, or whatever kind of fishing you are doing, boat control, especially along weedlines, is very important. And most fishermen don't worry about boat control as much as they should.

Al Lindner woke up the fishing world to the importance of boat control. If you are running a fifty horse power motor, he said, you should run it backwards. Why? Because you can stay on the weedline better, and that's where backtrolling originated.

One of the things that I cannot stand is to fish with someone who doesn't know how to control a boat. He's not staying on the weedline; he's in the shallow water; then he's in the deep water, and so on. And this is one of the reasons many fishermen don't like to fish with other fishermen. They take their fishing so seriously that they want to spend every second right on that weedline. As long as you are out there doing it, you might as well do it right.

Besides that, boat control isn't that hard to learn even if it's windy.

Name some of your favorite largemouth bass lakes in Minnesota.

Capra: Let's start with the metro area lakes. Out of all the lakes that I have fished throughout the country, Lake Minnetonka is my favorite lake for largemouth bass. Lake Calhoun and Cedar Lake which are right in the heart of Minneapolis are very good bass lakes, too. And Forest Lake is good, and Clearwater Lake near Annandale ranks right up there with Lake Minnetonka. It's loaded with largemouth bass and northerns.

Also there are all kinds of good largemouth bass lakes around the Mille Lacs Lake area. That one hundred mile radius around the Twin Cities extending into Wisconsin has some of the most fantastic bass fishing that you will ever find.

How about the lakes out of the Twin Cities area?

Capra: I'm not too familiar with the lakes in southern Minnesota, but I'm sure there are a lot of good bass lakes down there. Then you get up around the Leech Lake area where the muskie fishing is fantastic, well, the bass fishing is also fantastic up there.

Al and Ron Lindner and I were fishing on Leech Lake this spring and Al said let's go look for some bass. Now this is Walker Bay on Leech Lake which is noted for its tremendous walleye and muskie fishing.

We went in there and the three of us smoked the largemouth bass. I'm talking about bass up to four and a half pounds who probably never had seen a spinner bait or a plastic worm before. Al said, "Can you believe this?" Everyone goes up there fishing for muskies and walleyes, and here all those bass are sitting in shallows.

What is the range of your success regarding largemouth bass fishing in Minnesota?

Capra: I would consider it to be a poor day if I only caught a couple of fish. And a good day would be anything over ten to fifteen nice bass.

If you catch eight to ten largemouth bass in the two-plus-pound range, I would consider that a pretty good day on the lake.

What has been your best day for largemouth bass in Minnesota?

Capra: I had my best day on Clearwater Lake. I actually caught fifty some bass over two pounds in one day. It's one of the few lakes that you can get into a school of bass and catch fifteen to twenty of them without moving your boat.

How about your largest bass?

Capra: Six pounds. I caught it on a Big O crank bait on a little hump in Spring Park Bay on Lake Minnetonka.

I've caught a lot of big bass on crank baits even though many bass fishermen will tell you that crank baits aren't a big bass lure.

Will there ever be a new state record largemouth bass caught in Minnesota?

Capra: Eventually the state record will be broken.

Where will this new state record bass come from?

Capra: From a river system or a lake in southern Minnesota. Although the average bass in our rivers is smaller than the average bass in our lakes, there has got to be some tremendously big bass in our rivers since they are so underfished. And in southern Minnesota, I'm told, there are some very fertile lakes which are also underfished. When I say underfished, I don't mean exactly that. I mean they have much less pressure than the lakes in the metro area and most northern lakes have.

What's special about Minnesota fishing?

Capra: In Minnesota and Wisconsin we've got such a fantastic opportunity to do whatever type of fishing we want to do. If you want to fish shallow water, there are many lakes where you can do that successfully. There are lakes like Gull Lake where you can deep water fish. There are just thousands of good fishing lakes in Minnesota not to mention that there are many species of fish to be fished.

Chapter 5

GRANT HUGHES ON SMALLMOUTH BASS

The transition that Grant Hughes made from the "let's talk about it over drinks" sales world of suburbia to becoming a resort operator and patriarch of smallmouth bass fishing on Lake Vermilion, perhaps, isn't as complex as a caterpillar becoming a butterfly, but it does seem to be more of a metamorphosis than a simple career change.

"It's what I've always wanted to do," Grant said, referring to running his own resort with an emphasis on fishing. Nevertheless, while running the resort has given him the opportunity to catch many trophy fish (many five-plus-pound smallies and one that tipped the scale at seven pounds two ounces), this writer suspects that catching trophy smallies may also be one of Grant's motives for running a resort.

Grant was born and raised in Minneapolis, Minnesota where he spent much of his youth playing hockey. He attended Saint Thomas Academy in Saint Paul, Minnesota where he graduated from high school; then he went on to earn his bachelor's degree from the University of Minnesota.

Like many other young men Grant was well prepared for a traditional career. After spending several years as a buyer/manager of a two million dollar department for a large retail store, he became a sales representative for a national cosmetic company. Accordingly, he was well on the traditional road to success.

However, this life style had many frustrations, and Grant was not realizing any of his boyhood dreams so he and his wife Judy decided that they would give up suburbia and become resorters. "One day I called Judy from Chicago," Grant stated, "and asked what she thought about buying a resort on Lake Vermilion. She said, 'That sounds absolutely fantastic.' "

Well, that was fourteen years ago, and, by all appearances, becoming the proprietor of Muskego Point Resort has worked out very well for the Hugheses.

But the desire for this change in life style, from the fast lane to the dirt roads of the great north woods, was a dream of Grant's that had been dormant since his youth. As a youngster Grant had spent his summer vacations on Lake Vermilion and had learned there was life, and perhaps a better life, "Far from the centers of ambition," as the poet Robert Bly put it. These summer vacations in his youth were spent at his parent's cabin which is located only a mile from Muskego Point Resort. During these vacations he earned spending money by working at various resorts on the lake and by guiding inexperienced fishermen. Yet, who would have thought that this youngster would someday be guiding for nationally recognized bass fishing experts like Roland Martin.

Sometime after the Hugheses bought Muskego Point Resort, they met Al and Ron Lindner. After the Lindner's first visit in the spring of 1975, Al returned that fall because he thoroughly enjoyed fishing on Lake Vermilion. If any one single event has helped Grant become the fisherman he is today, it would have been his opportunity to share a boat with Al Lindner. Since that first visit Grant and Al have become good friends and have fished together on many occasions. "Al doesn't say a lot while he's fishing," Grant remarked, "but if you watch him, you have to learn something. And while fishing with Al, I decided that I wasn't going to be out-fished by anyone on my lake. That was my goal. I took Lake Vermilion as a challenge. And, of course, this has helped me succeed in my business since our guests have trust in me and my fishing knowledge."

Grant's ability and willingness to help fellow fishermen brings to mind a story that Joel Hafermann, owner of Riverside Sports in Shakopee, Minnesota related to me. He said, "If there are any fish to be caught in Lake Vermilion, Grant Hughes is the guy that can help you catch 'em. In fact, once when I was fishing on Lake Vermilion, I was having terrible luck. I couldn't even catch a bullhead. So I stopped at Grant's place and asked him for help. He gave me a few suggestions, and I tried again with little success. Well, after I had returned to Grant's place for the third time, he took me out fishing and showed me exactly what to do. We caught walleyes, smallies, and northerns. And the surprising thing about this guy is I wasn't even staying at his resort."

Muskego Point Resort is a deluxe fishing resort. If you would like further information, phone 218-666-5696 or write to: Muskego Point Resort, Cook, Minnesota 55723.

SMALLMOUTH BASS BEHAVIOR

Have you noticed any cycles in smallmouth bass behavior?

Hughes: There are cycles which probably have much to do with the predator/prey relationships including fishing pressure. On lakes where fishermen have raped the smallmouth, the walleye population will probably increase because both smallmouth and walleyes use very similar structure, and their food choices are very much the same.

For instance, fifty to sixty big smallmouth can put a lot of pressure on a bar, but if half are removed, the walleyes have a better opportunity for any food that might be there.

I see this relationship on Lake Vermilion where the walleye fishing is getting better because in the past few years the pressure on the smallies has been heavy.

Does smallmouth bass behavior vary from lake to lake?

Hughes: Provided that the structure and water temperature is adequate for them, I don't think their general behavior would vary much from lake to lake. Over a period of a year they will go through the same behavior cycles. Of course, they might have to go a little deeper in one lake as opposed to another, but if the structure is there, they will behave the same way.

I should qualify that by saying, I am referring to most Minnesota lakes and not lakes and reservoirs down south, for example, where other variables enter into the picture.

What are the smallmouth's feeding requirements?

Hughes: I don't know how much they feed. Of course, in warm water they will feed more heavily. But I can tell you that I have caught ninety percent of my five-plus-pound smallies during the evening hours. Not at night, evenings. And once the sun has gone down forget fishing for smallies until it has been dark for awhile.

Can you qualify evening?

Hughes: The last three hours of light and probably the middle hour and a half is the best. Then again about ten or eleven o'clock you can hammer those fish in warm water with a crayfish on a slip bobber rig.

How highly developed is the smallmouth basses memory?

Hughes: They condition to certain presentations in fishing, etc., but I wouldn't call it memory. And it's not just smallmouth bass either.

In fact, I think we're about due to see the return of the old Mille Lacs Lake Cocktail—the Flat Fish and crawler since most walleyes alive today haven't seen one. Although we would probably use a little different presentation than we did when they were first used, I think they would probably again catch a lot of fish. In the heyday of the Flat Fish and Lazy Ike lures everybody just trolled the whole lake with them at different speeds.

Is the smallmouth bass basically a shallow or deep water fish?

Hughes: It has been written many times that smallmouth bass never go deeper than twenty feet. That's bull crap! I've caught smallies in forty to fifty feet of water. Not very often, but I do know that they go deep on occasion. I think, rather than going down into deep water to eat, they go there to suspend. And they will suspend in deep water, during colder water periods, like dead wood. You could practically slap them in the face.

In Green Lake near Willmar fishermen take a lot of smallmouth in deep water. They are definitely not just a shallow water fish.

Smallmouth seem to have a territory. Maybe it's a sunken island or a couple of sunken islands or an extended point. You might have fifty on one extended point.

Furthermore, a smallmouth bass lives his whole life in a relatively small area. I don't think a smallie migrates ten miles to spawn, for example. Usually these home areas have everything a smallmouth needs. The spots that I usually fish and try to put people on have everything that a smallie needs—gravel, silt, sand, weeds, and rocks that vary in size from bowling balls to Volkswagens. Most of them will top between three and five feet in the shallowest places and they will also have quick access to deep water.

Tell me about the smallies spawning behavior.

Hughes: They do not necessarily spawn near shore as many people believe. They can spawn on a sunken island with twenty feet of water all around it. Also, I get the impression that most people feel that all fish that are of spawning age, spawn. I don't think so. On an exceptional year sixty to seventy percent of the smallmouth will dump their spawn. The rest of them will absorb the spawn. And in most years, I would guess that, only fifty percent or so will actually complete the spawning cycle.

You'd better elaborate on that statement.

Hughes: Fifty-six degree water temperature is the ideal temperature for female smallmouth to dump their spawn. Well it isn't very often when we have fifty-six degrees that lasts very long. In a typical spring the water temperature gets warm and then cold and then warm again. They are ready to dump their spawn, and then they have to hold on because the water temperature has changed before they have had a chance to spawn.

In fact, I can't think of a year when in July and August I haven't caught smallmouth bass with spawn left in them. It doesn't look like spawn because it has deteriorated and looks mushy.

The water temperature doesn't stay stable long enough. Usually, it warms too fast, and they aren't ready. But I don't think water temperature is as important with regards to spawning for other fish as it is for the smallmouth bass. For instance, the years we have had late ice-out, northerns have spawned under the ice.

You mentioned spawning size. What is spawning size for smallmouth bass?

Hughes: In Minnesota it is about a four year old fish which would be ten to twelve inches long.

Comment on your "dominant fish theory", if I may call it that.

Hughes: I have a live box which extends into the lake where I have kept smallmouth bass all summer, and there is always one dominant fish in the box that dominates when the fish feed. There probably will be some biologists that will say I'm nuts, but I have seen this happen enough that I would swear to it:

One fish eats first. When that fish is done eating, he regurgitates the last thing he has eaten. Then every other fish in that live box will go on feed the instant the dominant one regurgitates. It is not necessarily the biggest fish either. But pull that dominant fish out of the box and another will take his place. Then the new dominant fish eats and regurgitates the last thing he has eaten whether it's crayfish, leeches, or minnows. And when he regurgitates, the water just boils when all of the other fish go on feed.

I have changed these fish throughout the summer, and the phenomenon continues. Of course, the largest amount of smallies I have ever experimented with was six at any one time.

Also, this phenomenon doesn't just happen in my live box. How many times have you hooked a smallmouth and he regurgitates four or five little minnows, crayfish, or night crawlers, and all of a sudden you've got ten to fifteen smallies fighting to get the bait that was in the hooked fish's mouth. You bring the fish up to the boat, and there will be twenty fish just banging him to get that food. [How this phenomenon affects fishing is discussed in the presentation section of this chapter.]

How does the smallmouth bass differ from his cousin the largemouth bass?

Hughes: Largemouth bass are more adaptable within greater ranges and seem to be able to adapt to almost any water temperature or conditions. Being they are from the same family it is surprising that there are so many differences between them. Although smallmouth do enjoy warm water, basically they need colder water for more of the year than a largemouth does. But during Indian summers, for instance, when the water temperature gets cold (fifty-six to fifty-seven degrees) and then we have nice sunny days warming the water, by the third day the smallmouth are back in shallow water again. At this time of the year, they love it when they can find warm water.

LOCATING SMALLMOUTH BASS

Comment on locating smallmouth bass.

Hughes: They're home bodies. And by being home bodies, I feel, they are usually easy to catch. If you locate them at the right time, you can slaughter them. Here is where you should use good judgment—don't over-bag.

Also they school by size. Although you might have one or two big fish mixed in with four or five medium sized fish, usually they will be schooled by year-class. Very seldom will you find a bunch of small fish mixed in with big fish.

Do smallmouth bass follow schools of bait fish?

Hughes: They don't get very far away from their food supply. But that's not necessarily bait fish.

Do smallies relate to weeds as much as other game fish do?

Hughes: Oh yes! Basically they are a weed fish. They prefer the cabbage types of weeds provided it is not full of northerns and muskies.

When you are fishing weeds, don't fish the real long, shallow bays that are full of weeds. Fish the outer edges and preferably fish where you have an extended point coming out of a shallow bay with good deep water access on one side. Also, between two points is a good place to fish, and if there is a good weed growth between the points, that will be much more productive than the big, massive weedbed areas. And always fish any stickups or structure that might be mixed in with the weeds.

Comment on timber with regards to locating smallies.

Hughes: Timber is a good place to locate smallmouth bass. Preferably submerged timber and timber that has been under water at least one year. It seems like there aren't any fish on new cuts. And timber with a few rocks around it is even better. If you have stickups in the middle of a shallow, silty bay, it might hold a straggler, but he'll be a small one.

How important are rocks to the smallmouth bass?

Hughes: Rocks are the key. As far as I'm concerned, they are the overall most important locational factor in the smallmouth basses habitat.

And it's not just any kind of rocks. It's not the flat table rock, etc. It's bowling balls to Volkswagens. Rounded rocks with lots of nooks and crannies and not all bowling balls and not all Volkswagens either. A mixture of the two and preferably with a deep water access nearby.

All year 'round?

Hughes: They are using that as their association point. They might not be on it all times of the year; they might be out ten feet from it in thirty feet of water suspended at the twenty foot level, but their food chain will be there. Ninety percent of their feeding will be done right there.

Are all points good places to fish?

Hughes: Some points look so good. And some of them produce some of the time. But I don't know of any points that produce all of the time unless they are extended bars with good structure adjacent to them.

If you've got two points coming together with a mixture of bowling balls and Volkswagen size rocks, they will be better. A plain point just doesn't do it. You have to have the necessary rocks, weeds, etc.

Also, a point doesn't mean anything unless you know what's under the water. IT'S NOT THE ROCKS YOU SEE WITH YOUR EYES. IT'S THE ROCKS YOU SEE WITH YOUR LOCATOR THAT ARE IMPORTANT OR THE ROCKS YOU FEEL WITH YOUR LURE. Put that in big letters.

It's the good rocks under the water with good breaks very nearby that smallmouth will relate to all year long.

Let's go through a typical season with location in mind.

Hughes: Let's start with opener because nobody should be fishing smallmouth before that anyway.

A normal opener is usually relatively cold, maybe even a few snowballs. And during this colder water period the smallmouth bass, unlike some other species of fish, will be quite inactive. They will probably be suspended off of the breaks in twenty to twenty-five feet of water and will only move to shallower water if there is a warming trend on the surface. Usually by opener, which is mid-May in this part of Minnesota, the surface water temperature will be forty-six to forty-nine degrees. At this surface temperature, smallies will very seldom come into shallow water.

As the surface temperature warms to the mid-fifties, the last of May or early June, they will move up into shallow water. You will have that pre-pre-spawn movement: the smallmouth will move up into shallow water and then go back down again.

Why would they go back down before completing the spawning cycle?

Hughes: They are coming up to feed. And the females will feed aggressively for about ten days before they spawn. Then they will go back down into deeper water and come up about two days prior to spawning.

During this two day period the surface temperature will be sixty to sixty-one degrees, and in ten feet of water the temperature will be about fifty-six degrees. There will be less than a six degree temperature difference between the surface water and the water ten feet down. They will go on a feeding binge during this two day period, and I feel very strongly that they do this. And, at this time, they will hit almost any lure you've got. They will blast it! Also, they will be relating to the sandy parts of their home area rather than the rocky parts. That will be the sandy part closest to shore. If there is a piece that goes out and comes back up, they will be on shore side of it and not on the hump side.

Run that by me again.

Hughes: If you have a point coming out with sand and gravel that breaks to twenty feet of water and then comes up on a sunken island, and the sunken island has rocks, and so forth, on it, rather than locating on the sunken island the smallies will be on the shore side of it. But remember, they are still relating to that piece. They locate here because that area will have a relatively soft sand bottom, and that's where they prefer to make their nests and dump their eggs.

Once they dump their spawn the females will be inactive for about ten days. But you will still have some activity from the young bucks in the spawning area.

After the females drop their eggs, they will go down into deep water again and suspend, but when they come up—ten to twelve days after spawning—into the shallow water again, it will be on the sunken island part of the piece on the edges of the rocks, and they will spend their summer there.

Do smallies go on a post-spawn feeding binge like other species of fish do?

Hughes: I have never noticed any real feeding binge after spawning. They come back on feed of course, but it is nothing like a pre-spawn feed. Also, the bucks are much more active after spawning than the females. In fact, they will attempt to move anything off of the spawning beds—lures, salamanders, etc.

Let's finish seasonal location.

Hughes: During the summer period they will be near the closest access to deep water from the food shelf. They will spend their whole summer there. That is, the closest access from deep water to the rounded boulders unless they are driven off by fishing pressure or a big northern or biological and weather factors.

In the fall, about the last week in August, when the water temperature is near sixty degrees again, the smallmouth bass will make a move to the outermost part of their home area, and that is where they will stay until late fall—the ice-over period.

During this fall period they will move up to feed if there is a warming trend, and they will hit crank baits like you wouldn't believe.

Comment on the fall turnover period.

Hughes: Lakes can turnover more than once in the fall and especially shallower (lakes with an average depth of less than forty feet) bodies of water. Cold, windy weather and then a week of nice weather can cause a lake to turn over more than once.

In fact, during one year that I am aware of, Lake Vermilion had three fall turnovers, and Gull Lake had two fall turnovers.

But, in general, after the fall turnover period, the smallmouth bass will be scattered and can be found at any depth in the lake. At this time of the year catching smallies is no more difficult than other times of the year, but locating them can be much harder since they are scattered.

And this brings us to the ice-over period when the smallmouth bass are very, very inactive. In fact, I believe, they remain inactive almost twenty-four hours a day during the ice-over period.

What are some other locational clues?

Hughes: If birds, particularly loons and gulls, are working an area, they are working bait fish. When you see four or five gulls sitting over a piece of structure, you know they are not there because they are enjoying the water. They are there because there is something there to eat, and the smallies might be there for the same reason.

Also, look for minnows in the water and take notice as to what the fish you've caught might be spitting up. If they are spitting up minnows, use minnows for bait because that's what they're feeding on at that time. And be aware of what kind of bugs are on the water.

What will the presence of bugs tell me?

Hughes: I don't "match the hatch" [Choosing a lure that represents a bug.] the way trout fishermen do, but bugs are a food source for smallies. Hellgrammites and water beetles are like gum drops to smallies. The bugs are a locational key—find the bugs and very likely you will find the smallies.

Another locational clue that I pass on to my guests who like to fish for walleyes around opener is: Drop your temperature gauge into the water and if the warmer water is on the top, that's where the walleyes will be. And, conversely, if the warmer water is on the bottom, that's where the walleyes will be. But if the lake has already turned over (spring turnover, that is, just before opener), the water temperature will be the same temperature in the upper part as it is in the lower part, and the walleyes could be at any depth. In this situation, you know it's going to be tough fishing since the fish will be so scattered.

How important are topographical maps in helping locate good structure to fish?

Hughes: They would certainly be helpful if you could find one that was accurate. But I have never seen a good one, and most of them aren't even close. If they showed one one-hundredth of what was there, it would be a miracle.

Well, maybe the worst map is better than no map at all, but usually you are going to have to run through some water to determine the productive and nonproductive areas of a lake.

Any final thoughts on location?

Hughes: Yes. I didn't mention that I try to never run the same water when I'm coming or going on the lake. Even if I know exactly where I'm going, I might run twenty feet from shore going and run thirty feet from shore when I'm coming back. And tomorrow I might run forty feet from shore going and fifty feet from shore coming back. Of course, this doesn't help you if you don't watch your locator.

Even as much as I've been up and down Lake Vermilion, I will still find some things I hadn't seen before. Look at the structure in between your fishing spots. Try not to run the same path twice and you will often find new things to fish. It might only be an old stove or refrigerator, but it might hold a big smallmouth bass or an eight pound walleye. And the beauty of most of these finds is you can fish them in a couple of minutes.

PRESENTATION FOR SMALLMOUTH BASS

Do you prefer live bait to artificial lures or vice versa?

Hughes: There is a time and a place for both. I feel very strongly about both. I'm not a purist.

Unfortunately, the biggest problem with live bait is the amount of fish killed with it because it's very, very difficult to predict where you are going to drive that hook.

Comment on lures from opener throughout the season.

Hughes: I start out the season with artificials: single spins, Beetle Plus, and the Fuzz-E-Grub Plus, etc. I use small lures around opener, nothing bigger than a quarter ounce and often an eighth ounce size until those fish go into pre-spawn patterns. The only exception would be a jig and pig where you might want to go a little bigger.

I should mention that in the Lake Vermilion area, opener for smallmouth bass is the closest Saturday to the fifteenth of May. Now that's not true for most of Minnesota where lakes aren't open until the end of May for smallies.

Getting back to lures. I will usually use artificials until the surface temperature of the water reaches about forty-nine degrees. Then there will be a brief period where I will use leeches and night crawlers, but for the most part it will be a jig and eel combination. This is still pre-spawn I'm referring to.

Then the short period immediately before spawning is topwater heaven. Any minnow or stick type bait all the way up to six inches will really turn them on.

What lures do you use during the spawning period?

Hughes: Right during spawning I'm still using topwater lures. Mostly stick baits—minnow imitations.

Most of the summer months, post-spawn on, I'll use live bait. Although I can catch a lot of smallmouth bass on artificials during the summer, I can catch many more using live bait.

What live baits do you prefer during the summer period?

Hughes: Jumbo leeches. The true jumbos that are about an inch and a half across the back and four inches long. Also, they should be firm and black, and the smallies will eat them like popcorn. They love 'em! Night crawlers and minnows are good, but if you use a minnow, it better be a red-tail chub. Smallmouth will take a red-tail chub a hundred to one over any other kind of minnow. And, you might have guessed, red-tail chubs are the hardest to get.

But, I have no doubt, crayfish are the smallmouth basses number one staple in his summer diet. Crayfish are a son-of-a-gun to fish with unless you are using a slip bobber rig to keep them from getting hung up in the rocks. They will crawl under the rocks, and you will rip them off of your hook, and they are also very expensive. But on a slip bobber rig they can just hang there in front of the fish's face without getting hung up. And smallmouth bass will eat crayfish in any stage of the crayfish's development; that is, they don't have to be in the soft shell stage although soft shell is preferred. And I don't recommend using large crayfish.

Comment on your choice of lures in late summer and early fall.

Hughes: That's the crank bait season. This would be about Labor Day on or until the water surface temperature is in the low fifties. The water surface temperature during this period will be about fifty-six degrees, and I will continue throwing crank baits until it gets down to fifty-two degrees.

We haven't discussed crank baits.

Hughes: My favorite crank baits are the old Big O's, Bombers, and Bagleys in the shape of crayfish in all shades of orange. There is a period around Labor Day when I do very well with chartreuse and no orange on that lure at all—it's the small fry crank bait in the baby bass pattern. And most of the time I throw deep divers with a tight action.

What is the best crank bait for big smallmouth bass?

Hughes: The 7600 and 7800 series Big O has probably turned more smallmouth over five pounds for me than any other hard bait I have ever thrown. They have a clear lip which is very important. I don't know why, but smallmouth bass seem to hit those much better. I have thrown numerous painted lip crank baits, but I don't have anywhere near the success with them that I do with the clear lip cranks.

Many of the bait companies are no longer producing the natural colors in cranks, but I feel very strongly about those natural patterns. They're darn good. But fishermen like to have something new all the time, and I'm no exception.

Comment on lure size.

Hughes: I don't necessarily believe you need a smaller lure during cold weather for smallies. In fact, I have caught some of my better fish on the bigger size crank baits in colder water in the fall. I just don't seem to take quality fish on smaller lures. Other than spring, as we discussed earlier, I prefer larger baits and large lures.

How large is large?

Hughes: For example, I like a three and a half inch to a four inch redtail chub on a quarter to a three-eighths ounce jig.

Is there anything else about lures? Plastic worms, salamanders, etc.?

Hughes: Plastic worms aren't very good for smallmouth bass. And salamanders aren't at all as good as they are supposed to be either.

Many times when I have used salamanders for smallies, I have caught six ounce bluegills, and that doesn't make much sense does it. Water dogs, or whatever you call them, just cost too much and don't produce very well.

I thought one of your largest smallies ever was on a salamander?

Hughes: That's true. The second largest smallie I ever caught was on a salamander. But it was the only good fish I have ever hooked on a salamander, and I think it probably would have preferred another bait.

At this point in time, I don't think there is any dynamite bait around. We have shown them the same lures and the same leeches long enough.

Are there any seasonal differences in presentation that we haven't covered?

Hughes: When using live bait, your retrieve should always be made slowly, especially in cold water conditions. With artificial lures a slow retrieve isn't as important. It's much more important that artificials are running true, and that you are getting down deep enough.

On a typical opener I would fish with a small, soft bodied jig: a Fuzz-E-Grub or an Ugly Beetle Plus. Or, perhaps, a jig with rubber legs or maybe maribou. That's because it's the prime time for the first insect hatches. I particularly like using black Fuzz-E-Grubs with white legs and not tipped with a minnow and jig 'em at a moderate retrieve and the smallmouth will hit them on the drop.

In early June or so you can use more surface baits—topwater lures. And with topwater lures you'll very seldom take a fish on the retrieve. They will hit when the lure hits the water or when you twitch the lure, not on a straight retrieve. After it hits the water, put some action into it. Twitch it six inches or so. Twitch it four or five times like it's a crippled or an injured minnow. Then wait a few seconds and do it again.

Then during the summer period I will pick my location and fan cast it with a crank bait real quickly. With cranks you will take the aggressive fish first.

I'm moving all the time. I don't like to throw an anchor unless I cannot possibly hold the boat without one. I'll move around the edge of the contour and cast all the prime locations with a crank bait. On my second pass I will use live bait and work off of the top and down the sides.

Even with live bait if I take a fish, I don't plant myself and work the heck out of one particular rock. Also, unless I'm taking fish on every two to three casts, the maximum time I will spend on a particular piece is fifteen to twenty minutes.

Do you feel that you have worked an area thoroughly in that short of time?

Hughes: I have worked it enough to take any hawgs that might be there. I'm sure I leave a lot of fish behind, but by doing that I can go back the next day and take a few more. And I can do it year after year. If you raise too much commotion on a piece, the next day will be negative city.

Comment on your technique for fishing a crank bait.

Hughes: If I'm fishing a five foot hump, for example, I will use a crank bait that will run eight to nine feet deep because it will hit a boulder and deflect off and often that's when the fish will hit the lure. I don't know whether it is the noise or the change in motion, but they are probably following the crank bait and that's when they choose to strike it.

The bills on crank baits should be just plowing into those rocks which will tear up a lot of lures, but that's part of the game. Also, when fishing a crank bait properly, you will get hung up a lot. If you are not hung up a lot, you are not fishing a crank properly.

What other types of structure or cover is a crank bait effective on?

Hughes: Lots. But, especially in the fall, I like to crank the tops of rock piles and extended points. I will work the sides of those dead weedbeds where there is a long extended rock point coming out. Crank baits are also very effective in the fall where you have two points coming fairly close together with weeds off to one side and rocks in between.

Is most of your fishing in shallower water?

Hughes: Most of the time I fish in ten feet of water or shallower for all species with the exception of crappies.

There are times when I see fishermen drowning a minnow in fifty feet of water in the month of August when I'm catching walleyes in a foot of water. You can catch three pound walleyes in a foot of water in the middle of the day in August. And that's probably true of many lakes, but I know it's true for Lake Vermilion.

What is the best live bait presentation for lunker smallies?

Hughes: The one key presentation that has turned on more big smallmouth bass is a number eight hook with four pound test line with a number five or number seven split shot up about fifteen inches above the hook. Minnows, crayfish, leeches, and night crawlers all work well on this rig.

How do you present it to the fish?

Hughes: I'm more or less flipping it to them. I flip it in just behind the rocks. If they don't hit it immediately, I don't move it. I drop it to the bottom and force myself to leave it there laying in the rocks for about ten seconds. And when I move it, I only move it a couple of inches. Usually the second you move it, you'll get blasted. Otherwise you are snagged.

And the best thing to do when you are snagged, is to rip it off and retie. Never go up for it because you will spook the fish, and besides that, a hook and a split shot are only two or three cents anyway.

You can use the same technique with jigs, but it's a little harder because jigs get hung up much more often. And when I use jigs, I use the lightest possible jig I can use to get the bait down to the fish.

What size range of jigs are you referring to?

Hughes: A sixteenth to three-eighths and that will vary depending on depth, wind, and bottom content. You are not going to throw a three-eighths ounce jig in the junk since it would just disappear in that stuff. And to maintain control of your lure when it's windy, you may have to use a large jig.

After you have made your initial cast, the key is a slow retrieve bringing it back and letting it drop, and so on. Let it sit down there for a little while, and the strike will usually come on the drop of the lure so don't lose contact with your lure. I always stress a slow retrieve when fishing with live bait.

Earlier we discussed your theory that one dominant smallmouth bass will always feed before the others in a given school of bass. Does this theory have any applications in presentation?

Hughes: Oh yes! Indeed it does! For instance, if you hook a smallmouth bass and he regurgitates four or five little minnows, crayfish, leeches, or crawlers, and then all of a sudden you've got ten to fifteen smallies fighting to get the bait that was in the hooked fish's mouth, you can catch all fifteen of them. To do this, you do not boat the hooked fish until your fishing partner, if you are not fishing alone, gets his line in the water.

Al Lindner and I did this on Trout Lake, and we couldn't believe it. He had hooked a smallie, and there were all kinds of other smallies right around it. But before he boated his fish I threw my lure right near the hooked fish and within a second I had hooked a fish. Then he boated his fish and threw right back at the one I had on and he hooked another one. It was just boom, boom so fast we had fish after fish on.

And this phenomenon happens often. The theory has to be correct. It happens and happens very regularly. When you get 'em like that, they'll slam anything—a stick bait, a jerk bait, anything.

Are you saying that if I'm fishing and hook a smallmouth bass, I shouldn't land him until my partner has a chance to cast near the fish I've hooked and then he'll probably hook one, too? Then after I've landed my fish, I should cast at the fish he's hooked, and I will hook another one, and so on?

Hughes: Yes. That's exactly what I'm saying. But, of course, it has to be a situation which I described where you have other fish following the one that you have hooked. If you take that fish out of the water, the others will leave. It seems that once the activity is gone the others will leave. Also, there is a dominant fish in each school no matter what size the school is, and the dominant fish isn't necessarily the largest fish in the school either, which is something I do not understand.

If you doubt me, I know Al Lindner will verify this phenomenon. You can totally wipe out a school of smallmouth bass in five minutes.

But I hope no one uses this technique to overbag or rape a given area of good sized smallmouth bass. Catch 'em and enjoy it, but release them.

After that bit of information, I don't know if anybody will care if I ask this next question or not, but I'll ask it anyway. How effective is a bobber system in fishing for smallmouth bass?

Hughes: A bobber fisherman can catch a lot of smallmouth bass. He has perfect control over his bait. He has perfect control over the depth he is fishing. And he can keep from being snagged. I'm referring to a slip bobber system, that is.

And late in the fall a slip bobber system may be one of the better presentations. A slip bobber with a crayfish (when crayfish aren't hibernating) on the hook and as little weight as you can get by with, may be the presentation that will take the next state record smallmouth bass. Also, it's a good presentation to use in late summer or early fall at night. Midnight to about three o'clock in the morning.

Earlier you said that you don't troll for smallmouth bass, but trolling can be productive.

Hughes: You can take a lot of fish trolling using live bait or a Shad Rap—something that will stay at one level should produce some good suspended fish.

I don't troll, per se; I just move. But sometimes I might pull a rig with live bait in twenty to twenty-five feet of water just off of the side of a piece of structure.

How important is boat control?

Hughes: Very important. It's half of the battle. You should move your boat along the contour and don't forget your partner. You could be fishing in twenty feet of water, and he might be fishing in four feet of water.

And to troll properly, you must backtroll or pull your boat with a front mount electric trolling motor. Actually, most people know what to do, but they get careless.

Is there anything that you would like to add to this section on presentation?

Hughes: One thing that comes to mind regarding lures is color and action are much more important than shape and texture.

WEATHER AND BIOLOGICAL FACTORS AFFECTING SMALLMOUTH BASS

Let's start with wind.

Hughes: It's important. During the first six to eight hours of wind, smallies will locate on the windy side of structure, and after eight hours or so, they will be on the lee side.

Why is that?

Hughes: I don't know. Possibly the bait fish move. All I know is that smallmouth bass will move to the back side of structure; they won't put up with the wind for more than six to eight hours.

How about the old barometric pressure affect?

Hughes: I don't know. All I know is that it can raise hell with my fishing, but I don't know why.

Comment on water temperature.

Hughes: I don't think smallmouth bass will leave their home area unless they are forced to by undesirable water temperature. Possibly undesirable pH levels and oxygen levels, too. Only the drastic changes can get them to leave because they are very much home bodies.

They will use a piece of structure differently depending on water temperature, too. For example, during Indian summer if it is cold, they might be down in twenty feet of water, but three days later if the surface water temperature warms, they will be right back up in the shallows feeding again. They're using a particular piece of structure by locating in different places on it. They will go up, down, or around it.

Take a very large piece like Niles on Lake Vermilion which has probably sixty tops. Sometimes they will be on the five foot tops, and sometimes they will be on the seven foot tops, and then sometimes they will be on the twenty foot tops depending basically on the water temperature.

If you find a school of smallies on the twenty foot tops, for instance, then fish all the twenty foot tops. It isn't very often that you will find good fishing on the five foot tops and good fishing on the twenty foot tops also. Very, very seldom will you find that, and if you do, it is perhaps during a total lake change.

Are cloudy days better than bright, bluebird sky days for fishing?

Hughes: Not necessarily. A bright sky can be an advantage or it can kill you. The key factor would be the time of the year, and the wind plays a part, too.

For instance, in the spring a bright sky will warm cold water, and fish are eager to get into warm water. Smallmouth will make a move to shallower, warmer water. In this case a bright sky would be an asset in fishing.

Later in the year as the water gets quite warm, a bright sky can be pretty tough to fish, but it isn't as critical as it would be if you were fishing walleyes. Also a bright sky condition won't hurt fishing at all after four o'clock in the afternoon.

How does rain affect smallmouth bass fishing?

Hughes: Rain is great! Just so it doesn't rain on the day I want to go fishing. It makes me uncomfortable. Although I have caught some good size smallmouth in the rain, it hasn't happened very often.

Fishing just before and during a lightning storm is supposed to be great fishing.

Hughes: Just get off of the lake regardless of all of those notions about great fishing during a lightning storm. I've had a couple of bad experiences with lightning and never again. It's just too dangerous to be out there.

How about the old cold front excuse for not catching fish?

Hughes: A big Canadian cold front goose stepping in can screw up your fishing really bad. But it's simply because we're not versatile enough to switch to whatever it is we need to do to catch them after a cold front. We don't know enough to accept it. We are catching fish today and tomorrow after the cold front, we're not catching fish. Do we look somewhere else? No! We blame the cold front because it's an easy excuse. I don't know what the answer is, but I think it screws up our heads more than it screws up the fish.

How does the fall turnover affect smallmouth bass fishing?

Hughes: Whether you have a thermocline or not, you are going to have turnover. And once a lake turns over the smallmouth fishing is darn tough.

After turnover, the smallmouth will be highly negative, and they will usually suspend over deep water near their home structure. If there's a warming trend, they will completely reverse their location and come into shallower water again.

If it continues to get colder after fall turnover, the smallmouth will continue to suspend, and I don't think anything changes that, even during ice-over. They will stay there until spring. Now I could be wrong, but immediately after ice-out, they seem to be where they were just prior to ice-over.

Recently we've read a lot about pH levels in water. What are your thoughts about it?

Hughes: I don't know enough about it yet. Certainly it is important, but I'm not certain of the smallmouths' preferred pH level. But we may find that it is more important in fishing than water temperature and oxygen levels.

Oxygen was the next topic that I was going to ask you to discuss.

Hughes: It's definitely important. The upper twenty feet of water in a shield lake will almost always be very thoroughly oxygenated. Very seldom will you have much oxygen depletion above twenty feet.

Oxygen depletion will occur below twenty feet and also in the cabbage beds when the weeds start to brown out and use oxygen in the fall. At this time of the year smallmouth will leave the weeds and go back to the rocks; if in fact, they have left the rocks.

How does the thermocline affect smallmouth bass?

Hughes: They will always stay above the thermocline. But Lake Vermilion, for example, doesn't have a very definite thermocline since it is a shallow lake. You'll never pick up the thermocline on a graph on Lake Vermilion.

On Vermilion Trout Lake in August you can read the thermocline on a graph like a second bottom because it's so defined. If there are game fish below the thermocline, they are probably big northerns, trout, or whitefish.

Do you see any relationship between moon phases and fishing?

Hughes: I have done my best on the first day of the full-moon, that is, not quite full-moon. Then fishing gets worse as the moon becomes more full. I'd rather have no moon than a full-moon.

Comment on water clarity.

Hughes: If you have gin-clear water, the fish will be quite a bit spookier than if you're fishing dingy or dirty water. And smallmouth bass have to have relatively clean water to live in. It doesn't have to be clear water, it can be stained, but they don't do well in cloudy or dingy water. When I'm fishing for smallmouth in clear water, I use light line and I have a tendency to use darker lures on bright days and brighter lures on dark days which is the opposite as I would do for walleyes. For example, I like fluorescent orange on a cloudy day because, I feel, the contrast helps.

EQUIPMENT AND TACKLE FOR SMALLMOUTH BASS FISHING

What are your preferences for colors in lures?

Hughes: In general, anything that's got orange on it. A brown bait with a white belly and an orange stripe is good. And in crank baits it has to have some of the crayfish colors on it. In spinners I prefer brown and orange skirts and sometimes browns or blacks. I have also done well on white spinners. When I use single spins, I prefer black, brown, grape, and some brighter colors in the Lake Vermilion type of water.

Do you use snaps or swivels?

Hughes: Other than on a Lindy Rig, I don't use them. But if you are trolling and getting a lot of line twist, I don't think it would hurt to use them if you use the black colored ones.

You said that you prefer light line; is that for sport?

Hughes: I'm a great believer in light line. It is more sporting. Also, it should increase your strikes two to one over the next size heavier line, especially in clear water.

I once caught a nineteen and three quarter pound northern on eight pound test line, and I had broken my rod when I set the hook.

How did you get that northern in?

Hughes: I took my time.

What length snells work best?

Hughes: There's no best length; just so it's not too long. I don't use those prefabs because I never know how long I want my snell to be until I get to the location that I'm going to fish. You might need an eight incher or a four footer.

There's a six foot prefab snell on the market today and how anybody has any control over a six foot snell is beyond me. I never use a snell longer than forty inches. And I usually use them with a floating rig or jig.

What are your preferences in rods and reels?

Hughes: I hate the buggy whip type rods. I like a fast taper rod with enough backbone to set the hook. I enjoy playing a fish, but not until he is so tired he will die when I release him. Don't play with a fish until he is exhausted. And even with ultralight rods, I prefer one with some backbone.

My favorite reel for an ultralight rod is the old Zebco Cardinal Three.

What is your preference in boats?

Hughes: Ranger.

Comment on electric trolling motors.

Hughes: I have a Mercury Thruster which I'm not satisfied with. The best electric I ever owned was an Eagle twenty-four volt unit. It had lots of power and was very quiet.

Is there anything that you want to add about equipment and tackle?

Hughes: Yes. I've never been able to put together any kind of a pattern in a shield lake for smallmouth bass with plastic worms. I've used all colors and sizes, too.

MISCELLANEOUS INFORMATION ABOUT SMALLMOUTH BASS FISHING

Earlier you mentioned that you fish Lake Vermilion as five different bodies of water. How do you divide those bodies of water?

Hughes: Wakemup, Norwegian, and Head of Lakes I fish as one body of water. Then the Narrows including part of Niles Bay is another lake. Also, Niles to the east and Oak Narrows and Smarts Bay for another grouping of water. Frazier Bay is a totally separate lake in itself. And last, the Big Bay area, including the area behind Pine Island, as another lake.

Why do you separate Lake Vermilion into these areas for fishing purposes?

Hughes: The water temperature will vary as much as seven degrees from area to area in Lake Vermilion. This is probably due to varying water depths. Also the oxygen content and the bottom structure varies tremendously.

The Tower end of the lake is like the Appalachian Mountains and from Frazier Bay on up to the west end of the lake is like a hike through the Rockies. Lake Vermilion has smooth and rough jagged structure which can make it a very difficult lake to fish. For example, when I mark a topo map for a guest, I have to be sure to tell them exactly where to fish, say a sunken island, because that particular area may have a hundred sunken islands within a square mile. And all of them might top within a foot of each other, but that particular one might have the fish on it that week. It's a confusing lake because so much of it looks the same, but isn't the same.

Go into more detail on the differences in the lake.

Hughes: Lake Vermilion is a shield lake and also a mid-meso lake. So many of the shield lakes are just barren rock bottom lakes. The glacial shield lakes are relatively shallow rock basin lakes. The average depth on Vermilion, for instance, is only forty feet deep. It's a shallow lake with its basin silted in, and it has areas of mid-meso type weed growth, etc. Some of this is because of where it is located.

Lake Vermilion is just north of the Laurentian Divide and has no pollution running into it. The Laurentian Divide is the place on the continent where the water shed changes: the water south of it flows south and the water north of it flows north. Just thirty miles south of here the water flows south, and here it flows north. On land you can't even notice the Laurentian Divide, but by air it looks like a mountain range. So anything we put in our water Canada gets.

Lake Vermilion does have a low pH which is common to shield lakes. It isn't critical though. And because the lake is somewhat silted we are somewhat protected from the damages of acid rain.

Do you enter fishing tournaments?

Hughes: I don't have the time to fish them because of my business. I like competition, but I don't know if I would enjoy big tournaments. Besides, we should fish for fun, not money.

Comment on "catch and release" and the future of fishing.

Hughes: Something that my friend Al Lindner has preached for the last few years has to be driven home: The public has a tremendous amount of fishing knowledge so it's pretty easy to catch fish, but it's hard to stop catching them. It's really important that we release fish and learn more about releasing fish properly so they don't die later as a result of being released improperly.

So many guys claim to be "catch and release Joe" when, in fact, they are "catch, kill, and release Joe". We need to be very aware of how lucky we are and be very, very wary of those who over-fish a species. We have to deal with the guy who takes home his limit every weekend. We need to fish for fun, not for food. I actually beg some of my guests to release fish.

People who know better, have come to Lake Vermilion and kept over two hundred smallmouth bass. I don't care if they catch a thousand smallmouth bass, they should only take home six of them, and, preferably, they don't take home any, unless it's one to put on the wall.

Smallmouth bass are a very special fish and have more heart than anything that swims. They don't deserve to be butchered.

Where will the next state record smallmouth bass come from?

Hughes: It will come from one of these shield lakes, and I don't think we are very far from it. I'd be surprised if it came out of a river, although it might.

There are many lunker smallmouth bass in these mixed shield-meso lakes and combining that with the light fishing pressure up here, I would be surprised if it didn't come out of Lake Vermilion, Basswood, or La Croix. One of these lakes right along here.

How much of fishing is luck?

Hughes: Sixty/forty. Sixty percent of fishing is knowledge and forty percent is luck, and I know that makes luck pretty high, but how much do we really know about fish anyway. Not very much at all.

What's your largest smallie to date?

Hughes: Three years ago I caught a seven pound two ounce smallmouth bass on Lake Vermilion. I had four pound test line on with a leech for bait and was fishing on Breezy Point in Frazier Bay. It was seven o'clock in the evening late in July, and I hooked him on the first cast.

I've had a couple of bigger smallmouth bass on and lost them both. In fact, I know I have lost a ten pounder on Lake Vermilion or, at least, a new state record.

Name some of your favorite lakes in Minnesota.

Hughes: There's lakes up here full of smallmouth bass. Basswood Lake has many smallmouth and Rainy Lake is very good, too. Vermilion Trout Lake is a nice lake to fish because it has the story book type of structure you've always read about for smallmouth bass fishing with gin-clear water and lots of timber. You can see the fish and cast right to them. They are stacked up around every log. It's great fun!

Shagawa Lake near Ely is an excellent smallmouth lake, too. In fact, many of the lakes near Ely are good smallmouth bass lakes.

But I also like many of the small lakes that most people don't know about. We've got some little ones in this area that you can sneak into for a day and take a nice stringer of fish. They don't have the average size that Lake Vermilion does, but you can catch fifty to sixty of them in a day.

Also Rainy Lake out of International Falls has very large smallies. Crane Lake and Sand Point in this area have excellent smallmouth bass, and they are seldom fished properly for smallmouth bass.

To what extent should a fisherman be concerned with the smallmouths' ability to smell and taste?

Hughes: I hear many fishermen say that the human scent on a lure can turn fish off. But how do we know that fish don't like the smell of humans.

I'm a cigarette smoker, and I've had guys in my boat who aren't smokers, and one day they might out-fish me, but the next day I out-fish them. Smell and maybe even taste plays a part in fishing, but how much of a part I don't know.

To what extent do smallmouth bass move and migrate?

Hughes: They move within their home range or region, but I don't think smallies migrate. Maybe in rivers they migrate. Basically, they are pretty much home bodies.

What types of people do you like to fish with?

Hughes: I like to fish with people who feel as I do—a day on the lake is super and if we catch fish, it's a plus. I have my favorite species of fish to fish for, but I enjoy fishing for all species.

What do you know about acid rain?

Hughes: I don't claim to know a lot about it, but it's very disturbing. I understand that within ten years it could kill many of the lakes in the northeastern part of Minnesota.

Do you use those fish scent products that have recently come on the market?

Hughes: They mask the human scent, and some of the new ones have proven to be a definite aid in some circumstances.

What is your range of success regarding smallmouth bass fishing?

Hughes: What do you mean?

Would you be satisfied with six smallies in the three pound range on a given day?

Hughes: No. I'm spoiled. I guess if all I caught was six smallmouth bass weighing three pounds each, I would be disappointed.

You would!

Hughes: If I caught twenty-five smallies ranging between two and three pounds, I would say I had a fun afternoon. But to be successful, I would have to catch one over five pounds.

You are spoiled!

Hughes: I am. And I'm the first to admit it. I've probably caught as many five pound smallmouth bass as anybody has, and I didn't even know I was doing anything special.

How many?

Hughes: Many, many of them. But my goal now is to catch the state record smallmouth bass, and I want to catch it in Lake Vermilion. I know she's here, and I'm going to get her!

Comment on negative -vs- active fish.

Hughes: When fish are negative, you must fine tune your presentation. You can locate negative fish, but the difference between a few fish and a successful outing would be presentation.

Actually, most of the time, I don't think we are fishing anything but neutral to negative fish, so presentation is very, very important almost all of the time.

What do you do when fish aren't active?

Hughes: When fishing gets tough, you have to be versatile, trying different lures and locations. I work many different locations—I'm a jump fisherman. I don't fish in-between spots. With smallmouth bass I never continue on down a shoreline looking for a straggler like I might if I were fishing for largemouth bass.

If I don't turn a smallie after fishing a half a dozen spots that are similar types of structure, I'll switch to another type of structure.

If I haven't been out for a couple of days, to put together a pattern I work several different types of structure, but I always work several of the same types of structure before I switch to the next type because of the error possibilities in fishing just one or two.

What do you find special about Minnesota fishing?

Hughes: We should feel very privileged to live in a state with so much water and so many species of fish to choose from.

Chapter 6

MARK WINDELS ON MUSKIES

How many muskie fishermen do you know of, or have you heard of, that can boast a legal size muskie boated for every day they have fished for muskies? Well, two years ago Mark Windels caught thirty-seven legal size muskies in forty-five days of fishing, and last year he boated thirty-five legal size muskies in as many days. That's not a legal muskie a day, but for most Muskie Hunters it would be the stuff dreams are made of.

It is not surprising that Mark Windels and his muskie fishing techniques have been the subject of many magazine articles and books. He is also a sought after seminar speaker since he is one of the most successful muskie fishermen in the country today.

Among his other accomplishments in the fishing world, Mark is a successful tournament fisherman. The Indian Head Pro Muskie Tournament is a challenge for any muskie fisherman and a good example of Mark's ability to catch muskies. This annual tournament is held on Deer Lake and Bone Lake in Wisconsin. It is a two day tournament that consists of one hundred and forty fishermen, seventy fishing on Bone Lake and seventy fishing on Deer Lake the first day, and then the fishermen switch lakes on the second day.

Over the years Mark and his various partners have finished fourth, fifth, sixth, and in first place twice. In two of these tournaments Mark's team has landed the biggest muskie. In 1983 he and his partner, Harley Ogata, were the only team with more than one muskie in this two day competition. In fact, they had four legal muskies out of the twenty-one caught by the one hundred and forty anglers competing.

Initially, Mark had carved out his reputation as a muskie expert by consistently catching large muskies, and, I might add, by releasing most of them. He never keeps a muskie that he doesn't intend to mount.

I asked Mark to do the muskie chapter of this book for several reasons. First, of course, is his ability to consistently catch large muskies; second, he is a conservationist believing in "catch and release"; third, having been trained as a scientist, his perspective on fishing goes far beyond just being a fisherman; and finally, he is also a manufacturer of fishing tackle which broadens his outlook on the sport of fishing.

However, no one becomes a great fisherman over night. Mark started fishing the Mississippi River near his boyhood home in Saint Cloud when he was a youngster. At that time, most of his fish catching was limited to rock bass, bullheads, carp, and an occasional smallmouth bass. When the Windels vacationed at their cabin on Daggett Lake on the White Fish Chain, Mark spent most of his time honing his fishing skills on northerns and bass.

Then about thirteen years ago when he was in his mid-twenties, he began specializing in muskie fishing. Although Mark is pleased to catch twenty pound muskies, today he devotes most of his fishing time to hunting trophy muskies. He won't keep a muskie under thirty pounds since he is not a meat fisherman and doesn't believe a fish as rare as a muskie should be taken to ultimately become someone's supper.

Mark's entry into the fishing tackle industry was somewhat unintentional, if not accidental. That is, he was dissatisfied with the lures and leaders that were available, and since he was continually having to modify them to meet his standards he decided to make his own. Eventually, he began selling his own line of panfish jigs and a bucktail spinner for muskie fishing. Apparently, there were other fishermen who were unhappy with the quality of lures available since there was an immediate demand for his products, and soon he left his job and became a full-time tackle manufacturer.

Windels Tackle Company is located at 121 Mill Street in Crookston, Minnesota 56716. Many bait and tackle shops in Minnesota carry Mark's lures and stainless steel leaders, the most popular being Panfish Snacks, Rabbit Hair Jigs, Walleye Snacks, Bass Harassers, and several models of the Muskie Harasser.

MUSKIE BEHAVIOR

How do muskies spawn?

Windels: They spawn at random. The male muskie swims alongside of the female muskie and when the female drops her eggs, the male drops milt over them. They randomly strew their eggs along the shore. As a result, they seem to be rather poor spawners which is one of the reasons they never seem to be overly abundant in any one area. This is probably their form of population control which is important since they're on the top of the food chain. And muskies do not stay in the spawning area to protect their eggs the way bass do. Also, since they do spawn late in the season (late May to early June) much of the hatch is eaten by perch and northerns, etc. They're very poor survivors which is another of the reasons they're not abundant. Of course, once they reach a certain size their survival rate is very high.

Do muskies school and, if so, do they school by size the way many other species of fish do?

Windels: Yes they school, but not by size though. I have found two or three muskies using a particular piece of structure and there might be a couple small ones mixed with a big one. Those three muskies or so would constitute what I would call a school. If they do school, they school in small numbers, but they're not strictly solitary, and you can definitely find big muskies mixed with smaller ones.

Do muskies mix with northerns?

Windels: Very often you can catch muskies and northerns on consecutive casts. They are not necessarily mixing or schooling together, but they are using the same area to feed. However, muskies will eat northerns so you won't often see a small northern in the same area as a large muskie. A northern will eat anything smaller than itself. In fact, a northern is a somewhat more aggressive feeder than a muskie.

Comment on how and when muskies feed.

Windels: Feeding is going to vary with water temperature. There is going to be less feeding when the water is cold since it takes a long time for a fish to digest a large meal, and most muskies eat single large meals like a one pound sucker, for example. It takes a long time to digest a one pound sucker in cold water so they are going to feed infrequently during colder water periods like spring and fall. And, conversely, they will feed more frequently in the warmer water periods.

How does that relate to the theory that fish feed heavily in the fall?

Windels: While I have no facts to back it up, this notion that fish put on the feed bag in the fall makes no sense at all. When you have cold water, if anything, the fish are feeding much less than they do in the summer.

The reason fall fishing is good, I would guess, is the lack of fishing pressure, and the weedbeds are dying out. Quite simply, fish are more vulnerable. Anytime a fish is moving and frequenting shallow water it becomes vulnerable. They are moving along shorelines stopping at various places to feed and at those times they become easier to catch.

Further, muskies do not seem to be very active in the winter, and they are seldom caught by ice fishermen. Walleyes, for example, are active in the winter, but that is not to say they are eating more, they are just catchable.

We know fish have instincts, but do muskies also have habits?

Windels: I think since muskies are usually found in shallow water you could term that shallow water frequency a habit. Very often you can motor through shallow water and see them in one or two feet of water. In these shallow waters you would be hard pressed to see any other good sized fish like a northern. Very often muskies are in only knee deep water.

Does anything intimidate a muskie?

Windels: Not much. In fact, they have a strange behavior of not being spooky. You can approach a muskie in shallow water, even motor right over them, and they will stay put where a bass or a northern would spook and leave. This is also demonstrated in their following behavior where they will follow a lure right up to the boat, and if you swish the lure back and forth in the water, they will actually follow the lure and continue following it. Bass, northerns, and walleyes will flash away at the sight of the boat. Muskies swim right behind the lure up to the boat and swim away slowly.

This lack of caution—muskie fishermen call it a lack of fear perhaps to make the fish more glamorous—is very important in my approach to fishing. Since I know that they aren't spooky and they frequent shallow water, I fish shallow and I do not worry about working the boat in shallow water. Also I use a heavy line and tackle. Heavy tackle will not deter them from striking. If they are not afraid of a boat and motor, they are certainly not spooked by thirty-six pound test dacron line as opposed to twenty pound test monofilament line. Twenty pound test mono is hardly thin line anyway.

Do you concern yourself with the muskie's ability to smell and taste?

Windels: I'm not concerned about it at all. I do not think they are important senses in the muskie. There are some people who think differently—those that believe in using fish formulas, etc. I am somewhat skeptical about products like that for muskie fishing, and I do not use them myself. In fact, I'm not one who washes his hands after touching gasoline, for instance, and I haven't seen any effects on my catching fewer fish than someone else because I don't take those precautions.

Are big fish lazy fish?

Windels: I think big fish are lazy. A big muskie has a maneuverability problem, too. Although they move well, they are not good at cornering forage like smaller fish are. A muskie that gets large and fat is an opportunist that takes the easy meal. It doesn't get big by chasing small perch. It grabs one pound suckers, etc.

How does this notion (big fish are lazy) relate to your theory that a bucktail spinner is the best lure for taking muskies?

Windels: The bucktail spinner is easy for a muskie to catch since it travels in a straight line, and it does not have an erratic action. When fish zero in on a bucktail spinner, they've got it. With a jerk bait or a lure that wobbles from side to side, the muskie has to be more precise in its strike or it will miss the lure.

What does the bucktail spinner represent to a muskie?

Windels: When you are retrieving a bucktail, the resistance given off in terms of blade vibration gives the illusion of something very large in the water.

And there are other special advantages of the bucktail spinner—it is a very efficient lure to use, and it has a very high hooking percentage.

To what extent does the muskie have the ability to remember? Lures, for example.

Windels: In the Midwest the bucktail spinner has always accounted for the most muskie catches. Black with a silver blade being the most popular color. Of course it is the most widely used muskie lure, and that keeps its reputation going. However, you can't get away from the fact that it is still working. If it were not producing, it probably would have died out. So the need to switch lures every few years or so has not been demonstrated in muskie fishing. Further, with "catch and release" in muskie fishing, if it were a learned behavior, it would start showing up. There is no indication, from what I've seen, that muskies become lure wary.

On the other hand, I have seen some instances where muskies did recognize lures. I've caught muskies on a given lure, released them, and later had those same muskies follow the same lure on subsequent casts. Then by changing the lure, I've been able to catch those same fish again.

Once I hooked a thirty-five pounder and lost him right at boat side. I returned to fish that spot every half hour for the rest of the day, and the muskie followed nine times, but the only lure he would follow was that same purple Harasser I had hooked him on earlier. I had this muskie pin-pointed very well. I would pull up to the spot and throw a jerk bait or a surface plug, and the fish would not follow those lures. But as soon as I would throw that purple bucktail, it would follow it as though it were running it out of its territory. Since it had been hooked on that lure earlier that day, it is possible that it did recognize it.

What motivates a muskie to strike a lure?

Windels: Most muskies we catch have empty stomachs; that is, when we catch a big fish and kill it, the taxidermist will usually find the stomach empty. So I assume they are motivated to strike a lure when they are hungry.

Explain movement and migrational patterns of the muskie.

Windels: There have been some radio telemetry studies showing that there is a major muskie movement in the spring, which you would expect. They are moving great distances into marsh bays where they spawn. Then there can be considerable movement after they disperse from their spawning grounds. In the summer they move very little; they stay in what is called their home range. But occasionally in the summer, they will take off and swim great distances and very often return to the same spot. And then in the fall there is a big movement that takes place in September and October. This movement probably has to do with the changing water temperature, weedbeds dying out, and a changing food source.

Define a muskie's home range.

Windels: A muskie's home range might be a fraction of an acre, and it will change with the change in seasons.

Comment on active and inactive fish.

Windels: An inactive fish is probably a fish that has taken a meal and is probably not looking for anything more to eat at that time. He is just not on the prowl. I have a hunch that when a muskie has taken a meal, he probably goes into a state of relaxation and becomes rather immobile staying in a weedbed digesting his meal.

An active fish would be one looking for a meal and, no doubt, more catchable.

What do you do to find active muskies?

Windels: Find the food shelf areas—the very shallow areas where they are going to do their feeding. Muskies love to do their feeding in shallow water, and they will get right up in the weedbeds. So I generally look for shallow water feeding territories for active muskies.

LOCATING MUSKIES

Comment on locating muskies from a seasonal standpoint.

Windels: In the spring they are spawning in the marsh bays—the muck bottom, backwater bays pretty much like the areas where you will find crappies in the early spring. Therefore, in May and June, I'm going to be fishing those bays and areas nearby.

Then, the first pattern muskies relate to (after they leave these marsh bays) is weeds. Once the weeds are up, you will find muskies relating to them. Cabbage type weeds are the most preferred by muskies. All you have to do is locate a cabbage bed, and it will hold muskies provided you are fishing a lake that has a good population of muskies. And that pattern will hold through July and even later as long as the weeds stay green.

In August the muskies tend to have a preference toward rocky reefs and boulders, etc. Generally, during August and September, you should fish boulders, bulrushes, and green weedbeds.

In October most weedbeds are dead and you should fish rocky reefs, rocky points, and bulrushes. Also, October is the time of the year when muskies start to move around. This is a mass movement due to changes in water temperature and their food source. They are particularly vulnerable to fishermen at this time of the year.

Can you narrow down their location to a particular side of a rock pile, for example? The deep water access side perhaps.

Windels: Muskies definitely prefer a particular sight on a rock reef, but not that you could say it is always on the deep side. They will use a specific ambush point that is successful. Very often on a rock reef they will be on a certain end of the reef, but it has to do with the overall configuration of the reef itself and not so much the access to deep water. Quite often you will catch muskies on a certain side of a reef, but there is not a pattern to it. Each reef is different. It is probably a matter of how the rocks are laid out.

In late fall you want to cover a lot of shoreline since muskies seem to do a lot of roaming at this time of the year. You can work a shoreline pattern and you will run into fish.

What do you do when your usual patterns aren't working?

Windels: If I have fished my usual pattern of covering all the food shelf areas and shallow water where I would expect to find fish and I have caught nothing, I have to assume that they are not there or they are inactive. In that case, I would either change lakes or spend a little time fishing deeper water.

But deeper water is difficult to fish efficiently. One method is to troll since you can cover a lot of water quickly. Although I do not enjoy trolling, I might resort to that since it is often a way of putting a fish in the boat.

When you have fished all the areas you would expect to find fish and you have not caught any, it is time to experiment. But those are usually unproductive days.

I have found that when muskies are hard to catch in shallow water, they also are hard to catch in deeper water. (Deeper water is the water beyond the weedline.) If you are not catching muskies in shallow water, it will be tough to catch them in deep water since they go into shallow water when they are active.

What is the secret to catching a lunker muskie?

Windels: The lure is not the secret. It's the location. To catch a lunker you are looking for a fish that has not seen a lot of lures. You are going to have to fish areas that are not heavily fished.

You start by looking for marginal spots—places that are passed over by the average angler. This spot could be a hump that nobody fishes because it is too deep and too hard to fish, and so on.

How valuable are topographical maps in locating areas to fish?

Windels: The most important time of the year to use a topo map is in the spring and the fall when you are looking for the warmer areas of the lake to fish. If you look at a topo map, you can figure out general areas of a lake that have to be warmer because of the depth of the water.

So when you are looking at a map of the Lake of the Woods, for instance, where there are hundreds of miles of shore to fish, you can find these areas that have a heavy concentration of water of twenty feet or less, and you know that part of the lake has to be the first to warm up.

Some small lakes might have one or two sunken islands and this is, of course, very important in locating fish, too.

What are some other locational clues?

Windels: After awhile you do get a sense of conditions being right. And that has to do with the lay of the land, what you see in the water, the formation of weedbeds, and so on. Perhaps it is just the way the weeds look that have a special familiarity to them, and you just know it looks good. I guess that only comes with experience. Spots look like spots that have produced for you before, and that is something you cannot really teach someone.

What is the most common mistake made in locating muskies?

Windels: In muskie fishing, it is the infatuation some anglers have with deep water. It is not that deep water isn't productive; it is just more difficult to fish. Of course there are times to fish deep water, but in doing so, you are passing up better action in the shallows. Since active muskies have a definite preference for shallow water combined with the difficulty in deep water fishing for muskies, deep water is relatively unproductive.

If you took a person who worked at being a deep water muskie fisherman, who did nothing but cast humps in twenty to twenty-five feet of water, he would occasionally come in with a super big fish and could probably stake out a reputation by that alone. But he would also have to be the kind of fisherman who would be happy catching only a few muskies a year. Actually, the big thing he would have going for himself is that he is fishing water that most fishermen completely avoid. So, very likely, if a muskie does use that hump, he would have a crack at catching him. But most people I know that are successful at catching muskies do so by working the shallow water where muskies are most vulnerable and available.

That is not to say that in the future we won't have good methods for working deep water, but right now fishing deep water is inefficient.

In thirty feet of water, for example, is that fish five feet down, or is he on the bottom? It just becomes a difficult problem in trying to catch muskies in deep water. When you throw a lure in shallow water, you do not have to worry about depth control of your lure. In deep water you spend a great deal of time getting the lure down to the fish if he is on the bottom, and more time pulling the lure back up. If you are trolling at the right depth, it could be a very productive method of fishing, but if you are at the wrong depth, you are completely wasting your time. Furthermore, most of the lures we have today don't work in those deeper depths very well. By the way, my three largest muskies [thirty-eight pounds fifteen ounces, thirty-seven pounds twelve ounces, & thirty-seven pounds even] all came from water less than five feet deep.

Earlier you mentioned that it was not uncommon for muskies to suspend at the five foot depth, for instance, over thirty feet of water. Please elaborate on that.

Windels: When a muskie leaves the shallow flats, it will often suspend at nearly the same level. He just swims straight off of the flats. That is, he won't go off of the food shelf and swim down into deeper water. He is relating to the food shelf and swims straight off and suspends, perhaps, a hundred yards away. And when he is ready to come in again, he will swim straight in.

Why would a muskie leave a food shelf if he is relating to it?

Windels: I don't know. Some of what I have said is speculation, of course, and many muskies seem to just stay shallow. But sometimes muskie fishermen will troll at about the five foot depth all over the lake and they will occasionally catch a muskie. But using this method can burn a lot of gasoline, and it is a very boring and frustrating method of fishing.

There are always lots of rumors about giant muskie being sighted and caught. Do you follow up on any of those rumors?

Windels: Although sometimes the rumors are accurate, I tend not to believe them, and I don't get too excited about them.

There was a muskie lake I had heard about a few years ago, but I was skeptical and did not bother checking it out. When I finally did fish the lake, I was very surprised to find out that it was a great muskie lake. I guess, with rumors, you have to go and check it out yourself.

What lake was that?

Windels: It was Wabigoon Lake in Canada. To give you an idea of how good it was when we did finally fish it, we caught and released two thirty pounders, a twenty-seven pounder, and three fifteen pounders in one day. That was two of us. When the word got out about the lake, it really got out.

That same day we ran into some friends of ours who had a thirty-eight pound muskie in the boat, and they had caught a thirty-four pounder the day before. It was a situation where the lake had been unfished, but when the word got out that it held big muskies, people burned it out. It is one of the last lakes I would want to fish now.

Is there anything that you want to add regarding location?

Windels: Spots where you have caught or seen muskies should be fished repeatedly. A spot that holds a muskie will, more than likely, hold a muskie again.

Good spots have special qualities that draw lots of fish. There are areas that always hold muskies and areas that only occasionally hold muskies.

Perhaps in location the most important thing is covering lots of water. Always fish more spots quickly than fish fewer spots thoroughly. I would rather cover ninety percent of several spots and leave, then cover a hundred and twenty percent of fewer spots. I know I have hit the highlights. The percentages are with you if you fish for aggressive fish—the easy fish to catch.

PRESENTATION FOR MUSKIES

I'd like you to discuss presentation for muskies beginning with the seasonal differences in presentation.

Windels: Fish are cold-blooded creatures, therefore, in the spring and fall presentation.

How much line is there between your rod tip and the lure when you make this presentation?

Windels: Basically, it is just the length of the leader. You should reel right up to the leader. Usually I use a one foot leader and combined with the length of the lure we are talking about eighteen inches.

What happens when a thirty pound muskie hits a lure that is only eighteen inches from your rod tip?

Windels: It can get hectic! A friend of mine once landed a thirty pounder by just lifting it into the boat when it hit on a figure eight presentation. That is, he just worked it into the net and lifted it into the boat. But very often when a muskie strikes a lure, it will S and head shake.

Unlike northern pike, a muskie's strike is often light. Northerns hit a lure and then turn, thus the fierce strike. Muskies, on the other hand, hit and follow through. They overtake the lure and sit there and shake their head. When you get a strike on a figure eight presentation, it isn't really a strike. The muskie kind of latches on to the lure and, generally, what you do when he head shakes, is lead him through the water to keep some tension on your line. Occasionally, if he has a lot of power, he might take off swimming. In that situation you will have to hit the free spool on your reel and feed him line.

It can get tense, but it is not as sudden of a strike as you might imagine. It is not a line breaking type of strike or a jolt like that of a northern pike. If anything, it is generally a soft strike since the muskie is simply overtaking the lure.

Many people will miss the strike because it is so soft. All of a sudden their spinner blade is turning again and the fish has dropped the lure and he's gone.

Does the figure eight presentation account for many of your catches?

Windels: Perhaps ten percent and more each year. I would say it could add a good ten percent to your catch if you are good at it.

Why does figure eight-ing work better than perhaps a circle presentation?

Windels: You can do circles, but the figure eight method keeps the lure's action much better. In fact, some fishermen will take the lure and walk around the boat. Although that works, sooner or later you will stumble, ruining your presentation. Even beginners should learn to figure eight. It is a natural action to do and not too hard to learn.

Perhaps figure eight-ing imitates a trapped minnow like in a situation where a predator fish has a minnow or minnows trapped up against a rock pile or a drop off. It is probably a typical escape pattern for bait fish, and predators are conditioned to seeing something going back and forth.

Do you ever use a flutter down presentation for muskies?

Windels: It does not seem to work for muskies. If you stop or kill your lure you must use a slower retrieve and a faster retrieve in the summer. But sometimes with too fast of a retrieve you might miss some of the really big fish who are the opportunists who only take the easy meal. Slowing down your retrieve might be better for taking big fish even in the summer. But big muskies are so few and far between I don't know if you can afford to fish that way very often. Generally, you should fish for that average muskie and, perhaps, with a little bit of luck, you will catch that good sized one eventually.

If you are fishing on big waters, sooner or later, you will get a crack at a big one. But fishing for big fish all of the time can be very boring and takes the patience of Job. Personally, I still need to catch a fish now and then to keep it fun.

Many people have trouble slowing down their retrieve in the fall after fishing fast all summer. One trick that works well to help you slow down is to take some line off of your spool. If you take off fifty yards of line, your line take up will be much reduced. Also you can go to a slower retrieve ratio reel. But be careful not to go to a larger spool size since spool diameter is every bit as important as gear ratio is when it comes to taking up line.

Does your lure choice change with change in seasons?

Windels: Some muskie fishermen believe in using different lures for each season of fishing; I don't. For instance, there is a widely held theory that jerk baits work better in the fall than bucktail spinners do. Well, I think, I have been able to reason that down. With a jerk bait, you jerk and retrieve, jerk and retrieve, so you are only retrieving half of the time. What you are doing is cutting your retrieve speed way down. And that is what you want to do in the fall—use a slow retrieve. But I maintain that if you use a slow retrieve on a bucktail spinner in the fall, you will have the same general results.

If you notice that the muskies are hustling to catch up to your lure at boatside, then often missing it, you are probably retrieving too fast.

Elaborate on that.

Windels: If you are getting to where you are pulling the lure out of the water and getting ready to cast again and then you see the fish, you are retrieving your lure too fast. That will often happen. Sometimes you are just pulling the lure out of the water and the muskie will take a shot at it.

To avoid this situation I make an L movement along the side of the boat. An L movement is simply making a right angle with your lure just before you would bring it out of the water. This will give you one last look at anything that might be following your lure.

Do you make this L movement on every retrieve?

Windels: Yes. I don't go back and forth; I just make the one L movement, and then I pull my bait out of the water and cast it again. This L movement sets me up to go into a figure eight presentation if I see a muskie following my lure. All I have to do is continue the L movement on into a figure eight during the presentation, it will turn a muskie off. A following muskie seeing a lure stop will not hit it. About all you can do on a follow to entice him to strike is to speed up your retrieve; that will often trigger him.

For instance, in doing a figure eight presentation if you miss a beat when making a corner, that is, if your lure skips, it will turn the muskie off, and I don't know why. They seem to want to see the lure getting away. What seems to work effectively in figure eight-ing is trying to take the lure away from the muskie making it difficult for him to catch it. That will turn a muskie on. A good figure eight-er can have a following muskie in a neutral mood and entice him into striking by speeding up his presentation.

How long will this take?

Windels: Up to one to two minutes sometimes.

What does the muskie do when you are figure eight-ing?

Windels: He follows the lure the whole time. He is swimming and following the lure. In fact, what many people do is to slow up when the muskie gets behind the lure, and that is not what you should do. You want to make it look like the lure is trying to get away so you are ripping the lure through the water, and, all of a sudden, the muskie will get aggressive and start snapping at the lure.

You can tell when he is getting ready to strike on a figure eight presentation, so you can set him up. Get a long pass going where he gets behind the lure and you can just slow up a little bit and he will overtake the lure and grab it. But you have to be able to tell when he really wants it versus when he is just looking at it, otherwise when you slow up your presentation, he will turn off and swim away.

When do you set the hook?

Windels: You always set the hook immediately with artificial bait. It is usually a matter of trying to take up line and getting resistance built up as quickly as possible. It is not so much a matter of sinking the hooks deep in the fish's mouth as it is a matter of eliminating slack in your line.

Many muskie fishermen have this misconception that you really have to bury the barbs. To some extent that may be true if you are using monofilament line, since there is so much stretch in it. But most muskie fishermen use dacron line which has little stretch so there is no need to set the hook more than once. By setting the hook more than once, all you will accomplish is to tear a bigger hole in the muskie's mouth increasing the chances he will get away. Set the hook once quickly and maintain even pressure.

Comment on trolling as a method of presentation.

Windels: It can be very efficient since your lure is in the water all of the time. But you will learn less since you won't have any information on follows, etc. Whereas, with casting as a method of presentation, you might see as many as thirty follows in a day so you have learned a lot about muskie behavior and location. And it is not uncommon to have as many as twenty follows in a day and not catch a muskie. But, nonetheless, trolling is a very efficient way of working the deep water and the water that is hard to fish by casting.

Also, trolling is a good method of presentation to use when you are motoring around on a new lake trying to locate the food shelves. On a new lake I will put a lure in the water and start trolling around making mental notes of the weed flats I have found. Then I will return later and cast those areas. I also troll when it is too cold to cast, and my hands cannot take the cold any longer.

But, I'm afraid, I find trolling boring. Of course, if one can catch a forty pounder trolling, there is nothing wrong with that.

Trolling is like when a group of hunters drive deer. It is very efficient, but probably not as much fun as tracking one down. I can't argue with the efficiency of trolling, but there is more to be desired because catching the fish is not the only thing. It is the experience, too! How you catch the fish.

How efficient is it to use bucktail spinners when trolling?

Windels: The bucktail spinner is a lure you would use when trolling over the tops of weeds in shallow water. Generally, you are limited to trolling a bucktail in the weed zone motoring right over the weeds and running the bucktail spinner in the prop wash.

Muskies seem to be somewhat attracted by a passing boat, and they will get into the boat's wake when it goes by. It might be that they are attracted to the bubbles rising up to the surface, and quite often you will see them roll in the wake.

But they are not afraid of a boat, and they will often key in on it. There are some muskie fishermen who troll with their lure right in the prop wash ten feet behind the motor, and muskies are even attracted to that.

If your lure is only ten feet behind the boat, how tightly would you set the drag on your reel?

Windels: When casting, I have my drag set very tightly with no give at all. But in trolling you are going to want to loosen it up because quite often the boat is going faster than the fish. When a muskie hits, thumb the reel hard until there is good tension built up in the rod and then loosen up a bit and let some line out as you start to slow the motor down.

Another thing you should do is keep the motor going forward since this will enable you to keep some tension in your line if the fish starts coming at you. Use the motor to help you get control of the situation.

Generally, how far behind the boat should my lure be when I'm trolling?

Windels: Seventy-five feet or so.

What lures would you recommend for trolling deeper water?

Windels: When you are outside the weedline, work the deep water near the bottom. In this situation I would tend to use a diving plug.

Have you ever used downriggers for muskies?

Windels: A few people have played with them with little success, and I think it is a rather futile way of fishing for muskies. The percentages of muskies using deep water as opposed to the food shelf is a very small population.

How do you vary your presentation from stained to clear water?

Windels: I use Harassers with fluorescent blades and bright bucktails in stained water because it is easier for the muskie to make eye contact with brightly colored lures. Many of your strikes are visual, and the quicker you make eye contact with the lure the more alert you will be; that is, by using oranges and chartreuse you will see the lure at a greater distance so once you have made eye contact you can follow it better.

Eye contact also is important in figure eight-ing since you have to keep ahead of the fish at all times. When they strike, you will see the lure disappear, but you won't immediately feel anything. Remember he is overtaking the lure so visual contact is more important than feel in this situation.

I have seen many people who did not set the hook when the lure disappeared, and an instant later the muskie opened his mouth and they had lost the fish. They just did not react in time.

How would your presentation change in a clear water situation?

Windels: Since fish can see greater distances in clear water there might be some advantage to a longer cast. Other than leaning toward using a silver blade on a bucktail spinner, I wouldn't pay too much attention to color. Although I do have a preference for lighter colors, I don't have a good reason for it.

Do you ever fish the slop for muskies?

Windels: Oh yes! And here a buzzer might be the best choice for a lure. You will need something that will ride over the top because muskies can get into some real heavy slop just as a bass can.

Anytime it is open enough to use a bucktail spinner without having to pull weeds off after every cast, you are probably better off with the bucktail. But there are conditions that are thicker than a bucktail can handle. Then a buzzer is good, or at least, they are the only thing that will work efficiently.

Muskies lay in the weeds in ambush, or sometimes they will lay right on top of the weeds. In either case if you have a foot of water above the weed tops, you have plenty of water to work a bucktail spinner.

Is there anything that I have forgotten to ask regarding presentation?

Windels: One important thing. Boat control. Because my approach is to cover as much new water as possible with every cast I usually rely on my outboard motor rather than on an electric trolling motor.

I use a fifty horse power Mariner with a tiller handle. It is very convenient to steer the motor with the tiller handle between your legs while you cast. It keeps both hands free for fishing, and I can guide the boat and keep cutting across the flat while casting.

Are you going in reverse?

Windels: Yes. And it gives you more speed and boat control than you can get out of an electric trolling motor. There are times when you are using an electric trolling motor in the wind so you are not moving very fast, and you end up making two to three casts to the same spots which is not an efficient way to fish. Then your partner is really fishing used water!

I always like to move fast enough so my partner is making his cast beyond where I just cast so he is always fishing fresh water, too.

Using the outboard also saves the time of turning your outboard off and going up to the front of the boat to use the electric motor. When I pull up to a spot, I immediately put the motor in reverse, and, bang, I'm casting.

WEATHER AND BIOLOGICAL FACTORS AFFECTING MUSKIES

How do cold fronts affect muskie fishing?

Windels: Cold fronts make fishing very difficult. If a cold front has just passed through, I might very well opt for staying home and working instead of going fishing. It does dampen my enthusiasm knowing weather does affect probable results. That does not mean you can't catch a muskie on those days, but it does mean you are going to have a hell-of-a-time catching fish.

Does your fishing technique change during cold front conditions?

Windels: The only exception being I know I'm going to have to work harder. I don't give a lot of credit to fish; I find them rather dumb animals. Therefore, I am not one to change lures or line just because the weather has changed.

So many fishermen panic during a cold front and make all kinds of changes in their game plan. Cold front or not, it is still a matter of locating a muskie that is in the right mood, and with the proper presentation you will catch him.

Does rain affect your chances of catching a muskie?

Windels: I like fishing in the rain mainly because it keeps the novices off of the lake. And generally when you have rain, fish are very active.

If you are willing to brave the rain, how about lightning?

Windels: I tend to avoid fishing when there is lightning about. Of course, in tournaments I have fished in terrible lightning storms and have taken fish. I guess common sense or old age keeps me from fishing during those kinds of storms a little more each year.

I recall one tournament where there was so much lightning that only fifteen of forty boats entered in the contest went out. We took our chances and headed right across the lake. I pulled up right near a marker buoy that I wanted to fish. I stood up and pitched out a jerk bait. When I looked up there was a swirl by my lure, so I set the hook and caught a legal muskie.

Well, the lightning was so bad that we didn't go back across the lake to find a tournament official to witness the catch. And that fish hit right in the middle of all that lightning and it had been lightning most of the night.

Lightning does not spook muskies period. But it's damn stupid to be out there while it lightnings.

How did you come out in that tournament?

Windels: We finished fourth. And that was partially because I lost a muskie about forty inches long on a jerk bait when a screw came out. The upsetting thing about it was we would have won an additional $1500.00 if we would have boated that fish.

How do rising and falling water conditions affect muskie fishing?

Windels: In some water systems, such as rivers, rising water will put the muskies up in the mouth of the river as it draws most game fish in. In general, with rising water, fishing will get poorer and vice versa. Also in a river when you are talking rising water, you can expect more current so fish will have to get up in shallow water.

Do you use pH levels in locating active muskies?

Windels: I have a pH meter and it helps me establish patterns and learn about where and when to find muskies. I check the pH meter whenever I have a follow or catch a muskie to have a reference point for finding other likely spots. I have found muskies in quite a range of pH and have not found any hard and fast rules. Muskies are more active in the more moderate pH readings (closer to the high sevens).

How about water temperature?

Windels: I use a water temperature gauge in the spring and fall. That is, in the spring the active muskies will be in the water that is the warmest. In June and July I try to find sixty-five to seventy degree water temperatures for active muskies. If I find an area of sixty-two to sixty-three degrees, for example, I would expect to find little activity.

This past fourth of July on a fishing trip to the Lake of the Woods four of us caught four muskies in three days of fishing. It was absolutely terrible. But the places we did find muskies were the warmest places possible and without any concern for water temperature we probably would have done worse.

I don't know anything about upper temperature levels causing a problem, but wherever there is weed growth, there is a cooling effect so I don't think weedbed areas of a lake ever get too hot.

How does sunlight affect muskies?

Windels: Some people would have you believe muskies avoid sunlight. While that may be true for some species of fish, it is not true for the muskie. They love sunlight. In fact, they will often lay in the sunlight in water a couple of feet deep.

We hear a lot about wind: Coming from one direction it can mean good fishing and coming from another direction it can mean poor fishing. Do you have a preference for which direction the wind is coming from?

Windels: I prefer a west and southwest wind which for Minnesota means somewhat of a stable weather system—a warm front condition. It's the way the weather systems move through Minnesota. Actually, it's not so much the wind as the wind is a result of the weather that has gone through. What you are looking for is steady weather with no extreme changes.

With regards to locating muskies in the spring, I avoid the side of the lake that has the wind blowing cold water up against the shore because that cold water off of the top of the lake is going to cool the water on the windy side and muskies will not be there. Whereas, they will be on the quiet side of the lake where the sun is warming the water. In fact, the water on the quiet side could be several degrees warmer than the water on the windy shore.

But if I were fishing a tournament in the summer, I would fish the wind side of a lake since there would be fewer fishermen using that water.

How does the barometric pressure affect muskies?

Windels: I don't even look at the barometer. I do know that when a storm is coming conditions are such that fish activity is good, and after a storm has passed, fishing will slow down.

Comment on sky conditions.

Windels: I prefer to fish when the sky is cloudy, but steady weather with a clear sky is not bad either. Actually, three days of steady weather seems to be the key. That third day will be good fishing, and very often with steady weather you will have a buildup of clouds.

In the fall I look for those sunny days when the sun warms the shallow water and provides some muskie activity in mid-day. A warm protected shore, for instance, where the sun is shining may be five degrees warmer than the rest of the shore. In October it is definitely something to key in on.

But, generally, I like clouds, a little rain, and wind from the southwest. On a day like that you might see thirty muskies and catch two or three of them, and that would be a great day of fishing.

On a cold front day after a weather system has passed through, very typically, you may see two or three muskies, and you might still catch one.

Don't let cold front conditions dampen your enthusiasm because any tournament will teach you that someone will always catch fish. If anything, I pray for tough conditions during a tournament since I know it will psyche out many fishermen, and they are going to give up or quit early. So if I can pump myself up and stay at it, I will have a much better chance of winning. I never quit a tournament early and that gives me an edge. When you fish a tournament and the conditions are perfect, your chances of winning are less because all of the contestants are catching fish and are in the running.

Does the thermocline affect muskies?

Windels: I don't really know too much about it. Most of the lakes that I fish are shallow (thirty-five feet in the deepest part) so there is good mixing of water the year 'round. In general terms, it is not something that Minnesota muskie fishermen need worry too much about since most muskie lakes here are shallower bodies of water.

Earlier you said that stained water usually produced better fishing. Why?

Windels: Stained water is often more fertile and contains a lot of nutrients, good bait fish, and often carp and suckers. Any time you have an abundance of bait fish you are going to have fat fish that feed often; they are going to get big quickly.

When I see water that is very clean, I tend to think of an environment that is sterile with less bait fish so the predator fish will be fewer in numbers and smaller in size. Of course, there are clear water lakes that also have good bait fish numbers and good muskie growth.

How do moon phases affect muskie fishing?

Windels: There is some evidence that moon phases are very important when trying to catch big fish. It may not make much difference in the long run as far as numbers of fish caught, but there is a great deal of strong evidence to show that during the full-moon and the dark of the moon some of the biggest fish are caught, bass in particular.

Although there could be something to this notion, I don't pay any attention to moon phases. I feel, if there is something to it, other variables are more important and will usually override the moon's affect anyway. I just fish when I can.

EQUIPMENT AND TACKLE FOR MUSKIE FISHING

What type of rods do you use for muskie fishing?

Windels: My rods are custom-made by Thorne Brothers in Fridley. I have them custom-made because I want a certain size, a certain length, and a certain stiffness to handle my style of fishing which is mostly throwing bucktail spinners. You need a heavy rod, but a rod that bends also.

Many women and children will catch their first muskie because they just kinda hang on and the hooks stay in since the main key is keeping pressure on. Taking up the slack as quickly as possible and then maintaining the tension can be difficult with a rod that does not bend.

With a rod that does not bend, you do not have any room for error. When the fish jumps, the rod straightens out. But the rod has to be stiff enough to throw the heavy lures used in muskie fishing; that is the reason stiffness is important.

What kind of reels do you use?

Windels: I use a Garcia 7000, but many people find it to be too large. The standard muskie reel is the Garcia 6500 and would be the reel I would recommend to people. I happen to like the 7000 better because it holds up better and has a little better drag system.

The new small reels on the market today are definitely the wrong way to go. I cannot see any advantage to them. And if it gets to be a matter of reel weight, that is ridiculous.

What kind of line do you use?

Windels: Monofilament stretches twice as much as dacron so I consider mono a poor choice. Braided dacron is the best I have found, and, generally, I use thirty-six pound test.

What makes a good leader?

Windels: A good leader has to be strong, of course. Breaking was a big problem with the leaders I used to use. I would buy seven strand leader material and make my own. But everytime I got a northern on, those leaders would wrap up and kink. If you use a leader with a kink in it, it is just a matter of time before it will break. Every time the wire flexes and straightens, it weakens it.

Knowing that and being a strong believer that you cannot spook muskies, I made one out of spring stainless steel. It worked so well I started manufacturing them for sale. They are made of wire that is fifty-thousandths of an inch spring stainless steel with a ball bearing swivel and welded split rings. They are actually welded rings, not split rings, so they cannot come apart. The swivel tests at one hundred and thirty-five pounds of pressure, and the snap is built-in so it has no weak points. Spring steel can take the flexing.

Do you always use a leader?

Windels: Yes. A big fish will not nibble; it will take the whole bait so a leader is necessary. There is no reason not to use a leader. If muskies are not afraid of a boat or a fisherman, they are certainly not going to be nervous about a leader. But even though I am using a leader, I do retie, at least, every two or three hours.

Let's talk about lures.

Windels: Let's start with jerk baits. They have no lips on them so there is no built-in action. If you reeled them in, they would come in, in a straight line. So you have to jerk them to get them to dive and dart. You will get a lot of strikes with jerk baits, but you will miss a lot of fish, too, since their hooking efficiency is poor.

How well do topwater plugs work for muskie fishing?

Windels: Topwater plugs for muskies are very popular in areas of shallow water and flowages as in Wisconsin where there are a lot of stumps.

Muskies love topwater lures just like smallmouth bass do. They love to bust things on the surface. But the problem with topwater lures for muskies is the same as it is for bass—they will often miss the lure. They often strike at the bubble trail as opposed to striking the lure, and if they do get hooked with a big plug, it is usually on the outside of their mouth which results in losing many fish. But the gurgling action on the water does stimulate fish and will turn muskies on in spite of water temperature.

How about buzzer baits?

Windels: They have their applications and they are exciting to fish with. Early in the spring when muskies aren't active, you can turn on a negative muskie with a buzzer bait.

Tell me about bucktail spinners. How you make them and why you feel they are the best muskie lure.

Windels: The bucktail spinner that I manufacture [the Muskie Harasser] is geared pretty much for this part of the country. They are rather specific for the muskie fisherman in this area and are suited for his waters and his fishing conditions.

All the lures I sell are designed by me, and they are lures I have perfected to the point where, basically, they do not need any improvements to catch fish.

Many companies manufacture fishing tackle, and they are more concerned with price than they are with how well the tackle works or how well it holds up. My approach has been to make the best possible lures for fishing and not worry about price. I guess the main thing about the way I make a bucktail spinner is that it has no weak point. Nothing to come apart when you have hooked a big fish.

And to answer the last part of your question, they are the best muskie lure for several reasons: they have the highest hooking and holding percentage of any muskie lure; they are easy to use at most depths that you will find active muskies; they give off a vibration that attracts fish, and with a large blade they give the impression of something very large coming through the water; they are easy to cast; they are the best lure for figure eight-ing; and you can cover a lot of water with them.

In a word bucktail spinners are efficient. They are by far the most efficient muskie lure available. And muskie fishing is a game of odds; that is, the more water you can cover quickly, the more muskies you will catch. The fewer that shake loose or miss the lure, the more you will catch.

What size lures do you use?

Windels: Length of a lure is a more important consideration than weight. I firmly believe that you should use as large a lure as possible in muskie fishing. Since big fish take single, big meals you should therefore approach the size meal they are probably eating. But anything more than a foot long or heavier than four ounces is just too big to cast.

There is probably something in the muskie's behavior that tells him he will not get big by chasing little fish. A small lure will not often entice a big fish.

What are the standard size muskie lures?

Windels: In jerk baits and crank baits the standard sizes are six and eight inches. With bucktail spinners, seven to nine inches are the most common sizes.

Do you have a preference for any particular brand or type of boat?

Windels: I use a sixteen foot Crestliner Muskie Pro model. Since I fish large lakes in all types of weather, I want the extra depth and width to handle rough water. The Crestliner is well built with a good, dry design. The flat floor makes casting easy, and I like the open boat design.

I gather that the fifty horse power Mariner is by far your favorite motor?

Windels: Yes. That or the fifty Merc since they troll so smoothly and have plenty of power when you need to run ten to twelve miles on a big lake.

You didn't say anything specific about depth finders.

Windels: I use a Si-Tex depth finder with a depth alarm. I set it at three feet. This alerts me to rock reefs I might otherwise hit, and this is important since I'm usually backtrolling in shallow water.

Is there anything you want to add about equipment or tackle?

Windels: Polaroid sunglasses are a must. I know it doesn't sound like much, but they will enable you to see under the water much better which will aid in seeing follows and spotting rocks.

MISCELLANEOUS INFORMATION ABOUT MUSKIE FISHING

What is the best way to land a muskie?

Windels: You have about three choices: a net, a club, or a gaff. I don't like gaffs since they are dangerous to use, and it is hard to lift a fifty inch fish over the gunnel of a boat when it is thrashing on a gaff. And, of course, a gaffed fish cannot be released. Clubbing works very well and is a very effective way of landing a big muskie.

Frequently when using lures like a jerk bait, the fish will be hooked on the outside of his mouth. You should not lead that fish into a net since it would very likely get hooked on the net leaving half of the fish still outside of the net. So you almost have to club a trophy fish if the lure is hooked on the outside of his mouth.

Where do you club 'em?

Windels: Right where the meat joins the base of the skull. That will work very well. But netting is by far the safest way to land a muskie. This is another reason I'm a strong proponent for using bucktail spinners since it is hooked inside the fish's mouth, and he can be led right into the net. You should be able to lead him in, and he will swim right down to the bottom of the bag. Then it should be a simple matter of lifting him aboard.

What size net do you use?

Windels: One with about a thirty inch diameter and deep enough that if you stood in it, you could bring the rim up above your waist. You have to think big since someday you might hook a five footer. And once you get him into the net, don't panic, just hoist him into the boat carefully. Once he is in the net he can't get enough power to do anything anyway.

I would also recommend using a Hook-Out Tool. It is a device made for removing hooks that has an off set handle. I started using it routinely after I had been hooked for the third time. Once on Wabedo Lake I was hooked in the thumb and the lure was still in the fish which was still in the water.

Ouch!

Windels: It gets scary. Who knows what could happen. The pain is just unbelievable. So in releasing muskies you can't get too concerned for the fish since you have to be concerned with your safety first.

The best way is to brace the fish across the back and use the Hook-Outs to remove the lure.

How about the old fingers in the fish's eyes method?

Windels: That is very bad for the fish, and I never do it. If you brace the fish across the back to steady him and remove the hooks with a Hook-Out while the fish is in the water, both you and the fish will come out in good shape.

Does pattern fishing apply to muskie fishing?

Windels: It does apply to muskie fishing, but not the way it does to bass or walleye fishing.

You can establish some patterns in muskie fishing, but since so few fish are caught you cannot firmly establish a color pattern, for example. You would really be jumping to conclusions if you based a color pattern on one or two fish.

Locational patterns can be established. In spring look for warmer pockets. You might be looking for toppers sticking out of the water as opposed to submerged weeds. You will find toppers in the warmer water areas since the weed growth is more advanced in warmer water in the spring. You don't have to look at a temperature gauge if you can see toppers.

Other patterns that you can look for are patterns that will eliminate other fishermen. For example, if the weed growth is too thick, they won't bother fishing it. Get in there and fish it because you might hit a large muskie that no one else has ever thrown a lure at.

When should I hire a guide?

Windels: A beginner or a person who cannot catch muskies should probably hire a guide. Or, if you want to learn a particular lake quickly, a guide should be able to show you locations and the proper presentations to take muskies.

What lake, lure, conditions, etc. will the next Minnesota state record muskie come from?

Windels: If a new state record muskie were caught, it would probably come out of a river system. Quite possibly the Mississippi River because of the lack of fishing pressure on some stretches of the Mississippi.

A new state record muskie would have to be around twenty years old, and the chances of catching a muskie that old out of heavily fished lakes are very slim. It will have to come from marginal waters where fish have a chance to grow and get big.

In Minnesota the only areas that are not heavily fished are areas below dams on rivers. In spite of some rumors of enormous fish, I doubt that the Minnesota state record will be broken.

Actually, I don't think the current state record will be broken. Many people believe in sixty pound muskies, I don't. Not in Minnesota anyway.

Comment on "catch and release".

Windels: Muskie fishermen have taken care of their sport by "catch and release". They are way ahead of most other anglers in that they fish for sport. They have been doing a good job of taking care of their sport largely through the efforts of Muskies, Inc.

Today, ninety percent of the muskies caught by Muskies, Inc. members are released. The remaining ten percent are injured fish or thirty-plus-pound muskies which are mounted.

Since a very high percentage of Minnesota fishermen are releasing their catch, the fishing in Minnesota is getting nothing but better. You can see the effects on Leech Lake—the average size of a muskie is larger, not smaller than it was a decade ago because people are releasing twenty-five pound fish. This is not true in most other states where if a large fish is caught, it is kept.

Do you fish for muskies at night?

Windels: I have tried some night fishing for muskies and have been rather unsuccessful. But it does work and it might be a good method to try on lakes that are very heavily fished.

How big is your largest muskie from Minnesota waters?

Windels: My largest muskie is a thirty-nine pounder, and I have only seen one fish that I believe was bigger. At the time, I felt it was about a forty-five pound fish.

Where and how did you catch this thirty-nine pounder?

Windels: It was October 15, 1972 and I was fishing on the Mississippi River. The air temperature was thirty degrees, and it was snowing. I was fishing out of a ten foot jon boat on the Mississippi River, and I had just caught a thirty-four inch muskie. I took three more casts, as I recall, and then I hooked something. It was a fish! It came right up to the boat and swam past. And when it went by, it turned the boat right around.

It didn't fight really hard, probably because the water was cold. Then I made ready by putting the landing net on the front seat. It was almost as if she didn't know she was hooked. She was a real sluggish, slow fish just power swimming with big, wide movements with her tail.

After she made one good run, she then started coming back to the boat. As she neared the boat, I guided her into the net with my rod, and she swam right down into the bottom of the net.

When she was in the boat, I killed her with an oar. A thrashing muskie is pretty dangerous, especially in a ten foot boat! You get hooks flying, etc.

She was fifty-three inches long and weighed thirty-eight pounds and fifteen ounces on a state certified scale.

What is "Muskie Fever"?

Windels: Muskie fishing has so much going for it. Frequently you will see the muskie following your lure so you can estimate its size. And, obviously, overestimate. There are stories about muskies as big as the boat—you can see the head on one side of the boat and the tail on the other side of the boat. You can't talk about walleyes or other fish in those respects. Thus legends are born.

Also their following behavior is intriguing and since the muskie is the biggest fish around it has a special viciousness attached to it. It looks so mean and it will strike out at anything, even baby ducks. It also has a special magic to it since it is so rare.

Some people claim they have fished all of their lifetime and cannot catch a muskie which perhaps only says how poor of a fisherman they are. The whole design of it makes the muskie a very special fish in that way.

How difficult is it to catch a muskie?

Windels: Actually, it is not that difficult of a fish to catch. Give a good muskie angler three or four days on good water and he should be able to land a twenty pounder.

Where would you go in Minnesota to catch a twenty pound northern, and how long would it take you? A hell-of-a-long time!

Muskies are very predictable and to catch a twenty pounder is not that difficult. In fact, by catching thirty fish or so I would expect one of them to hit the thirty pound mark.

What should be done to improve Minnesota's muskie fishing?

Windels: We need more muskie lakes since the interest in the muskie is much greater than the resource.

Our D.N.R. is starting a program where they are going to be stocking more of the Wisconsin and Mississippi strain of muskies which is a faster growing strain.

Also, we need many more muskie lakes. Wisconsin, for example, has several hundred muskie lakes, and Minnesota has only a couple of dozen. That hurts! Of course, we have the acreage because Leech Lake, Cass Lake, and Lake Winnibigoshish are so large, but as far as the number of lakes, Minnesota muskie fishing is rather limited.

What happens to the other species of fish when a lake is stocked with muskies?

Windels: Many non-muskie fishermen get concerned when they find out their lake is going to be stocked with muskies since they feel the muskies will eat all of their walleyes, etc.

Actually, the muskie is just another predator fish which tends to keep other populations from getting too high. Muskies will help keep the balance of the lake a little healthier. Everyone knows that Lake Winnibigoshish, Cass, and Leech Lake have good walleye and northern populations, and they are natural muskie lakes, too. So muskies obviously aren't hurting other fish populations there. If you look at other lakes that have muskies in them, fishing for other species is also good.

Muskies might compete with northerns to a small degree, but a lake cannot be overrun with muskies. Stocking a lake with muskies is not going to ruin the fishing for other species, that's for sure! And it would very likely help.

You'd better elaborate on how it would help.

Windels: It won't increase the populations of other fish, but it will increase the average size of those other species because it will help them not to overpopulate. You may have few numbers of panfish, but their average size may be larger.

Name the best muskie lakes in Minnesota.

Windels: There aren't many lakes in Minnesota that have muskies in them, so there are no secrets. The top ones would be: Leech, Cass, Winnie, Wabedo, Inguadona, Little Boy, Girl, Baby, Woman, Deer and Moose which are near Grand Rapids, and Pike Bay which is south of Cass Lake. Also, the Mississippi River, the Saint Croix River, the Little Fork River, and the Big Fork River.

There are a few others like Lake Independence and Rush Lake, which is near Rush City, that have good numbers of stocked muskies, but they don't seem to produce any large fish. Only the lakes that have native muskie populations produce any real trophy muskies in Minnesota.

Chapter 7

GARY KORSGADEN
ON CRAPPIES

Most fishermen, professional and amateur alike, were weaned on panfish, and many of them have caught more crappies than there are lakes in Minnesota. Yet how many of them have ever caught a two-plus-pound crappie, and, more to the point, can they catch them with any regularity?

Well, not only has Gary Korsgaden caught lots of crappies in the two to three pound class, he has caught them in the middle of July when the water surface temperature is ninety degrees, and it is dead calm with a bluebird sky.

But since the crappie fisherman doesn't enjoy the status that, for example, the walleye fisherman does in the hierarchy of sport fishing, Gary is occasionally kidded about being a "crappie expert". Nevertheless, Gary Korsgaden has the respect of every professional fisherman I have spoken with. These pros feel that Gary has few equals, if any, when it comes to understanding the crappies' behavior patterns and what the best methods are to catch crappies, especially the large, adult crappies which perhaps are the most elusive sport fish in Minnesota's lakes and rivers.

During Gary's adolescent years he would spend summer weekends at his parent's cabin on Toad Lake which is located north of Detroit Lakes and has a large population of huge crappies. "A gentleman by the name of Cy George who had a cabin nearby taught me how to fish for crappies," Gary said. "We fished on Toad Lake and several other area lakes."

Cy taught Gary two methods of fishing for crappies. The first method, and the one they had the most success with, was casting the weedlines with a one-sixteenth ounce yellow maribou jig tipped with a minnow. The second method was trolling using a Bass Buster on a cane pole. Both methods work well and are early morning and late evening patterns.

In those days, when he was tagging along with Cy, Gary didn't have any desire to become a professional fisherman, or, for that matter, an authority on the subject of crappie fishing. In fact, he didn't realize that other crappie fishermen weren't catching one to two and a half pounders with the same regularity that he and Cy were catching them.

When Gary realized that these large crappies he was catching were something special, he began entering them in contests sponsored by the local tackle shops. For his efforts he won fishing tackle and his catches would make the news on the local radio station. This recognition is perhaps what motivated Gary to pursue his interest in crappie fishing.

After completing high school, Gary continued fishing and worked as an engineer, but he was soon lured back into fishing full-time by the Lindy Rig. More specifically, it was about the time that Al Lindner became well known for his successful methods of catching walleyes using the Lindy Rig, and Gary tried Lindner's methods for walleyes and says he caught ten to twelve everytime he went fishing. "That's when I really got hooked on fishing," Gary stated.

With this renewed enthusiasm for fishing and since Gary already enjoyed a reputation as a very good fisherman, he decided to attempt to make his living as a guide. Later on when the guiding business was doing well, he organized a fishing school. Thus, it was during these years that he worked as a multi-species guide and a fishing instructor that he fine-tuned his fishing skills. Also, during this time, he began writing for fishing magazines and doing radio talk shows.

When I asked Gary why he excelled as a fisherman, he said, "It is because I made a decision to go into guiding which means I had to produce fish for my customers day in and day out no matter what the weather conditions were. Also, I have an unquenchable thirst for any information about fishing. I follow up on any new techniques and try to determine if they work, and if they work, I try to figure out why they work."

Currently, Gary is a part-time professional fisherman. He conducts several seminars every year, and he is an instructor for "The Fishing Institute" at Mankato State University in Mankato, Minnesota. Also, he is planning to author a book on crappie fishing. But during the week he is on the road selling cosmetics to retail stores in a three state area for the "Charles of the Ritz Company". All things considered, by not being involved with fishing seventy to eighty hours a week, Gary feels, he won't overdo it, and, consequently, spoil his enjoyment for fishing.

CRAPPIE BEHAVIOR

Is it necessary to distinguish between the black and the white crappie?

Korsgaden: No. Basically, it is just a difference in color and size. The black crappie will tend to be somewhat larger.

What are some of the crappie's traits?

Korsgaden: The crappie is a forage fish. It will eat anything from a small mayfly to minnows two inches in length. A crappie is very adept in open water and in deep water. He can be a bottom feeder, a surface feeder, or he can feed anywhere in between. Also, he adapts very well to the weedline areas of a lake. And after spawning, as many species of fish do, their activity will revolve around the weedline.

Because of his basic needs and schooling tendencies the crappie is an open water forager. They feed the way sheep do—grazing from point to point. The crappie is equally able to secure food using his open water abilities as he is able to secure food using his ambush abilities on the weedline. And because of the large numbers of crappies in a typical school they can ambush a very large school of minnows.

Is this ambush technique a coordinated effort by the whole school?

Korsgaden: Yes. Crappies work very well as a team in securing food. Most of the time the bigger crappies in a school are on the bottom of the school and the smaller crappies, which are the more aggressive ones, will be on or near the surface when the school is feeding. The bigger ones are somewhat more lethargic and that is probably how they grew to be that size.

Why do the bigger crappies position themselves below the smaller ones while feeding?

Korsgaden: The bigger crappies lay below and catch the wounded minnows; therefore, they expend much less energy than the more aggressive, smaller ones. And if they expend less energy filling their food needs, they will put on more weight and become larger. To say the larger ones get a meal without doing much work is an oversimplification, but it is essentially correct.

What are some of the crappies locational habits?

Korsgaden: They are a weedline origin fish keeping very tight to the weedlines during the early morning hours and the late evening hours. So the best time to catch crappies is in the mornings from sunrise to nine o'clock and from three o'clock in the afternoon to dark since they are easier to locate during those hours.

During midday they will often suspend in open water in twenty-five to thirty foot holes.

Once the cold water and warm water has stratified, crappies will not go below the thermocline. They will be forced just slightly inside of the weeds at the base of the weedline.

You also have to remember that the crappie is a forage fish, but not the dominant forager. If there is a population of northerns or bass working a weedline, which happens often in mid-summer and through August, the crappies will suspend the whole day because they cannot compete very well with those large fish.

Their locational pattern will also depend on the lake. If there is an overbalance of walleyes or northerns, for example, that can change the crappies location on that lake.

Do crappies school by size?

Korsgaden: To a degree they do school by size because crappies of a similar size have similar forage needs. For instance, a three pound crappie will not have the same forage needs as a quarter pounder will.

Do crapies follow schools of bait fish?

Korsgaden: They will most definitely follow schools of minnows. Whether this means anything to the crappie fisherman or not, I do not know.

How often do crappies feed?

Korsgaden: Probably daily. And feeding can occur at any time of the day. They feed less frequently in colder water periods, and colder water feeding will be for shorter periods of time.

How does the spawning cycle affect the crappies feeding requirements?

Korsgaden: Prior to spawning crappies feed very, very heavily at any opportunity they have. Of course, when I say feed very, very heavily, that is relative to pre-spawn water being colder than summer water. Also you must remember that there is less food available during the pre-spawn period.

Does the crappie's behavior change from lake to lake?

Korsgaden: Oh yes! In a shallow water lake the crappie will change his location more by moving horizontally, and in deeper water lakes he will change his location more by moving vertically. A crappie might change his location ten feet vertically in a deeper water lake to work a food source, and in a shallow water lake he might change his location fifty feet horizontally to work a food source.

Are there any myths about the crappie behavior that you would like to comment on?

Korsgaden: I'd like to comment on a myth, but it doesn't have anything to do with the crappies behavior.

Go ahead.

Korsgaden: The notion that you can never fish-out a good crappie lake is false. A population of big crappies can be fished down to almost nothing. I feel our Minnesota lakes are getting fished out. Fishermen have to realize that they don't have to take home a limit everytime they go fishing to enjoy the sport. And worse than that is the guy who fills his freezer.

LOCATING CRAPPIES

Is the crappie an easy fish to locate?

Korsgaden: Generally, a crappie is only easy to locate in the spring. The rest of the year he is harder to catch than a walleye. Big crappies, that is.

Since the crappie is not a bottom origin fish that expands the area you will have to fish to locate crappies; therefore, a crappie can be hard to locate and catch. A crappie can be in almost any geographical area on a given lake at any time of the year.

And working the small lures needed to catch crappies can be much more difficult than dragging a Lindy Rig, for instance. And, of course, the typical crappie fisherman takes a more lackadaisical attitude about his fishing technique.

Comment on location in general.

Korsgaden: Crappies relate to weeds very heavily in the spring because that's what they seek out for spawning. Generally speaking, for spawning purposes, crappies will seek out clumps of weeds and bulrushes in two to three feet of water.

Then as the season progresses, they will move out into the lake, and they will congregate very heavily on the weedline. They will use the weed-lines all summer until the weeds start to die. When the weeds start to die, the crappies will rapidly exit the weedline because weeds are no longer producing oxygen; they are producing carbon dioxide.

After the lake has turned over, they will move to deeper water and suspend. And because of forage they will relate to rocky areas and rock piles. Rocks and rock piles are a key locational factor at this time of the year in deeper lakes—mainly mid-mesotrophic lakes found from Saint Cloud north.

Also the small rocks that are slightly larger than a softball with crevasses and creases will harbor smaller forage fish, larva, and, in some lakes, fresh water shrimp. Devils Lake, for example, has a lot of fresh water shrimp in it.

Let's go through location from ice-out to ice-over.

Korsgaden: Beginning with ice-out you will find crappies in very deep water, thirty to thirty-five feet, if it is available to them. Then as the water warms, they will move into shallow water (two to five feet) to spawn.

When spawning is completed, in about mid-May, they will move into deeper water. As the weedline starts to develop, crappies will move to the weedline and start relating to it. They will use the weedline all summer into the fall period.

After the fall period, they will move to the deeper structure areas; that is, the rocky areas, rock piles, etc. And during the ice-over period they will locate in the deeper holes. The ones with sharp drop-offs will hold large concentrations of crappies.

What is the best time of the year to locate a lunker crappie?

Korsgaden: The springtime is when lunkers, as well as smaller crappies, are the most vulnerable to the angler since you can actually see them swimming in the shallow water.

Of course, the key to catching a lunker is to fish a lake that has lunker crappies. Lunker crappie lakes are mid-mesotrophic lakes usually having a very good walleye population and a good forage base (high fat forage) of ciscoes and shiners.

The best time of the year to catch a lunker is just before spawning takes place. Usually this would be mid-March to April, and the water temperature will be from the high forties to the mid-fifties.

Once I've located crappies, is there anything special I can do to take the larger ones in the school?

Korsgaden: If you see crappies surface feeding, drop your lure down a little and often you'll be able to catch the larger ones below the main school.

Do you use topographical maps to aid you in locating fish?

Korsgaden: Just to get a general understanding of how the lake looks. Its structure, that is.

Comment on night fishing for crappies?

Korsgaden: The night shift is definitely a good time to fish for crappies. In fact, many old-timers I know hang Coleman lanterns over the side of their boats to attract minnows which in turn attract crappies. And when night fishing, fish the same locations you would fish during the day.

PRESENTATION FOR CRAPPIES

How does your presentation vary throughout the year?

Korsgaden: In the spring you are fishing a lot shallower water using a bobber and jig combination. Then as you move out into deeper water, you have to use a casting presentation while counting down your jig and minnow. Of course, when the fish move off of the weedline, you can still use a bobber and jig combination, and when the fish are suspended out over deeper water that presentation will work well, too.

Early mornings and late evenings in the summer you should be fishing right on the bottom, especially if you are fishing rock pile areas. In the fall of the year you are also fishing right on the bottom with a sixteenth ounce jig tipped with a small minnow using a casting method rather than a bobber system.

What are the best colors to use in clear and stained water?

Korsgaden: In clear water I prefer yellow or white jigs. And in dark water I use a lot of black colored lures. In cloudy colored water I like to use oranges, fluorescents, and bright blues.

Do lures imitate something found in nature?

Korsgaden: Sure. A lure definitely imitates some type of food source. Of course, I can't prove that, but a crappie wouldn't strike it if he didn't think it was food.

Comment on trolling.

Korsgaden: Always troll slowly and preferably with an electric trolling motor. Or you can hover over the fish and use a vertical presentation. Also, I like hovering better than anchoring since I can keep moving and anchoring takes too much time anyway.

Why would you want to move if you were on a school of fish?

Korsgaden: Because a school of fish will move almost as rapidly as you contact them. Fifteen to twenty minutes is the longest you can expect a school to stay put after you have started fishing them. And the more fish you take out of the school, the more you will scatter them.

When they move, is there any way of knowing which way they will move?

Korsgaden: They might move up or down the weedline, but the chances are they will move out over deep water and suspend at the same depth they were at when you came in contact with them. Many times this will be right off of the bottom edge of the weedline out into deeper water.

What do you do when you've taken all of the active fish in a school?

Korsgaden: When you are on a school of fish and the fishing slows down, change the color of your lure or tip your lure with a minnow. With this change in presentation you can often trigger four or five more crappies to strike. Maybe even more.

Comment on lure size, jigs specifically.

Korsgaden: The proper jig size will not change overnight unless there has been a change in weather. At most, it will probably change weekly.

For example, if you are not catching fish today with the same size jig you were catching them on yesterday, don't change your jig size right away since you may have only temporarily spooked them with too noisy of an approach, etc.

What is the best method of presentation when fishing crappies that are located under docks?

Korsgaden: Cast to the dock and free swim your jig back to the boat. Or you can use small spinners, and let them helicopter down, but watch your line for any sideways movement, or if the spinner stops sinking, you probably have a fish on.

Comment on lure retrieve speed and trolling speed.

Korsgaden: When trolling, to get the best action from a jig you will have to troll very slowly. This is also true of casting. When in doubt, slow down since you are probably retrieving too fast anyway. In fact, most people retrieve a lure much too fast.

What size line do you prefer for crappie fishing?

Korsgaden: Two to four pound test line and the heaviest you should ever use would be six pound test.

Comment on negative -vs- active fish.

Korsgaden: All fish have their negative periods when you just can't seem to entice them into striking. A positive feeding fish is active because of biological needs or external variables—weather, etc.

The fortunate thing about crappie fishing is there are always some active fish. In a school of one hundred crappies, for example, you will always have between five and thirty fish that are active no matter how poor the conditions are. The important thing to remember is that when only a few are active, you must fine-tune your presentation.

Can you make a crappie strike when he is not in the mood to feed?

Korsgaden: The strike factor is more significant in a predator fish like the northern or the muskie. But it is possible to trigger a strike in a crappie with a nice slow falling jig or a jig tipped with a minnow. It is more likely that the crappie is biting because he is hungry than some other motivation, but the easier you make it for him, the more likely he will bite.

If you have ever dropped a minnow into an aquarium with a crappie in it, the crappie will take the minnow when it reaches a certain point only; whereas, a bass will swim the length of the aquarium to eat that minnow. Crappies tend to be less competitive than most other species of fish.

What is the most common mistake crappie fishermen make regarding presentation?

Korsgaden: Not sticking to a proper presentational system, perhaps, due to their lack of patience. Also many crappie fishermen do not work an area as thoroughly as they should.

What do you mean by the proper presentational system?

Korsgaden: Sticking with a small jig and minnow combination with no leader, no snaps, no swivels, using two to four pound test line, counting down the offering properly. And a good deal of successful presentation is in your ability to concentrate.

WEATHER AND BIOLOGICAL FACTORS AFFECTING CRAPPIES

Let's begin this section by discussing water temperature.

Korsgaden: Since fish are cold-blooded creatures that live in water, water temperature is perhaps the most important variable in locating and catching them. Water temperature triggers many biological responses in fish and triggers changes in the lake itself.

If a lake is very deep and has clear water, it will not warm as quickly as a shallow, cloudy water lake will. Consequently, those fish in the deep, clear water lakes will spawn a week or two later, etc. And that time span will follow throughout the year, including summer locational patterns, and so on.

The biological trigger for crappies to begin spawning is water temperature. After that, it's open water play for them. And other than their movements due to predator fish and fishing pressure, most of their seasonal behavior patterns are also triggered by water temperature.

Crappies usually spawn in late March or early April when the water temperature reaches the mid-fifties. But some years spawning can even occur as late as late May.

How does wind affect crappie fishing?

Korsgaden: It is only a problem in the spring when it blows cold water in onto the crappie beds, forcing the crappies out into the main lake.

Are you a barometer watcher?

Korsgaden: Somewhat since high pressure follows a cold front which slows down the crappies' activity. And it will change their location scattering them a bit. On the other hand, a low barometer or slightly falling barometer is typical of a low pressure area and cloudy weather which usually means increased fish activity.

How does rain affect crappie fishing?

Korsgaden: I've had some real good crappie fishing in cloudy weather while it was raining.

How does lightning affect crappie fishing?

Korsgaden: I don't even want to suggest going out on a lake during a lightning storm.

Comment on foggy conditions.

Korsgaden: It's a low light condition and crappies, as well as other fish, seem to be more active during low light conditions, so it can be a very good time to fish.

Is the old cold front excuse for not catching fish a good excuse?

Korsgaden: I think the cold front is overplayed and many fishermen use it as a cop-out when they are not catching fish.

Crappies are a great fish to fish after a cold front since there are so many of them. If you have any expertise at all, you should be able to catch a few. Also, the crappie schools are so large, relatively speaking, that there are always some active crappies somewhere in the lake. Also, after a cold front, crappies are a lot more scattered, and they will frequently suspend over deep water.

Do clear sky conditions always mean poor fishing?

Korsgaden: A high sky in a clear water lake will force crappies to the shaded areas on the weedline, and on a cloudy, windswept, gray day you will find crappies scattered from right off of the weedline to twenty feet off of the weedline.

Contrary to what many people think, on a high bluebird sky day you can catch many crappies; the key is to locate them. Remember under these conditions they will be concentrated.

Dave Csanda and I have caught thirty large crappies from an area no larger than a good sized living room because of a shaded weedline break. The high sky conditions caused them to be stacked in there very heavily.

What are your thoughts on acid rain?

Korsgaden: Although I have an opinion, I would rather not comment on it since I don't have the information to back my opinion. But I will say this, we probably won't know the effects of acid rain until it's too late.

Comment on the pH concept in locating crappies.

Korsgaden: It is a new and developing concept in fishing, and there needs to be a lot more work done on the pH theory. Again the evidence is not in. Actually, I still don't think we have covered all the areas we should explore regarding water temperature and oxygen content.

Comment on oxygen levels and the thermocline.

Korsgaden: Lakes that thermocline do so from mid-June to very early July—the first few hot days of summer. But not all lakes thermocline, for example, a wide open, windswept lake might not thermocline at all since the almost constant wind action will cause water temperatures to stay pretty much the same from top to bottom. There will be no stratification of the colder water on the bottom and the warmer water on the top.

Further, crappies will not go below a thermocline since there is little oxygen down there. In fact, most fish won't go below the thermocline.

The thermocline is more important to the crappie than any other fish since he will often work the bottom edge of the thermocline because that is where the small microorganisms that attract bait fish are located at this time of the year. And, naturally, the crappie will follow the bait fish.

"The thermocline is more important to the crappie than any other fish." You better elaborate on that statement.

Korsgaden: Well, I think, it is because the crappie can go out and suspend over deep water and work those water levels. The colder water below the thermocline is denser; therefore, you will have a buildup of microorganisms on that layer of colder, denser water. This buildup of microorganisms will draw minnows which come to feed on these organisms. Consequently, you will have crappies coming to feed on the minnows. It is the way the food chain for the crappie works on some lakes [lakes that develop a thermocline] during this time of the year—about late June through fall turnover.

How do you determine how deep the thermocline is?

Korsgaden: If you don't have a graph, you can use a temperature gauge. Simply lower the temperature probe down into the water until you find a sudden drop in water temperature. That's the thermocline. For example, when you are lowering your temperature probe into about twenty to thirty feet of water and within a two to three foot range there is a five to eight degree drop in temperature, you can be sure that you have found the thermocline.

What is fall turnover and how does it affect crappie fishing?

Korsgaden: It is a stage of transition triggered by air temperature that cools the surface water which makes the surface water more dense. When the surface water is heavier (denser) than the lower layer of water, it begins to sink and mixes with the lower layer of water. When the upper and lower layers of water have mixed thoroughly, turnover is complete. At this time the water temperature is the same from top to bottom and the lower, oxygen depleted layer now is reoxygenated. This is, of course, a simplified explanation.

It is important to realize that when turnover is complete, the water temperature is constant from top to bottom and the oxygen level is also constant, so fish and bait fish can be found at any depths in the lake, but crappies will usually be found in deeper water.

During the two week or so period it takes a lake to turnover, crappies will be in a neutral mood and harder to catch.

Comment on the moon's affect on crappie fishing.

Korsgaden: At this point in time, most of the information we have regarding the moon's affect on fishing is mostly speculation.

How important is the crappie's senses of smell and taste regarding presentation?

Korsgaden: I believe all fish have a sense of smell, but I question taste. The crappie uses his sense of smell to find forage fish.

EQUIPMENT AND TACKLE FOR CRAPPIE FISHING

What type of rod do you prefer?

Korsgaden: I like a long, slow action rod, and in ultralights I like a five foot fast action Fenwick or Skyline as long as it is graphite. When I'm casting a jig and a bobber, I use a nine foot rod which eliminates that end-over-end problem, and your accuracy will be much greater with a long rod.

How about reels?

Korsgaden: A spinning reel. A Zebco Cardinal Three which I understand is no longer being manufactured.

How tight do you set the drag on your reel?

Korsgaden: I think it is important to get a good hook set so I tighten the drag all the way down and set the anti-reverse so I can back reel when it's necessary to feed line.

What is your preference in line?

Korsgaden: I like Berkley monofilament in the XL clear type. And I tie my lures directly to the line without any leaders or swivels.

Do you have a favorite graph or depth finder?

Korsgaden: I use a Vexilar 555 graph and I love it. It has a very clear print out, and it is a very dependable unit. My depth finder is a Humminbird since I like the thirty foot scale and they were the first one to come out with a thirty foot scale.

Name a couple of good quality temperature gauges.

Korsgaden: Wallers makes a good one called the Fish Hawk, and Lowrance makes one they call the Fish'n Temp. They are both good units.

Do you modify your lures?

Korsgaden: I thin the maribou hair on jigs and make sure it isn't too far past the end of the hook because if it is too far past, it can cause crappies to strike short. Also I use a hook hone to sharpen hooks since factory hooks are never sharp enough.

What electronic equipment should all crappie fishermen have?

Korsgaden: A surface temperature gauge to locate warmer water areas for spring fishing; some type of thermometer to locate the thermocline for summer fishing; a depth finder; and a graph if you can afford one. Other gauges and monitors (pH, etc.) might be important, but, I think, you can spend time working a rod and reel to eliminate dead water much faster.

What tackle should a crappie fisherman have in his tackle box?

Korsgaden: A crappie fisherman's tackle selection is very simple. He should have jigs ranging in size from one-thirty-second ounce to a quarter ounce, and he should have them in every color imaginable. Usually the size jig you will need to use is determined by the depth you are fishing and the wind conditions. In very windy weather you can still take some crappies if you use a quarter ounce jig. The basic colors are white, yellow, black, and sometimes orange or purple. Although some people do well with brown jigs, I have never really been satisfied that brown is a good color.

Another valuable lure is a spinner and hook combination in gold or silver and sometimes red and white can be productive. I prefer the Prescott brand spinners with the fingernail size spinner because they flutter so nicely.

And when I'm trolling, I prefer a pencil type bobber, and for casting I use a slip bobber, especially if I'm fishing deeper water.

MISCELLANEOUS INFORMATION ABOUT CRAPPIE FISHING

Name some of the best crappie lakes in Minnesota.

Korsgaden: Rainy Lake near Baudette, Leech Lake near Walker, Blueberry Lake near Park Rapids, and the Toad Lakes near Detroit Lakes are all excellent crappie lakes. Also the Fergus Falls and Perham area lakes have big crappies. But the farther south you go in Minnesota the smaller the crappies are with the exception of Lake LeHomme Dieu and Lake Darling in the Alexandria area. But down in southern Minnesota near Worthington and Mankato where you have shallower, farm fertile lakes the crappies are very stunted.

How about the metro area?

Korsgaden: Lake Minnetonka has fair sized crappies—a half to three-quarter pounders.

What are your favorite crappie lakes in the state?

Korsgaden: The Toad Lakes and Crystal Lake by Pelican Rapids.

What is your favorite time of year to fish for crappies?

Korsgaden: Any time. But June and July are the prime times. And you can take some nice fish into August, too.

What are your favorite conditions?

Korsgaden: Daybreak with a light ripple on the water and gray, overcast skys. And in August I prefer a bright, high sky so I can pinpoint crappies on the shaded side of the weedline.

How big is the biggest crappie you have ever caught in Minnesota?

Korsgaden: Three pounds and four ounces on Prairie Lake near Pelican Rapids. In fact, a friend of mine and I caught a bunch all about that size that same day. We had six over three pounds and some that were in the two to two and a half pound range. The lake was ripe for big crappies.

What do you mean by ripe?

Korsgaden: Generally, crappies are on a seven year cycle. A typical big crappie lake will peak with big crappies every seven years. On lakes with a population of stunted crappies this cycle will not exist.

How many crappies do you catch on a typical day?

Korsgaden: A good day for me is one crappie over two pounds. A fun day is seven or eight fish around a pound, and I don't really keep track of how many small ones I catch.

Do you use those fish formulas that are on the market now?

Korsgaden: I don't, but they probably would help especially on hair type jigs since the hair would retain the smell of the formula, and also I feel crappies locate forage by scent.

Do you feel the "catch and release" concept is important to the future fishing in Minnesota?

Korsgaden: In certain species I do. Definitely bass, etc. But I'm not sure it is necessary with crappies because there just aren't enough anglers that can proficiently catch big crappies the year 'round. The fishing pressure on crappies is not there. Of course, some lakes get pounded pretty hard, but, on a state-wide basis, the pressure isn't there.

What advice would you give to beginners?

Korsgaden: The best thing to do is to fish with somebody who knows how to fish for crappies and read every type of fishing book imaginable. Read during the wintertime and make notes. Plus you should be proficient with your tools and have a good boat, a good locator, good rods and reels, and know how to use them correctly. Also, learn how to handle your boat properly. Rig your boat with the best equipment you can find and have good tackle since it makes the sport more enjoyable and a lot easier.

Do you have any bad habits? . . . I guess I should limit that to bad habits regarding fishing.

Korsgaden: Since we don't have room in this book to cover all of my bad habits, I'll limit my answer to my bad habits regarding fishing.

Sometimes I get lazy and don't sharpen my hooks, or I might not take the time to select the best minnows. Actually, if I'm not in the mood to do it right, I prefer not to fish at all.

Do you still fish in lots of tournaments?

Korsgaden: No. I do not enter tournaments anymore. I have nothing against tournaments, but, I feel, always having to prove who is the better fisherman isn't necessary. That's not what fishing is all about. Tournaments are fine for the recreational fisherman, but not on a day in and day out basis.

When should I hire a guide?

Korsgaden: I would hire a guide when fishing conditions are tough, and only under the condition that you are going to learn from him. Also, don't value a guide by how many pounds of fish he puts in the boat but by what you have learned from him. Sit and watch what the guide does. Ask him what he would be doing if the conditions were different.

Comment on live bait and artificial lures.

Korsgaden: Artificial lures are by far the most challenging way to take fish, and live bait can really enhance an artificial lure. But there are certain conditions when fishing is difficult and live bait is a necessary factor.

Do you think there will ever be a new Minnesota state record crappie caught?

Korsgaden: I don't think so. If so, it will only be an ounce or two over the current record, and if it happens, it will probably come out of a river system on a jig and minnow in twenty to twenty-five feet of water in a remote pool.

Comment on luck -vs- knowledge in fishing.

Korsgaden: Luck is being able to go fishing and knowledge is second fiddle to being able to go fishing.

What are the psychological aspects of fishing?

Korsgaden: Fishing is no longer an ego booster for me. For instance, last summer I was very excited to catch big crappies, up to two pounds, on a rock pile when the water temperature was between ninety and one hundred degrees, and the water was glass calm. It's enough for me to learn new presentations for taking fish when they aren't supposed to be biting. I no longer have to display a stringer of fish to my friends to have enjoyed the day.

What is special about Minnesota fishing?

Korsgaden: Minnesota offers many challenges for the fisherman, and there are thousands of beautiful lakes.

Chapter 8

LAUN "E" ANDERSON ON SUNFISH

There is little recognition in being a field tester for the fishing tackle and equipment industry. Actually, it is nothing more than research work, but Laun "E" Anderson finds that being a fishing tackle and equipment field tester is pleasant part-time work. Perhaps that has something to do with the fact that he would rather be fishing than doing anything else.

Field testing is somewhat like being one of the Nielsen Families. [These families have their television sets monitored to determine what programs they are watching, and this information is compiled to determine television ratings which executives use to decide which programs will remain on the air.] But unlike the Neilsen Families, a field tester for the fishing tackle and equipment industry is not selected at random. First, a field tester must be a knowledgeable fisherman, and, second, he must spend a great deal of time on the water—enough time to give the new prototype products a good workout to determine if they can "take a licking and keep on ticking."

Initially, an engineer designs a new rod, reel, lure, etc., and a tackle or an equipment company manufactures a few prototypes of that new product. Then the prototypes are shipped off to the field testers throughout the country. It is these field testers who, for the most part, by their report cards on these new products will determine whether or not a new product will eventually be marketed to the public.

In the past ten years if you have purchased a Lund, Heddon, or Creme lure, one of Gapen's products, or a rod and reel made by the Ryobi Company, you can be sure that Laun has seen it well before it was available on the market, and he has probably put it to the test, too.

When testing a new product, Laun looks for quality and ease of application. With lures, for instance, he tries to determine with what regularity that new lure will attract fish. "I'm not a man who mixes his words," Laun says, "if a product is of inferior quality, I tell the company they better send that one back to the drawing board."

Laun was born near Sleepy Eye, Minnesota and lived there until he was six years old when he and his family moved to Bowdon, North Dakota. In their free time his father would take the family fishing on the Cheyenne River. When they could manage to get away for a couple of days or more, they would go to the Detroit Lakes area and fish McDonald Lake, Rush Lake, and, occasionally, they would go to Canada fishing. Laun says his father was a good fisherman and taught him a lot about fishing.

When Laun was in his early twenties, he moved back to Minnesota and for the past seventeen years he has been a police officer for the City of Hopkins. Laun's rotating work schedule provides him with time to be on the water when there is little boat traffic on the lakes.

It's no secret that policemen have to deal with work-related stress that most of us can only imagine. To cope with this stress Laun goes fishing. "When I'm on the water," he said, "I'm relaxed. It's an individual thing—me against the critters." Laun sees fishing as a never ending contest since he is always trying to come up with the right technique that is going to outsmart those fish. "Sooner or later, the fish will make a mistake and let his guard down," Laun says, "and then he's yours."

Laun is a successful fisherman because of his positive attitude and hard work. He spends a great deal of time on the water paying attention to the variables that he feels affect fishing: time of day, season, water temperature, depth, lures, sky conditions, wind direction, and so on. Then he uses these observations the next time that he is confronted with similar conditions. Also, Laun says, "You need confidence and make every cast like it's the cast that will put one on the wall for you."

The yard stick used to measure your rate of success in fishing for sunfish is how long did it take you to catch a limit of thirty. For Laun it is a mighty poor day's fishing when he has to spend up to three hours for that limit. On an average day he will catch a limit in about two hours, and on a good day he can get the job done in less than an hour. However, he admits that there have been days when he has been skunked, thoroughly skunked. "Some days you are just not going to do very well," he said. "That's what makes it a challenge."

In addition to his work as a police officer and a field tester, Laun is active in the V.F.W.'s Cootie organization which assists patients in the Veteran's Hospital, and he is also involved with young people through Legionville which is a school patrol safety camp that is funded by the American Legion. But the list doesn't end there. He is a consultant for the

Lake Maps Company and a staff member of Ed Gercey's Outdoor Outline which is a weekly newspaper devoted to outdoor news. The topics Laun writes about range from fishing to how to use a metal detector.

With regards to Laun's fishing success, outdoor sports writer Art Perry probably said it best: "Laun is an excellent multi-species angler who specializes in catching sunfish. A specialty that takes no less knowledge and ability than it does to consistently catch walleyes, bass, or steelhead trout, etc."

In closing, Laun's motto is, "In the summertime, don't try to find me around the house because I'm probably fishing."

SUNFISH BEHAVIOR

In discussing the sunfishes behavior, is it necessary to distinguish between bluegills and pumpkinseeds?

Anderson: No. Generally, they are just a variation in the species. Bluegills and pumpkinseeds mix together and can be caught using the same techniques.

Have you ever got into a school of sunfish where they were all bluegills or all pumpkinseeds?

Anderson: No. They almost always run together. It would be somewhat rare to catch a limit of bluegills without having caught a few pumpkinseeds or vice versa.

How do bluegills vary from pumpkinseeds—size, quantity, etc.?

Anderson: There are more pumpkinseeds than there are bluegills in most Minnesota lakes. A mature bluegill is anywhere from six to eight inches long and will weigh from a half a pound to a pound. And a mature pumpkinseed will run about a third smaller than a bluegill. Of course, in some lakes their average size will be much larger.

What do sunfish eat?

Anderson: They eat small insects, larvae, algae, plankton, and the blossoms of most any type of vegetation.

What are the seasonal differences in the sunfishes feeding habits?

Anderson: The only seasonal differences that you will find will be mainly due to the availability of certain types of food, and, also, water temperature will change their need for food. Since they are cold-blooded critters, in the summertime, for instance, they will require more food to live. And in the summer they will feed for longer periods of time and take in much, much more food. Some biologists estimate that during the hottest periods of the year a sunfish will eat three times his own body weight in food daily.

What is the most important aspect of the sunfishes behavior that fishermen should be aware of?

Anderson: I suppose they should know that the sunfish is a warm water fish; that is, the sunfish usually prefers the warmest water that is available in a lake. And, generally, the warmest water in a lake is the shallowest water, so that's where they will usually be found. Emphasize usually.

Do sunfish school by size the way some other species of fish do?

Anderson: No. I've never found that to be the case. All sizes seem to school together, but the upper part of the school will hold the smaller sunfish, and the larger ones will hold in deeper water right below the smaller ones. Of course, this isn't true in each and every instance.

Why do bigger sunnies position themselves below the smaller ones? And I assume we're talking about when they are schooled in deeper water.

Anderson: The bigger sunfish take the best spots for food which is usually farther down, and they force the smaller ones to take the less desirable spots. And if you are catching a lot of small sunfish, then fish a little deeper and you should catch the bigger ones.

If you are fishing in ten feet of water and catching small sunnies, how far down would the bigger ones be?

Anderson: There is no general rule to cover that. It varies because of what they might be feeding on. It's really a matter of trial and error each time you are on the lake; that is, the theory usually holds true, but the exact depth you will find the big ones will vary too much to make any general statement about. What I do is lower my lure in about six inch increments until I find the bigger ones. And sometimes I don't find 'em.

Why are some schools of sunfish on a given lake active and others on that same lake are not active?

Anderson: Schools of sunfish in a shallower part of the lake are probably in warmer water which will usually increase their activity. And their food sources in various parts of the lake might be different, too. There are different variables acting and reacting in different parts of the same body of water at the same time. It can be like fishing on two different lakes.

What motivates a sunfish to strike or bite a lure?

Anderson: There are only two reasons a sunfish will hit your lure—anger or hunger. Hunger is obvious, but anger plays a part in the spring of the year when the males are protecting the spawning beds. If you throw a lure in a spawning bed, they will hit it because they are angry and trying to protect their eggs. It's the protection instinct.

How highly developed is a sunfishes ability to smell and taste?

Anderson: I feel, smell and taste are definitely important considerations for the fisherman of any species of fish, including the sunfish. If you are using any lure or bait that you touch with your hands, fish can pick up the human scent on that lure or bait. All deer hunters know the importance of scent when they are hunting. It's no different for the fisherman.

Are you saying that fish are repelled by the human scent?

Anderson: Definitely! They can smell and taste the human odor, and they don't like it.

Does the sunfish's behavior vary from lake to lake?

Anderson: Sure it does. Each lake is different with respect to water clarity, food sources available, depth, cover, vegetation, etc.; so the sunfish's behavior will vary accordingly. He is trapped in a body of water so if he can't find the exact environment he wants, he must adapt or die. For example, on a clear water lake where visibility is high and the sun's penetration is high, the sunfish will be spookier, and you will have to adjust your presentation to catch them with any consistency. And the greater the differences in lakes, the greater the differences in their behavior which is another reason why fishing is always challenging.

Why do so many of Minnesota's lakes have populations of stunted sunfish?

Anderson: It's a problem. When sunfish overpopulate, all you have is many, many little ones. It's not a matter of the availability of food; it's a matter of space. If you have a sunfish in a five gallon aquarium, he will only grow so big no matter how much you feed him. They need space to grow.

So a fish's eventual size is determined more by the space he has to grow in than it is determined by how much food he has to eat?

Anderson: Right! If you had half as many sunfish in some of these lakes, the half that remained would have twice as much room to grow. The remaining ones would indeed grow bigger, but exactly how much bigger, I don't know.

What can be done on lakes that have an overpopulation problem?

Anderson: If you have a lake that has stunted fish that are so small that they aren't even worth fishing, you can do one of two things. Either stock big game fish such as northerns or muskies to eat many of those small fish, or you can kill all of the fish in the lake with chemicals and start over. Killing off the whole population of fish in a lake and starting over with stocking programs has been done successfully in Minnesota before, but, I think, it should be a last resort.

How can you determine if a given lake has a stunted population of fish or if you are just catching the small fish?

Anderson: You can tell the fish's age much the way you can tell a tree's age—by the number of rings on the fish's scale. So if you've got old sunfish that are very small, the lake has a stunted population. Now if the scale samples you check turn out to be young fish that are small, you are probably just not catching the bigger ones.

Do you believe the theory that big fish are lazy fish?

Anderson: I don't know if it's that they are lazy or smart. The more wary fish live longer and tend to get bigger than the others. So if they can find a good spot for food without putting themselves in too much danger from predators, they will probably grow to be large. Big fish probably are the smart fish.

How highly developed is a sunfish's memory; that is, do you think they can become lure wary?

Anderson: Not anymore lure wary than a bass is of a purple worm. I think you can catch and recatch the same sunfish on the same lure over and over again. Maybe not the same day, but he's not likely to remember a lure he's been caught on two days ago.

Is there anything that you want to add regarding the sunfish's behavior?

Anderson: The main thing to remember in fishing for sunfish is that they do almost all of their feeding in the morning and in the evening. In the mornings and evenings they will move up into shallow water to feed. You can catch sunfish at high noon, but usually it will be more difficult to entice them into biting at that time of the day, and you will probably have to fish deeper water during the middle of the day.

Usually, you wouldn't fish at noon?

Anderson: I wouldn't fish at noon unless I could hear those lily pads snap from the sunfish pulling food off of the bottoms of them.

What?

Anderson: You can actually hear the snap when a sunfish sucks bugs, snails, or algae from the bottoms of lily pads. And when you hear that snapping sound, they are actively feeding and you can catch them quite easily.

Also remember that sunfish will use the weedline the way other fish do, so that can be a good place to fish for them, too.

LOCATING SUNFISH

Let's start this section by discussing the importance of weeds with regards to the location of sunfish.

Anderson: Weeds are an important source of cover for the sunfish. Being one of the smallest fish in a lake the sunfish has an obvious need for cover from larger, predator fish, and weeds provide that cover. Also the sunfish finds most of his food in weed areas. Almost all the fish activity that happens on a lake happens in the weeds or on the weedline.

Are any weed types more important than other weed types?

Anderson: Any type of weed that will provide cover and food is important. Lily pads, coontail. cambomba, cabbage, etc. are all important.

How important are rocks and rock piles in locating sunnies?

Anderson: Sunfish will feed in rocky areas, but since there is little protection for them in rocky areas they will spend relatively little time there. Rocky areas are important, but they aren't nearly as important as weeds.

Can the oxygen content of the water help you to determine where fish are likely to locate?

Anderson: In the summertime the oxygen content of most lakes diminishes as you go deeper. So during the summertime fish are forced to use shallower water because of the lack of oxygen in the deeper areas of the lake. As the season progresses, the lake forms a layer of water called the thermocline and sunfish will not go below that layer of water since there is almost no oxygen down there. Now after the lake has gone through turnover in the fall, the oxygen content is pretty much the same from the top to the bottom.

So to answer your question: Since we know that fish won't go below the thermocline that doesn't tell us where they are, but it tells us where they aren't. And that eliminates a whole lot of water. Then in the fall after turnover they could be found at almost any depth.

But in spite of all of this information, I don't know how important it is to the sunfish fisherman since the sunfish is a warm water fish and will most often be found in shallow water where the oxygen content is always good because the shallow water is usually the warmer water.

You started to say something about water temperature.

Anderson: Yeah. Sunfish spawn in the spring or early summer when the water temperature reaches seventy to seventy-five degrees which usually occurs by the end of May or early June on most Minnesota lakes, but that can vary by as much as two to three weeks from northern Minnesota to southern Minnesota. Also, shallow water lakes warm up earlier in the year, so the spawning period will occur sooner in those lakes. Then after the spawning period is over, I look for them in any weedy and shallow water areas of the lake up until the fall turnover period is complete.

What depth of water do sunfish spawn in?

Anderson: Anywhere from three inches to a foot and a half.

Comment on how the wind affects sunfish.

Anderson: When it's windy, sunfish will locate on the lee side of the lake or in some sheltered area of the lake.

How does the barometric pressure affect sunfish?

Anderson: When you are fishing during a falling barometer, you are going to have to really work to catch sunfish. But when the barometer is rising, sunfish seem to bite better, and they will even hit your lure harder.

How do sky conditions affect where sunnies will locate?

Anderson: It doesn't affect their general location at all. But I think when it's sunny, they will hold tighter to cover even in a dirty water lake, and they are probably more easily spooked by your presentation. And in a clear water lake they will tend to locate deeper than they would during an overcast sky condition, but, again, in the same general location.

There is one thing that all fishermen agree on: The fishing is always better when the skies are overcast.

How does water clarity affect sunfish?

Anderson: Most clear water lakes are not fertile lakes which means they don't provide the necessary ingredients for fish to grow large. In fact, I really don't like to fish lakes that have real clear water. I'd much prefer to fish stained or dirty water. I don't like to fish lakes like Clearwater Lake at Annandale in the early springtime since it is so clear at that time of the year you can see rocks in twenty feet of water. And if you can see rocks in twenty feet of water, you can bet that the fish can see you much better too which makes them harder to catch.

As the thermocline is developing in the summer, what does that indicate to you as far as locating sunfish?

Anderson: Briefly, because we pretty well covered this in the behavior section, you can eliminate a good deal of water since I don't think you will ever find sunfish below the thermocline. Not any that are alive anyway. And don't go looking for the thermocline on all lakes since many shallower bodies of water never develop a thermocline.

How does fall turnover affect the sunfish's locational patterns?

Anderson: I don't think it affects where sunfish will locate very much. In fact, I don't even worry about it at all. Just remember to fish slower in the fall as you should in any cold water period. Of course after turnover is complete, it might allow sunfish to locate in deeper water areas of the lake, but when they are in those deeper water areas, they are probably not active anyway.

What affects do seasonal changes have on fishing?

Anderson: As a season is coming to an end, fishing seems to get better. Then as the next season begins, fishing will slow down a lot. And during the middle of a season, it seems to be fairly constant—not great, not bad.

And these seasonal changes aren't necessarily calendar seasons. For example, summer begins on June twenty-first, but that doesn't mean that June twenty-first is the beginning of summer in a lake. The summer period in Minnesota lakes could begin anywhere from the middle of June to the beginning of July.

Let's talk about some specific locations where sunnies can be found—points, bars, docks, etc.

Anderson: The morning and evening pattern that I prefer to fish works well about ninety percent of the time around docks, points, bars, and so on. But docks are much better to fish for sunfish in the summertime than they are in the springtime or fall. And bridge pilings can be good all through the year.

Many times when I'm fishing for sunfish, I will catch largemouth bass since sunfish and largemouth bass use some of the same locational patterns. They like to locate around and under docks, near bridge pilings, and in weedy areas.

How important are topographical maps in locating sunfish?

Anderson: If I'm fishing a new lake, I would rather leave my depth finder on the beach than my map.

Can you eliminate a lot of unproductive water with a topographical map even before you go on the lake?

Anderson: Definitely! First of all, you are not going to be fishing for sunfish in forty, fifty, sixty feet of water, so that eliminates a good portion of many lakes. And don't fish any water that is deeper than fifteen feet any time of the year. Of course, there could be sunfish in water deeper than fifteen feet, but the odds are in your favor if you do your fishing in fifteen feet of water or less. Eliminate that sixteen-plus-feet of water right away. And when they are in deep water, (deeper than fifteen feet) they are in a negative mood. The catchable sunfish will almost always be in shallow water—the weedline into shore.

Are there any other locational clues that we should talk about?

Anderson: Most types of weeds are important because sunfish need vegetation for food and cover.

Also, if you find an area that seems to have all of the ingredients to hold sunfish, but there is no adjacent deep water, that spot will only, at best, occasionally hold sunfish. For a spot to be good most of the time, you need to have a deep water holding area nearby, so when they are through feeding, they can slip back to the deeper water.

Are large, shallow water flats very productive?

Anderson: If an area doesn't have good cover and deep water nearby, I wouldn't spend too much time fishing it. Those large flats just aren't very productive.

Earlier you began to say something about bridges and we got sidetracked.

Anderson: Bridges are real important to the sunfish fisherman because anytime you have structure in the water that collects algae on it, snails will live on it, and this makes for a good place for sunfish to feed.

Bass fishermen maintain that bridges with wooden legs are better than other kinds for attracting fish.

Anderson: Concrete and wood are better than steel bridges because algae will grow on them more easily.

What is the most common mistake people make in trying to locate sunfish?

Anderson: Getting to the point where they feel they know everything there is to know about fishing. And if you do that, you will soon find yourself not experimenting and not learning anything new, and that's when you will stop being a good fisherman.

Also, many people who fish for sunfish don't really make any effort to do more than fish off of the end of a dock. They should pursue the sunfish with the same effort they might pursue the walleye, and if they did, they would enjoy it every bit as much.

And, perhaps, the biggest mistake, since the widespread use of depth finders, is many fishermen feel that depth alone will guarantee success. Depth is only a good place to begin to locate sunfish.

PRESENTATION FOR SUNFISH

Let's go through a typical season from ice-out to ice-over with presentation in mind.

Anderson: Right at ice-out a golden rod bug or any of the larva type bait is probably the best choice. And if you are going to use an angleworm, only use about an inch or two of it otherwise a sunfish will steal your bait without even having the hook in his mouth. I prefer a number four hook with a long shank. With the long shank it is easier to release a sunnie without harming him since sometimes they will swallow the hook way down.

Then, as the season progresses about to mid-May, I prefer to use a Mepps Spinner or an Ugly Bug. And you can tip these artificials with live bait also.

About mid-June or so, you will need a lure that you can fish effectively in a little deeper water since after spawning sunfish will spend more time in deeper water. And if you do not have a large selection of lures, you can put a split shot sinker on your line about a foot before the lure which will make it run deeper in the water.

With these presentations are you still using a bobber?

Anderson: Yes. I almost always use a bobber. A clear bobber.

Then in the fall, I go back to lures that work well in shallow water since the sunfish now will spend most of his time in shallow water.

And for the person that likes to use a fly rod, the spring and fall can be great. I prefer those little poppers when I fly rod fish for sunnies.

But, I feel, the main thing is to use lures that you have confidence in because without confidence you are not going to do very well. This is not to say, that you shouldn't experiment with new lures, you should.

How heavy of a leader do you use on your fly rod rig?

Anderson: I use three to four pound Trilene green. And I tie all my lures directly to the line without using any snaps or swivels.

What length leaders do you use on your fly rod?

Anderson: Three to four feet seems to work best. And sometimes I tip the popper with an inch or so of angleworm.

How does your presentation change when the sunnies aren't active?

Anderson: When the fishing gets tough, I'll change my presentation by using different lures. I try to remember what presentation worked on a previous day with similar conditions. Also, I will experiment, but the main key when fishing is tough, is to fish many different locations.

Still thinking in terms of a tough fishing day, which would change first? Your presentation or location.

Anderson: I would change my presentation before I would change the location that I'm fishing, especially on a lake that I know well.

Changing presentation is more than changing lures. You may need to slow down your retrieve or make it more erratic or change the depth you are fishing.

With sunnies, presentation can be a bigger part of the game than location. Often you can see them in the water and put your lure right in front of their noses and they aren't buyin' it at all. Then I go through my tackle box to find out what they want.

With respect to the location/presentation game in fishing, are you saying that presentation is a bigger part of those two ingredients than it is in fishing for other species?

Anderson: Yes. I feel it is because it is usually easier to locate sunfish than it is bass, for instance. Often you can see a sunfish when you are fishing, but they won't take your lure without the proper presentation.

You tie and retie however many lures you have to, to get them to strike. That's the name of the game with sunnies. Remember, other than springtime when a sunfish will hit a lure out of anger when he's protecting his spawning bed, you must present him with a lure that he will want to take because you've tricked him into thinking your lure is something to eat.

Do you ever use trolling as a method of presentation?

Anderson: I never troll for sunfish, but I do like to drift fish for them. It seems to me that the sound of your motor running when you are trolling could easily spook fish. Often I will drift over an area to locate sunfish. Then when I get a strike, I will drop anchor and start fishing that area to see if I've located a good school of them.

Do you ever use topwater techniques for sunnies?

Anderson: Sometimes I use a Mister Twister floating jig head tipped with about two inches of angleworm. You can put a small split shot about eight inches above the lure if you want it to sink a little. Of course, you will probably have to use a bobber with the floating jig head to give you enough weight to cast that rig. So other than using a fly rod, that's as close as I get to topwater fishing for sunnies.

Comment on lure retrieve.

Anderson: I never use a fast retrieve for sunfish.

Comment on lures. Color, size, texture, etc.

Anderson: Just remember to use a small lure, and don't overdo it on the amount of bait you put on the hook. In dirty water I prefer to use a dark colored lure, and in clear water I use light colored lures—white or yellow. A good rule of thumb is: the darker the water, the darker the lure you should use. Also, in most lakes the water will get darker as the season progresses so don't forget to change the color of your lures.

As for texture, in plastics I prefer the softest I can find. And if a lure isn't working, experiment until you find out which lure will work.

Tell me about the plastic grub worm that the Creme Company began manufacturing at your suggestion.

Anderson: In the fall after the first frost, I pick golden rods and take the larva out of them which is a real good bait for sunfish. You can store these larva in sawdust in your freezer because they will stay dormant when they are cold. Then in the middle of July you can take them out of the freezer and use them for bait.

So a few years back I sent some of these larva to the Creme Company in Tyler, Texas, [The Creme Company is one of the largest manufacturers of plastic lures.] and because they thought it was a good bait they began manufacturing a plastic lure that resembles the golden rod larva. They call it a "grub worm."

Do you get a royalty on these?

Anderson: I wish I did!

When you are fishing a cold front, do you use a smaller lure as many bass and walleye fishermen do?

Anderson: No. Before I would go to a smaller lure, I would try a slower retrieve.

We've talked about how to use live bait, but you rarely use it except to tip artificial lures. Is that correct?

Anderson: About the only time I use live bait is when the water is real hot, and then I prefer a real small minnow. Little one inch bait minnows work the best.

How about waxworms?

Anderson: I don't use them, but they're a good bait.

Is there anything that needs to be said about boat control?

Anderson: Just don't drop your anchor in the middle of a school of fish. Anchor off to one side of the school.

Comment on versatility in presentation.

Anderson: It is very important if you intend to catch fish consistently. If you are a one method fisherman, there are going to be many days when you aren't going to catch fish. You need to be versatile and experiment a lot.

Is there anything that you want to add regarding presentation?

Anderson: When you start fishing an area, begin shallow and then if you are not successful, begin to fish deeper and deeper. And, frequently, you will be fishing the right spot, but you aren't fishing the right depth.

In what increments do you move your lure up or down in trying to locate the proper depth?

Anderson: Six to eight inches at a time. Also many people go to a spot where they've caught fish yesterday three feet below the water's surface and they leave if they don't catch them at that depth today. Although the fish may not be there today, it is possible they are just holding a little deeper, or, in some cases, they may be a little shallower, so try different depths on that spot before you go running all over the lake looking for another school of fish.

WEATHER AND BIOLOGICAL FACTORS AFFECTING SUNFISH

Comment on the barometer's affect on sunfish.

Anderson: A falling barometer will shut sunfish off. It shuts all fishing off for a time. The best time to fish, for any species, is on a rising barometer or if you have a condition where the barometer has leveled off for two to three days.

Any guess as to why?

Anderson: When the barometer is falling, fish go off of feed. The barometric pressure in the air changes the pressure per square inch in the water which affects fish, and the more sudden the change in the air pressure the greater the affect on fish.

How about the pH factor?

Anderson: The pH factor is definitely a factor in fishing. The best range on the pH monitor that I have found is six and a half to seven and three-quarters. The highest I've ever found is eight, but I've been on water where the pH was as low as one. When you find water with a pH less than that, you won't even find a fish, much less catch one.

Comment on sky conditions and how they affect sunfish.

Anderson: Overcast skies make for the best fishing because on bright, sunny days shadows spook sunfish easily.

How do moon phases affect fishing for sunfish?

Anderson: I don't know that much about moon phases—major and minor feeding periods, etc., but I do feel that they should be studied more by scientists and fishermen. But that doesn't mean if the major feeding period is at high noon, that I'm going to go fishing at noon. I'm probably still going to stick with my morning and afternoon patterns.

How does rain affect fishing?

Anderson: If there is a rain storm coming, I try to hit the lake. Fish have a tendency to feed prior to a storm so it can be a good time to go fishing.

How about during a rain?

Anderson: It can go either way. I've had good and bad fishing during a rain. But after a rain is over, the fishing is usually very poor.

How do cold fronts affect sunfish?

Anderson: After a cold front has hit, the fishing is somewhere between very bad and terrible. But someday I hope to figure out a post-cold front pattern for taking sunnies.

Do warm fronts have the opposite affect?

Anderson: During a warm front the fishing will usually continue to pick up until it becomes cold again. But even a slight drop in temperature will sometimes slow fishing down again.

Do you like to fish in the fog?

Anderson: Yes. It has the same affect as an overcast sky does.

EQUIPMENT AND TACKLE
FOR SUNFISH FISHING

Let's begin with line. What kind do you prefer for fishing sunnies?

Anderson: I use two to four pound Trilene in the green color which, I feel, is the hardest color for fish to see.

Why do you use two pound line; is it more sporting?

Anderson: I think using light line will increase the number of strikes you will get since it is harder for the fish to see than heavier line. And, of course, if you get more strikes, you should catch more fish.

What kind of a boat do you have?

Anderson: I've got a seventeen foot Smokercraft Pro Angler. Also, I fish out of a canoe, and when I have a lot of company, I use my pontoon.

But you really don't need anything fancy to fish out of. Just some basic equipment helps: anchor, locator, and trolling motor are the essentials.

What kind of rods do you use?

Anderson: I field test for Ryobi so I use their rods. And I would recommend using graphite rods over fiber glass since they are stronger and much more sensitive.

How about reels?

Anderson: The Ryobi 100 and the Ryobi MD 7 are the reels I use for most of my sunfish fishing. They're spinning reels. Actually, the 100 is my favorite because I like the "touch and trip" feature. You don't have to reach over with your left hand and release the bail before you cast.

What brand of electric trolling motor do you use?

Anderson: I use a Ram and I've been very happy with it. It's a good motor at a good price. They also run very quietly which is important so you don't spook the fish.

How about locators?

Anderson: I've got a Vexilar flasher and a Vexilar graph, and they both work very well.

What are some of your favorite lures for sunnies?

Anderson: I like the Creme worm which is a plastic worm rig with a leader and a spinner on it. It's about three inches long with two real small hooks on it and a small spinner with beads up front.

How do you rig and use it?

Anderson: I put a small split shot on my line just before it attaches to the leader. Then about a foot and a half up from where the leader attaches to my line, I put on a clear bobber. And a clear bobber is important. A clear bobber definitely won't spook sunnies as easily as a red or yellow bobber will. Then you cast it to where you want to fish, and don't begin your retrieve until all of the ripples disappear from where the bobber hit the water. Then start a real slow retrieve. Just enough to make the propeller turn and the worm will wiggle just a bit. With this lure you will also catch crappies and perch as well as sunfish.

Do you find that plastic baits work well throughout the year?

Anderson: Yes I do. The problem many fishermen have using plastic type lures, for any species, during cold water periods is that they fish them too fast. Slow down your retrieve and plastic lures will work very well in the fall, too.

Also I have had a lot of success with the Krappie Kat Jig and the Windels Panfish Snacks and Panfish Jigs. And the Lindy Floater Jig with about two inches of angleworm on it works very well, too.

A sunfish has a very small mouth so if you use too much worm, he'll just nibble it off of your hook and you'll miss him. He's a bait stealer. Put the angleworm on like a piece of yarn—just enough to cover the hook is best.

Which reminds me! Don't forget to sharpen your hooks. All hooks have a little ball on the end of the hook which is left there from the manufacturing process, and it is important to remove that ball by sharpening the hook.

Also, I like the zero size Mepps Spinner with the imitation minnow and treble hook.

If you are using live minnows, what size is best?

Anderson: The average size sunfish will not usually bite on a crappie size minnow. You should use minnows that are no longer than one inch.

Why do lures seem to run a course of popularity with fishermen?

Anderson: Mostly because of the marketing techniques used by the tackle manufacturers. They convince you that their new lure is superior to anything you've ever used before. And many lures become popular because of word-of-mouth advertising. If I tell you that I've been catching good fish on a purple grub made by a certain company, the next time you go into a tackle shop you will probably buy one of those purple grubs. We all do that. Besides that, it's fun to try new lures.

Do you modify lures before you use them?

Anderson: No. Other than I always sharpen the hooks before I use a new lure. I leave the modifications to the engineers back at the factory.

Are you referring to your situation as a products field tester?

Anderson: Yeah. I do recommend changes but only to the manufacturers.

What kind of comments or suggestions do you make to the manufacturers? Do you ever say to them that the product you are testing is a real piece of junk?

Anderson: You bet I do! If it's a piece of junk, I tell them it's junk. But I have a real good relationship with the companies that I field test for, and they are very interested in what field testers have to say about their products.

Of course, one field tester isn't going to change a product or decide whether a company should go ahead and market a new product or not. But if three or four testers throughout the country have the same complaint, a company will modify that product or not market it at all. We have comment sheets that we fill out on each product, and I tell them exactly what I think.

What do you expect, for instance, from a prototype reel?

Anderson: The obvious stuff: how smoothly the reel performs and does it stand up to continued use. Is the gear ratio desirable? With spinning reels, the bail and bail spring need to work well over a long period of time.

A few years back you were testing a Ryobi rod with an offset handle. How did that work out?

Anderson: I liked it. I felt I could cast more accurately with that offset style of handle. And it was more comfortable to hold in my hand for long periods of time.

What kind of knot do you tie?

Anderson: I tie the Trilene knot. We've tested it on Trilene's knot strength machine and it seems to be the strongest. And knot strength is important because, most of the time, when your line breaks, it breaks at the knot.

MISCELLANEOUS INFORMATION ABOUT SUNFISH FISHING

Is there any truth to the myth that fishing isn't any good during "dog-days"?

Anderson: Poor fishing during "dog-days" and most of those other wive's tales are just that: only myths. I've had great fishing during "dog-days" just as I've had poor fishing during "dog-days."

If people tell me they're not going fishing because the fish aren't going to bite, that's when I'm going to be on the water since it increases my chances of doing well when there are fewer fishermen on the lake.

Are there any "sleeper" sunfish lakes that are producing lunkers?

Anderson: The lakes that I've fished in the last five to six years have not been "sleepers". They may have been ripe because I usually fish a new lake because I've heard reports that there are good sunfish in the lake. And working with Outdoor Outlines, I usually hear when a lake is hot so I take advantage of that information.

What is your favorite lake for sunnies?

Anderson: Elk Lake in Sherburne County. But, I suppose, that's mainly because of the way I'm set up there with my camper trailer being there year 'round. Actually, you couldn't even begin to name the good sunfish lakes in Minnesota. If you are not sure of what lake to fish, go to a local tackle shop and they should be willing and able to help you.

In fact, the sunfish on Elk Lake are only of average size. But when I feel like fishing for a lunker, there are literally hundreds of lakes in Minnesota that produce sunfish up to two pounds.

Is "catch and release" an important concept for the future of sunfish fishing?

Anderson: It's important even with sunfish. If you add to the balance of nature, and only keep what you are going to eat, it will make for better fishing for every fisherman and even future fishermen. Keep it sporting, catch and keep what you are going to eat today; don't freeze them for eating next spring. Go out next spring and catch some fresh ones.

Earlier you mentioned that you always use a clear bobber. Why?

Anderson: I've used colored bobbers when I've broken my clear bobbers, and I didn't catch half as many sunfish after switching.

Really! Half as many?

Anderson: Yes.

What are your favorite conditions to fish for sunfish?

Anderson: I like the water to be as smooth as glass. No wind or very little. Then I go out and work around the lily pads. The sunfish will move up under the lily pads, and they will suck little bugs and snails off of the bottom of those pads. Many times you can actually see the lily pads moving when the sunfish are underneath them feeding. Also, you can hear the pads snap just like the snap of your fingers when the sunfish suck bugs off of them. An overcast sky helps, too.

How deep do you fish when you are fishing lily pads?

Anderson: About two to three inches below the lily pad.

Comment on acid rain.

Anderson: Unless they get off of dead center and do something about it, in fifteen to twenty years there will be no fishing in Minnesota since all the fish will be dead. The northern part of Minnesota has already been adversely effected by acid rain. And, contrary to current opinion, the lakes in central and southern Minnesota are also going to be hurt by it.

What lake has the best chances of producing the next state record sunfish?

Anderson: It will probably come out of Lake Minnewaska in Polk County. And I hope I'm the one who catches it.

Why Lake Minnewaska?

Anderson: I know a couple of fishermen that fish Lake Minnewaska, and they frequently come in with sunfish that average two-plus-pounds. A lake that consistently produces two-plus-pound sunfish has a very good chance of holding a state record. And it's the only lake in Minnesota that I know of that consistently produces big, big sunfish.

Any guess as to what lure or bait will take that next state record sunfish?

Anderson: No. But it will probably be a larger lure or bait than most sunfish fishermen usually use.

What would you recommend for beginner fishermen?

Anderson: Guides, seminars, and fishing clinics. Ron Schara puts on a beautiful clinic in Minneapolis during the Aquatennial which I help with because I like working with kids. Also, there's Camp Fish for kids which I recommend. It's a one week course—hands on type training.

How much of fishing has to do with luck?

Anderson: I suppose forty percent of it is luck on a given day, but in the long run it's mostly knowledge.

Would you fish differently if you were trying to catch a lunker sunfish?

Anderson: The name of the game when you are fishing for a lunker, is to fish the lakes that produce lunkers and be there when they are hitting.

If I'm going out to fish for a lunker sunnie, I spend maybe a week checking around with resort owners, tackle shops, and friends to find out where the big ones are hitting. Of course, you have to talk to people you trust and people that know what they are talking about.

If I know that one pounders are coming out of Lake Pelican and Lake Waconia is only producing half pounders, well, where would you fish? It's like anything else; you have to do your homework.

Also when you are fishing for large sunfish, you should use larger lures and larger baits. Generally, the large fish do not hit the real small lures.

What is the best time of the year to fish for large quantities of sunfish?

Anderson: Spring and fall.

Why?

Anderson: They are easier to locate because they will spend more time in shallow water. In the summertime sunfish spend more time in deeper water, and, consequently, they are harder to find.

What's special about Minnesota fishing?

Anderson: There are so many lakes in this state that are so well managed by the D.N.R. that fishing here is great. And almost all of the lakes in the state are multi-species lakes. You can fish for anything from northerns to bullheads in most of them. You can't say that for too many other places.

Chapter 9

DAN D. GAPEN, SR.
ON RIVER FISHING

Dan Gapen, to paraphrase a lyric from a Dennis Olson song, "is spread out all over this land like a handful of sand." A fisherman and a hunter here, a philosopher and conservationist there, and so on. He is made of the stuff that Woody Guthrie wrote songs about—the beauty of this land, man's need to enjoy it, and his responsibility to care for it.

Moreover, Dan is a fisherman, a hunter, an author, a columnist, a conservationist, an inventor and manufacturer of fishing tackle, a photographer, a radio talk show host, an editor at large for Fishing Facts magazine, and a member of the International Fishing Hall of Fame.

In 1974 Dan receives the prestigious Robert G. Green award as Minnesota's Conservationist of the Year. Then two years later he received the National Modar Conservationist Award and a special presentation from the Minnesota Department of Natural Resources. This presentation and these awards were given to Dan in recognition of his efforts to preserve running water and especially for his attempt to have the Upper Mississippi River placed under the protection of the National Wild and Scenic River Bill.

And like rivers, men have beginnings. For Dan it was on the shores of Lake Superior at Duluth, Minnesota. When he was six years old, the Gapen family moved to Nipigon, Ontario in Canada at "the road's end" as Dan put it. At that time, the road went no farther north. On the shores of the

Nipigon River the Gapen family ran a resort which catered to hunters and fishermen.

Dan's childhood was as much like a Tom Sawyer adventure as it was like a story about a young man having to grow up with many adult responsibilities. At the age of six he began tying flies in his father's fly shop, and by the time he was eight he was tying flies and selling them commercially. He had learned his craft well from his father, Don Gapen, who was the inventor of the Muddler Fly which soon gained worldwide popularity among fly-fishermen and is still used and imitated today.

As so many great fishermen have, Dan began guiding at an early age. When he was fourteen years old, he was guiding fishermen for brook trout, giant northern pike, walleyes, and lake trout. Then shortly after his fifteenth birthday, he began guiding hunters for big game—primarily moose, bear, and caribou. His hunting and fishing apprenticeship was under the watchful eyes of his father and the Indian guides that were employed by his family at their resort.

For the past twelve years Dan has made his home on forty acres in Sherburne County in Minnesota. Dan has restored this farm land acreage into a wildlife sanctuary where he raises Canadian honkers and wood ducks. In fact, one year he raised over three hundred wood ducks and released them to fly.

Currently, Dan holds records for several sizes of fish which include three of the top fifty northern pike ever caught and recorded in North America. And for a time he held the world's record for the spotted redtail gar and the short nose redhorse which were caught on the Mississippi River in Minnesota.

In the foreword of his latest book, "Fishing Rivers of the Far North", Dan recalls life on the Nipigon River. He tells of forest fires, howling wolves, the laughter of the Indian guides, a pet moose named Abdul, the lyrics of the loons, and other recollections of that period of his life which actually are poetic reflections of how Dan's values and attitudes were formed as a youngster.

"I wrote it for myself," Dan said of the new book, "I wanted to tell about the north country. The need for preservation since there is an encroachment by man that should be looked at very carefully, particularly in the Arctic. I wrote it for me, and I didn't care if I ever sold a copy. I just had to tell this story."

Well, with the reviews this Jack London style narrative has received, it no doubt will become an outdoor standard. The book has already inspired one television news department to do a week long series on the north country. From this book came an assignment from the Book of the Month Club where Dan is to author yet another book that will be about old-timers and Indian legends of the far north which are subjects that he loves to write about.

In closing, Dan Gapen is an intelligent and articulate outdoorsman whose background is rich in experiences. His influence has been irreversibly felt by this would-be author, leaving me somewhat regretful that most of this chapter is devoted to the catching of fish in rivers rather than the preserving of the rivers and waterways that Dan loves so much. May his lonely cry for preservation be joined by others.

Below is a list of books written by Dan D. Gapen, Sr. that are available by sending orders to: Dan D. Gapen, Sr., Route No. 1, Big Lake, Minnesota 55309.

Fishing Rivers of the Far North	300 page hardback	$18.95
Carp the Whiskered Walleye	125 page softback	6.95
River Fishing	300 page hardback	15.95
Big River Fishing	425 page hardback	18.95
Creeks to Love and Remember	230 page hardback	12.95
Why Fish Carp	125 page softback	6.95
Crappie	125 page softback	6.95
White Bass and Cousin Striper	90 page softback	4.95

Add $1.00 to cover postage and handling for each book.

RIVER FISH BEHAVIOR

I know smallmouth bass are your favorite fish, but what other species of river fish do you like to fish for?

Gapen: I love to fish for cats, too. Although they're not a favorite with most Minnesota anglers, there are only so many walleyes, and only so many northerns, and only so many largemouth I care to fish. I can't stand to make the number of casts it takes to catch a muskie because I grew up in an area where big northerns were so available. I just can't see myself casting three thousand times to get a swirl, so I'm not much of a muskie fisherman.

I love to fish the strange species, too. Contrary to what most people think, catfish are not that easy to catch, and they don't all like rotten bait.

Flathead catfish, for example, love live suckers, and you can even catch them on crank baits. Channel cats prefer fresh-frozen liver as opposed to rotten liver. They like fresh-frozen smelt or night crawlers; whereas, many people think you need rotten chicken guts, or worse, to catch them. In fact, the only catfish that really likes rotten bait is the blue cat which is most commonly found in the South.

How many different kinds of catfish are there?

Gapen: There are three basic species found in this country: flatheads, blues, and channel cats. The channel is the one that is very much like the walleye—he's found on gravel, sand, and in fast water slicks. You fish for them just like you would fish for a walleye.

Do river fish chase schools of forage fish the way predator fish do in lakes?

Gapen: In the spring large fish will run minnows into eddies, but it isn't as large a factor as it is on lakes.

Comment on the migration patterns of river fish.

Gapen: River fish migrate. Even river muskies. They'll migrate to spawn and so will smallmouth bass. But the smallmouth bass migrates as little as any fish will—they'll migrate a block or two off of a channel into a side channel.

Researchers in Tennessee have done a lot of research on the walleye, and the fishermen there call the walleye a jack salmon because they migrate like a salmon.

One of the greatest misconceptions in walleye fishing on the Lower Mississippi River here in Minnesota is the notion fishermen have that, for instance, only the walleyes in the area of Lake Pepin spawn at Red Wing. In fact, there may be fish spawning at Red Wing that came from Iowa.

In Tennessee they proved this by tagging walleyes, and they found that walleyes have run as far as two hundred and fifty miles to spawn. The researchers had to follow them through lock and dam systems. Also, they found that a river walleye goes back to spawn where he was born just like a salmon does.

Given that information why do you find so many of them behind dams?

Gapen: At one time they were blocked from movement up river for some reason or another. The water may have been too high or too low, but whatever the reason, they couldn't get through the lock system, and the females dropped their eggs behind the dams; therefore, the highest concentration of spawners on these rivers are behind dams because they were stopped there at one time, maybe generations ago.

Some of the Lake Pepin walleyes are found up at Hastings and all the way up the Saint Croix below Taylors Falls. If possible, walleyes will run like salmon back to where they were hatched.

In one study on the Wolf River in Wisconsin a nine pound female, which was one of several tagged, moved ninety-seven miles in a forty-eight hour period. I should point out that this female was held up from spawning and then released. Also, this spawning migration that she made was upstream, but the Wolf River is a slow moving river.

How fast do rivers flow; the Mississippi, for example?

Gapen: The Upper Mississippi flows about four miles an hour on the average, and the Lower Mississippi flows about half that speed.

Back to migration. How does this walleye migration information effect the fisherman?

Gapen: Let me comment on some other misconceptions about the walleye's spawning habits. Most fishermen aren't going to believe this, but walleyes begin their spawning runs in the fall of the year. The small males and larger females begin to move in on the Red Wing Dam, for instance, in November and December, but they don't spawn until April. During this time males eagerly await sex, striking any type of lure presented while the females lay off in deep channels about three or four miles downriver. In fact, river walleyes and suckers spend about six months of the year migrating.

Northern pike migrate very little. They go up creeks in the spring to spawn. And most muskies will migrate three to four miles to spawn. In Kentucky they've found that a muskie will migrate as much as fifteen miles to spawn. Some fishermen find that hard to believe, but it's true.

If a fisherman can adapt his fishing to the migration patterns of fish, he'll do a lot better with his stringer take. For instance, there is a return migration of fish on a river that occurs along the Lower Mississippi River at a speed of about one mile a day within the complex of a reservoir. In other words, if a big female spawns April 10th at Red Wing, Minnesota, twenty-one days later she will be at Wabasha which is twenty-one miles downriver. I had one knowledgeable old-timer really prove that to me.

He said, "Come down here May the 3rd and I'll put you on some big walleyes." Well, on May 3rd I arrived and he said, "These fish that we are going to catch tonight spawned at Red Wing twenty-one days ago." His theory was they were hungry, tired, and would stop on their way downriver to eat and then we'd catch them. Well, we went out and on three consecutive casts I caught three walleyes. One was ten pounds four ounces, another was nine pounds nine ounces, and the last was eight pounds even. These fish were spawned out females. I would guess that the ten pound four ouncer would have weighed fourteen or so pounds prior to spawning.

We were fishing under the Wabasha bridge. My friend said these walleyes come in here every year at this time and feeding lasts for four to five days. Later, he finds the same fish farther down river.

I can't argue with his theory; these fish were probably returning to the lower river system. Certainly some of the migrating fish will drop off prior to reaching my friend's feeding station, but the vast majority of them continue on down river after feeding. Were you to fish these spots at any other time of the year, you would probably not catch anything.

To what extent does fish behavior vary from river to river?

Gapen: Feeding will vary a lot from a clear river to a stained river. But fish will hold basically in the same areas—on the same type of structure, that is. So locating fish isn't much different from a clear river to a stained river, but your presentation should change.

Any time you are fishing a river in Minnesota and it has muddy or dirty water, the best time to fish is noon, high noon. This is particularly true on the Upper Mississippi, the Kettle River, the Cloquet River, and the Lower Mississippi.

A rule of thumb is: The best fishing is from eleven o'clock in the morning to one o'clock in the afternoon if the river you are fishing has dirty or muddy water.

When you are fishing a river that has clear water (this is running water that I'm referring to), the best time of the day to fish is early morning or late evening.

When lake fishermen come off of the lake at ten o'clock in the morning, that's when river fishermen should be going on the river to fish. And it's damn hard to catch a game fish before eight o'clock in the morning on the Upper Mississippi River. I don't care what time of the year it is.

Then there's another feeding surge about seven o'clock in the evening, but once it gets dark on these shallow rivers in Minnesota "forget it", get off the river. Of course, this isn't true of the Lower Mississippi River. Two o'clock to five o'clock in the afternoon is also a dead period on most rivers.

How hard is it for fish to hold a position in running water?

Gapen: Northerns will always pick the slow easy river bars. The slow stagnant water—the back eddy just at the edge where a point comes out and there is dead water with the current shooting past them. They don't like to work, they hold like an old alligator.

Walleyes and smallmouth bass can spend their entire lives not fighting the current. Remember they are designed in such a way that the current wraps around them. Go back to my boulder theory: An eight inch diameter boulder will hold an eight pound walleye. All he has to do is nose in on it with his chin along the bottom right next to the rock leaving his body and tail up off bottom. Current comes up around the rock and creates a vacuum behind it. Thus, the fish isn't working at all to stay in that current. He could stay there forever. And smallmouth bass do the same thing.

Are big fish lazy?

Gapen: There aren't very many of them; maybe that's why we don't catch them. That's number one. And big fish in rivers tend to feed a lot at one time where little fish feed almost constantly. That's why you will find little fish in the upper pools; they're in there feeding on insects and little crayfish, etc. Big fish in rivers will feed from eleven o'clock to one o'clock during the daytime and then they quit feeding. But this doesn't mean that you can't catch a big fish at other times of the day. It only means this would be the easiest time of the day.

Even when big fish in a river aren't actively feeding, you can entice them into striking. I've done it many times. Run a lure or live bait by him several times and he may pass it up, but put a night crawler, for example, right in front of his nose and pretty soon he will suck it in.

Are fish able to remember? Lures, for example?

Gapen: I don't know. I've often thought maybe smallmouth bass could, but I don't think northerns do. Possibly it's because northerns are so predacious; they strike at something without examining it first. But I really don't know, and you can say I don't know.

Is a fish's ability to smell and taste a factor in river fishing?

Gapen: It's important. A fish smells through his nose system, his lateral line, and his air bladder, too. Smell and taste are almost the same thing to fish, I believe.

But smell and taste are not as important when fishing for northerns and muskies as they are when you are fishing for smallmouth bass and walleyes, for example, since the northern and muskie are more strikers than they are biters.

In rivers smell might not be as important a factor in taking fish as it is when fishing lakes, since river species have to react faster to food possibilities. However, when a river fish hits your lure, there may be a lapse in time before you will feel the strike. It could be as long as four seconds. Therefore, if you have tipped your lure with live bait, it will give you more time to react to the strike since the fish will hold on longer.

Actually, in river fishing you don't usually get the strike you would from a fish in a lake. Many times all you will feel is weight on your line.

Do you find any differences in the walleyes' and the saugers' behavior?

Gapen: You have to fish for saugers a little deeper and a little farther out from structure than you would a walleye. As the season progresses, saugers always seem to be a little bit ahead of the walleye in their retreat away from heat and away from low water.

LOCATING RIVER FISH

Are weeds as significant in locating river fish as they are in locating fish in lakes?

Gapen: In shallow rivers, weeds are not an important locational factor, but they are in bigger, deeper rivers. Sometimes you will find northern pike holding to weeds, and in the spring you will find crappies holding in weeds. But hardpan structure is much more important than weeds are in locating game fish in rivers.

Comment on important holding areas for fish in rivers.

Gapen: Rocks are major holding areas in rivers. Gravel bars with a lot of rocky points are also good structure. But current breaks are the key structure in a river.

A current break is that shift of water which comes off a point, a fallen tree in the water, a log in the water, etc. where the main river current comes around the obstruction and creates a slice that you can see. Downstream behind these trees, logs, or rock points you have an eddying water effect. Right where the main river current and the eddy flow meet you have a current break. A current break can last from ten feet to two hundred feet downriver.

Fish will hold on a current break because there is food coming downriver from upstream. Simply put: Fish have the ability to hold close to a food market. They will hold along the inside of a current break where the eddy's slower currents revolve.

Many fishermen will fish a current break from the outside in and cast over the fast flowing water into the eddy, but that's the wrong way. You should go into the eddy and cast out to the current break so your lure and your line are not swept away by the current.

Fish upstream along the inside by casting upstream and retrieving downstream on the inside and your lure won't be swept away by that force on the outer current. Also, there is a lot of rock structure on a current break because pools of slow running water do not force loose gravel downstream like the outer current does. Thus, you've got a natural holding area for fish. There is also light diffusion on a current break. If it's a bright day, sunlight will be diffused just by the variance in those two currents—the outer current and the inner current.

At times, the two currents making up a current break will actually create a funnel; that is, an inverted cone effect with the small of the cone at the top of the current break and the wide open end on the bottom. This, in effect, will create almost stationary water along the eddy and mainstream current which fish hold in.

If somebody asks me where they should fish in a certain river, I would tell them about current breaks because you find current breaks off every kind of river structure there is. Current breaks are the key to catching river fish. They will hold all species of fish, too. Of course, in the fall, when the frog migration is on, fish are seen holding on the edges of the banks (the inner pools) feeding on frogs. But day in and day out, current breaks are the key to catching river fish.

Does the size of the current break have any significance?

Gapen: The size of the current break won't change the species of fish which will hold there. But the deeper the water, the larger the fish using that current break; that is, unless the stream has no deep water. Even in areas where there are beaver dams and stumps the current breaks will hold fish. Northerns will be on the structure and walleyes will be just off of it.

Can crayfish be a locational clue for locating fish in a river?

Gapen: Yes. Crayfish are a large part of the walleyes' and smallmouths' diet. Crayfish hide under rocks, they spawn under rocks, and they are part of the whole rock system, so if you find crayfish, the game fish will be nearby.

What are some of the better catfish rivers in Minnesota?

Gapen: This might shock you a little bit, but we have channel cats all the way up on the Cloquet and Saint Louis Rivers. Also, we have one of the finest catfish areas in the five state area on the Mississippi River between the Coon Rapids dam and Fort Snelling. That area is just loaded with cats. Actually, most of the channel cats caught in that area are accidentally caught by walleye fishermen. And channel cats will occasionally strike an artificial lure.

A few years back we made a movie about fishing for channel cats in this area (Coon Rapids dam to Fort Snelling), and in two and a half days and one night of fishing we caught over five hundred of them. Of course, this was "catch and release".

What type of bait did you use?

Gapen: Chicken liver and smelt.

Comment on where each type of catfish is found in Minnesota.

Gapen: We've got channels, flatheads, and blues. For the most part, the flatheads are found south of the Metro area in the southern part of Minnesota, the bottom third of the state. Channel cats are found on the Mississippi River and its tributaries which include the Saint Croix and its tributaries, such as, the Kettle and the Snake Rivers.

In Minnesota most of the blue cats are found in the Lower Mississippi River south of Minneapolis and Saint Paul. There are a few lakes in the Willmar area where blues have been stocked. However, the majority of catfish in Minnesota are channel catfish.

Comment on the basic location of panfish, northerns, etc. in rivers.

Gapen: Panfish are mainly a backwater fish. A pool area fish. You will find them in slow moving pools along the shoreline where the current cut begins up at the top of the pool. Bluegills can be found in stump structure.

Northerns, for the most part, will stage in two areas of a river. In fast water they will stage at the pool head right in that stagnant area where the eddy comes around from behind and joins with the main stream current. Then you can also find them at the downstream end of the pool where the water begins to carry on downstream—the slick surface area at the downstream end of the pool.

Walleyes can be found in the same slicking area of the pool where you find northerns. Northerns will be in close to the bank. The walleyes will be out on the far side of the eddy out along the edge of the current cut at the very lowest point in the pool. Generally, the bottom of the pool starts to come up at this point (the downstream side of the pool) from having been cupped out. But walleyes will be off shore along the edge of the current cut. It's the area right at the bottom of the pool. Actually, most people run over them; they never touch the walleyes in a pool.

As for largemouth bass, you will find them in stagnant areas, the back waters where there's heavy weed concentrations at the lower ends of islands, etc. Also you can find them on the inner circle of a slow revolving pool where there may be weeds. But in fast rivers, there usually are not too many largemouth bass.

Smallmouth bass are commonly found in amongst rocks and most fast water rivers have a tremendous amount of rocks. Look for the small smallmouth at the top side of the pools and bigger smallmouth will be out on the current cut about half way down the pool. And look for both of them above and below rock structure. Areas in and above rapids will hold big smallmouth.

With sturgeon, you will often see them breaking water below a rapids or in the rapids, but the best place to catch them is in very deep channels with slow moving water. Look for a silty bottom also. Although you will see sturgeon in shallow water during migration, when they feed, they will feed in deeper, slower water—a six to eight foot minimum.

I read in one of your books that if river fish are scared off a piece of structure or cover, they will return very soon.

Gapen: That's right. Unlike lake fish, if you scare river fish off a piece of cover, they will go with the current and within five minutes circle back to the cover that you scared them from.

PRESENTATION FOR RIVER FISH

How important is presentation?

Gapen: Presentation makes a fish strike a lure so that makes it important. And you can frequently get an inactive fish to strike with good presentation.

Take, for example, a walleye in six to seven feet of water and say he's holding behind an eight inch boulder. (Remember an eight inch boulder is large enough for an eight pound walleye to hold behind since all he has to do is nose in around it, and the boulder will create a current break with the water busting up around the fish.) As the food comes down the river with the current, all the walleye has to do is lift his head and go slightly sideways to catch food as it comes by him. Now walleyes tend not to leave their holding structure when they are feeding. In other words, they wouldn't go up even two feet if they are holding in six feet of water.

So if you are using a crank bait that runs four feet deep and you buzz that crank bait over him or you fish a jig crosscurrent or downcurrent, you aren't getting your lure down deep enough. Most people don't correctly judge the depth that their lure is running in this situation so they run their lure over the top of most of the walleyes, and the walleyes aren't going to come up to meet the bait. They stay down there and wait for the bait to come to them which brings us back to the theory of bringing the lure down along the bottom with the current or rather at an angle with the current. As a matter of fact, in this situation the lure is usually going too fast for the fish to strike it.

Of course, if a walleye, or other species of fish, is unusually hungry or it is spawning time, he will chase a lure. But when fish are in a neutral mood, you've got to put the lure or bait right in front of them.

Something else we should mention for your readers is that whenever they see a boil in a river, they should know that there is hardpan below. It is common knowledge among us who fish rivers that when you've got a disturbance on the surface, you've got hardpan below. And any hardpan (rocks, gravel, etc.) holds fish.

But often when people fish hardpan, they miss fish by three or four feet with a dozen casts. Then suddenly they hook the fish and can't figure out why. Well, that cast was the only cast of the dozen casts that was near the fish. More than likely they weren't getting their lure deep enough. Also, slack in your line as you are retrieving crosscurrent can cause the lure to swing out away from your target.

This seems like a good time to discuss lure size and comment on whether lure size should change from season to season.

Gapen: In rivers, lure size won't vary with seasonal changes. But your choice of lures should vary.

In the spring, for instance, a silver Rapala will do a good number for you because the fish are feeding mostly on minnows. And live bait behind a Bait Walker in the spring is also a good choice. That will work as well as anything. In general, something flashy in the spring works well.

How about jigs in the spring?

Gapen: Jigs can be very good in the spring and you can use a spinner on them, too. But once fish start feeding on crayfish, stop using the spinner. Use a jig without the spinner.

In July and August you will definitely scare off more fish with a spinner than you can believe. Then in the fall go back to using spinners on your jigs or use plugs or spoons.

And in the fall, fish are gorging themselves getting ready for hibernation, so to speak. In fact, smallmouth bass don't feed much in the winter at all; consequently, they have a need to gorge themselves in the fall. Therefore, September and October can be the best time to catch a big smallmouth.

What are your favorite lures for river fishing?

Gapen: I've got to go to one that I've invented—The Ugly Bug. I know that sounds crazy, but I made it for a purpose. It's got a wide head which allows it to fulcrum in and out of rocks easily. The point of pull is back behind the point of fulcrum. The eye of the lure is back beyond the wide point of the head. With this design you will lose seventy percent less jigs.

Also, I made it to represent hellgrammites, but it represents crayfish as well. With river walleyes you've got to get on the bottom and this lure does that well.

My favorite color in an Ugly Bug is brown. The reason for that is river fish feed on crayfish. In the spring, there's a rule of thumb, you should use minnows and as the crayfish shed their shells in mid-June or so, you begin using something that represents crayfish. Night crawlers also become a large factor in our rivers in June.

Why?

Gapen: I once had a biologist tell me that night crawlers and crayfish taste alike. Well, I've tasted crayfish tails, but I'll be damned if I'm going to eat night crawlers to prove his theory. But it must be true because minnows aren't nearly as important a bait after mid-June when the crayfish shed their shells. They shed their winter shell—that black shell—and become soft shell (brownish-orange in color) and then they scent better. Crayfish are the most important bait until early September. In rivers crayfish are as much as seventy percent of the smallmouths' diet and fifty percent of the walleyes' diet. Many fishermen talk about leeches, crawlers, and minnows and not very many Minnesota anglers use crayfish and they should!

In Indiana, for example, you can't go in a bait shop without finding hard and soft shell crayfish. They keep them cool (at thirty-four degrees) so they remain dormant. They have hard and soft shell crayfish available all year 'round. I prefer soft shell crayfish, but some fishermen do like the hard shell for fishing.

Rule of Thumb: In the spring use minnows, in the summer use crayfish or crawlers or something that represents those baits, and in the fall go back to minnows or minnow imitations.

This is where the Ugly Bug comes in. I tip an Ugly Bug with a little piece of crawler. Rather than using a whole crawler, I cut them in about five pieces. Put the hook through one time. It's there only for scenting.

Fish your lure from upstream to downstream since natural bait flows downstream with the current. I don't care what it is; it flows downstream. Have you ever seen a fish with his head facing downstream and his tail pointed upstream. Of course not! Fish always face into the current; they have to. So you have to assume that a fish would see a lure coming downstream before he would see a lure being retrieved upstream. Therefore, you will have a much, much better chance of visually attracting that fish.

Is there anything that you would like to add regarding the use of live bait?

Gapen: In rigging crayfish the best river size is about two inches, and I always declaw crayfish so they aren't grabbing something and hanging up when I'm trying to fish with them. Just pick the claws off and all they can do is walk. If a crayfish is over three inches long, there's nothing wrong with just using the tail for bait.

When hooking a crayfish, hook them underneath by the back of the tail. Run the hook up underneath the back of the tail and out the top; that way the crayfish or crayfish tail will be presented properly.

My second choice would either be a twister or a beetle type jig with an undersized spinner on it.

For example?

Gapen: An eighth ounce jig with a crappie size L spinner. I like small spinners.

Your third choice?

Gapen: A live bait rigged with a Bait Walker or something on that order. Preferably a crayfish or maybe a night crawler.

My fourth choice would be a french type spinner in a small size, say a number one or two Mepps type with a silver blade and a little piece of pork rind hooked on one of the treble hooks.

And fifth, I'd choose a crank bait in a crayfish color and not a deep diver.

Why?

Gapen: The deep divers will come to the surface erratically in a river because of the current. The short lip crank baits will work much better.

How effective are topwater lures in river fishing?

Gapen: I love to use topwater lures. Late in the summer and early in the fall during the frog migration, I use a popper and a fly rod for smallmouth. Also, a Heddon Baby Chugger on a spinning rod is a good combination. They're just one heck of a lot of fun to catch on topwater.

What are the best colors for topwater lures?

Gapen: Either yellow and green or, actually, any dark color because they will give you a better silhouette.

In one of your books you talk about rolling your lure. What does that mean?

Gapen: You have to work a lure less in a river than you do in a lake. The term jigging conjures up images of a fisherman jerking on a lure. To work a jig in a river you simply roll it.

Everybody over-fishes jigs in a river and most other baits, too. When you are working rocky areas, you control your lure's depth by the height of your rod tip. That is, by lifting it and by lowering it. I keep my rod tip in front of me, and I keep it high. If I need to get deep, as my lure is getting closer to the boat or coming down the slick (when I stop feeling the bottom), I will lower the rod tip vertically.

You lift and roll your jig. The current does almost all of the work for you. Rolling is kind of a natural action; it just happens. To roll your jig through an eddy—let's say you're casting up into an eddy on the edge of a current break—let your jig sink while you are lowering your rod tip and when you know it's hitting bottom, you reel as you lift and physically roll your rod tip. As you come back with your rod tip toward the water, take up your line as you're coming downstream or crossstream. What you are doing is rolling that jig right up off of the bottom.

Rolling is a much more effective way of fishing jigs than trying to jig it, per se. And it's much, much less tiring.

Are long casts necessary in river fishing?

Gapen: Most of your casts in a river are going to be short if you are going to be productive. You don't need to cast over thirty feet in a river unless you are fishing a big river.

Elaborate on your statement, "When fishing a river, you are always looking for walleyes."

Gapen: Where smallmouth bass are abundant (the Upper Mississippi, the Cloquet, and the Kettle Rivers, etc.), obviously, you can catch smallmouth bass, but why not present your lure in a two-fold manner so you can catch walleyes, too.

Smallmouth bass will hit a lure on the top, in the middle, and on the bottom; whereas, walleyes will usually only strike a lure when it is presented deep enough. So, even though, you are fishing for smallies if you always present your lure in a manner that gets it to the bottom (where the walleyes are), you will catch both smallies and walleyes. And the deeper you work your lure, the better your chances are of catching big fish. So, if you are always looking for walleyes, you will catch the smallies that you are after and quite likely pop a walleye or two in the process.

WEATHER AND BIOLOGICAL FACTORS AFFECTING RIVER FISH

Does water temperature affect river fish the way it does lake fish?

Gapen: Very little. River fish adapt much quicker to a change in water temperature than lake fish. And I never use a temperature gauge except for checking for the temperature that will trigger a given species of fish to spawn.

What affect does rising or falling water have on river fish?

Gapen: It's a big factor in all sizes of rivers. They both trigger feeding, but on different structure.

Both rising and falling water can be good fishing conditions; however, many fishermen don't know where to fish during a rising water condition. Where the hell do I fish is the question?

You go to the back end of the island or the back side of a point where you find flooded grass. Flooded grass makes insects available to minnows; minnows move into those areas to feed. And when you find minnows in an area, the game fish are not far away. It may only be two feet of water, but the game fish will be in there foraging on the minnows.

When rising water has attained its highest level and then stays at that level for a few days, fishing will become very poor.

Why?

Gapen: After a few days of high water, fish return to where they held before the high water, but the angler doesn't know where that is since the area is so inundated with water.

When fishing during a high water situation, many people cast the banks and complain because they aren't catching any fish. Well, in many instances, after that surge of feeding for a few days, fish have returned to their original location; therefore, you have to know where that original location is to catch them. Even if you know a river pretty well, there's still a good chance you won't find it.

How about low water conditions?

Gapen: Think about it! Common sense! You've got as many fish as before and much less water to fish. That makes fish much more vulnerable to fishermen.

How does sunlight affect fish in a river?

Gapen: They will avoid being in direct sunlight, especially in clear water. In a dark stream or a dark water river the affect will be much, much less. And fish in a river are usually very close to shade.

Also, running water will diffuse sunlight so if a fish is in three feet of water, the sunlight is totally diffused. Sunlight is reflected off of running water. Even heavy wave action on a lake doesn't diffuse sunlight like running water does.

How about the opposite, fishing during cloudy weather?

Gapen: It makes fishing somewhat easier, but it is not a big factor in river fishing.

How does rain affect river fish?

Gapen: When it rains, I don't fish. But I don't think it has a great bearing one way or the other on a river or a stream.

Once in awhile I don't catch a lot of fish, well, that's part of the game. I like to fish when it's warm and comfortable. I have fished during cold weather, but that was because I had to write an article for a magazine.

How about the old cold front conditions that plague lake fishermen?

Gapen: Cold fronts don't affect river fish as much as lake fish. Where lake fishing is shut down for three days or so, a river only shuts down for a half a day. A day at the very most. Often the little cold fronts that affect lake fishing, don't affect river fishing at all.

Is the oxygen content in rivers ever very low?

Gapen: Rivers are always moving so the oxygen content is always pretty good. And rivers don't thermocline like many lakes do.

There's a lot of talk lately about pH levels in water. What are your thoughts about how that concept affects river fish?

Gapen: I don't know anything about it. It's too scientific for me. There comes a time when you lose the "sport" in sport fishing with too many scientific variables. Besides, I don't think the hardcore scientific fishermen catch any more fish than I do anyway, and I probably enjoy the sport more than they do.

EQUIPMENT AND TACKLE
FOR RIVER FISHING

What kind of boat and motor do you prefer for river fishing?

Gapen: I use a fourteen foot Alumacraft (1457) jon boat which I like very much. But I am going to switch to the fifteen footer for the extra room. It runs very, very shallow and that's necessary for river travel. Also, jon boats are very stable, and they control much better than a keeled craft does in running water. I don't know why, but they do.

I don't use a big motor. In fact, a ten horse is as big as you need on a river. Motors with short shafts and a slip clutch with a neoprene prop are preferred. The neoprene props wear down evenly, and they work very, very well.

How do you rig your boats for the river?

Gapen: When you rig a jon boat for the river, do a couple of things. First, have an anchor on both the front and the back. Second, have a rod rack for your extra rods, and some pieces of rope about two feet long with a snap on the end which you can throw over a limb and snap it back to itself. These will work as a tie-off. Then a live well is a must.

Do you use an electric trolling motor?

Gapen: Generally, they don't have enough power.

Do you use snaps or swivels to attach your lures?

Gapen: No. I tie directly to the line because it's more sensitive. With snaps there's play between the lure and the line.

Comment on line.

Gapen: One key to river fishing is using eight pound test line since you will lose fifty percent less lures than you will with six pound test line. Ten pound test line is too heavy. Four pound test line is not necessary because the current will diffuse the visibility of the line anyway. Although I wouldn't use yellow or orange line, I really don't have a preference for a particular color or brand.

What kind of rods and reels do you use?

Gapen: Just make sure they are light since your casts are shorter and you'll make five times as many as you will on a lake.

I use a five to a five and a half foot graphite spinning rod with an ultralight reel with eight pound test line. I prefer a stiff action rod because you've got to be able to set the hook. I really don't have a favorite brand, but that size rod will handle any fish you catch in the river.

You've been a lure manufacturer so, perhaps, you have a theory as to why some days any lure will take fish and other days only one lure will work.

Gapen: I believe it's triggered by natural baits and how eager fish may be to feed. When fish are really hungry, they will hit almost any lure. But when they are finicky, maybe they'll only take the cherry pie. Fish are kinda like people in that regard. Or possibly they're feeding particularly hard on a certain natural bait and your lure is imitating that bait.

MISCELLANEOUS INFORMATION ABOUT RIVER FISHING

How would you categorize the rivers in Minnesota?

Gapen: Basically, hard or soft. A soft river has a lot of sand and runs slow with many bog areas and water depths of four to eight feet. A hard river flows fast and has a rocky bottom with lots of timber on its shore and usually has dark colored water.

The hard river is the one you really want to fish since it produces more fish. Of course, a soft river may have more suckers and other related fish than a hard river does.

Name a few of each.

Gapen: The Upper Mississippi can be both hard and soft depending upon where you are. The region below Brainerd is soft, and the area between Saint Cloud and Elk River is hard. And the area between Royalton and Rice is a little of both—hard and soft. The Upper Cloquet is a hard river and the Saint Louis is a soft river. The Kettle River is also both (hard and soft) with rocky areas and very sandy areas.

Why do the hard rivers produce better fish?

Gapen: The hard rivers have better reproduction because they have a better food base—more crayfish and hellgrammites and more protection, but not necessarily better spawning areas. And if a hard river is very shallow, it may not be productive. Considering that both a hard and a soft river have equal water depth, the hard river will be better fishing for game fish.

Are there any others that we should mention?

Gapen: The Minnesota River is a soft river with the exception of a few places. But it's getting better; the pollution has been cleaned up a lot, and how there's some pretty good walleye production. The Cottonwood River which flows through New Ulm has some pretty good smallmouth bass. And the Rum River which flows into the Mississippi at Anoka is a good little river and has good smallmouth, too. The Snake and the Knife River are good, and the Snake has some big sturgeon in it, but basically it's a small walleye river. The Snake is a soft river where the Rum is both soft and hard. The Snake River that I'm referring to is the Snake River that flows into the Kettle River just below the Saint Croix. Then the Elk River, which I live on, is about half soft and half hard and is a good river to fish.

Many of these rivers are arteries for the Mississippi. The Elk has smallmouth, walleyes, and northerns. Many of Minnesota's smaller rivers like the Snake and Crow have a lot of small walleyes. Otter Tail River out of Fergus Falls is a very good little river and has lots of walleyes, smallmouth bass, and good northerns and even some largemouth bass in it. Otter Tail would be considered a soft river with some hard river areas. The Willow River in the Iron Range is a dark colored river with small walleyes and many small northerns.

Most of the North Shore rivers are trout rivers with the exception of the ones that flow into the Saint Louis River—the Saint Louis flows into Lake Superior at Duluth. The Saint Louis and Cloquet Rivers have good fishing and they have catfish in them too as do their connecting rivers which is a real surprise to most people. The Stony River on the White Iron Chain near Babbitt is a good river with smallmouth, walleyes, and northerns. Island River near Isabella has nice walleyes in it. The Little Fork and the Big Fork Rivers in the Grand Rapids area are also good. Both of them have good populations of walleyes and fairly good populations of northerns. Also they have largemouth bass. They're both a soft and a hard river.

Sometimes a soft river will have some areas with a little deeper water, and walleyes will hold in that portion of the river. If it were August and I were fishing the Stony River, for example, and I couldn't find fish, I'd look for the big walleyes in the deeper holes in the soft part of it where the water is deeper and the channels are longer. And, once again, I'd look for anything that creates a current cut that goes out into the channel.

What are your favorite Minnesota rivers?

Gapen: Without a question, it's the Upper Mississippi. I like the Cloquet and I love the Kettle, too. And I fish many of the North Shore streams for trout. The Saint Croix produces a lot of fish, too. But for big walleyes and big smallmouth bass I prefer the Upper Mississippi.

The Upper Mississippi is pretty long, to say the least. Do you have a favorite portion of it?

Gapen: I fish it from Brainerd down to the Elk River area. That's a stretch of about one hundred miles, and the nice thing about it is every ten miles or so there is an access. A ten mile stretch of river makes a nice one day float trip.

When you are fishing rivers, figure about one mile an hour to fish it comfortably and take time for shore lunch.

What type of boats do you use for your float trips?

Gapen: The key watercraft on the river is a jon boat. And in a jon boat, or any fishing boat, you should have a live well. Not a mechanical live well, a gravity fed live well. The center seats of all of our jon boats have live wells in them. The center seat has two holes in the bottom of the floor where the water comes up. As you increase the speed of the boat, it sucks the water out. If the boat is tilted, water is circulated so you have fresh water all the time. You just don't need a battery operated live well.

If the boat manufacturers would put live wells in every fishing boat, we would preserve our fisheries by at least ten percent. That's because we all cull fish: when we have our limit on a stringer and then catch a larger one than the smallest one on our stringer, we throw the smallest one back and keep the last one we caught. This is not legal, but we've all done it on occasion. Ninety-nine percent of the time that small fish will die after being on a stringer. He's dead! Live wells would allow you to sort fish without harming them too much. Put the three pounder in and let the smallest one go.

How did you develop the technique of "River Slippin"?

Gapen: It was from the Indians that I learned the technique of "River Slipping". It's a method by which you point the bow of your boat into the current, while the propellant is trying to force you forward but you are going backwards.

In the case of the Indians (when they were guiding), there would be one of them in the bow and one in the stern and a fisherman in the center. They would portage to the top of the rapids, put the canoe in the river and begin to paddle into the current while their customer would fish. They went backwards while paddling forward. It's a good method of boat control as for speed and how far you stay away from the shoreline. They didn't call it anything; all I did was to give it a term—"Slipping".

Nowadays we point our jon boats into the current with our motor in forward gear idled down to the point where you are backing down the river slowly, and it's the best method of boat control in running water there is, and I learned it from the Indian guides at my father's resort when I was a kid.

What are some of the differences in fishing rivers as opposed to lakes?

Gapen: Half of my fishing is done on lakes, but I'd much rather fish a river. In Minnesota when the lake fishing is slowing up, the river fishing is getting hot. That's a good thing to remember. And July and August are the hottest times to fish a river in Minnesota.

Comment on trophy fishing.

Gapen: It will vary for every species. In a river work the deeper cut areas. Deeper water for big fish. And you won't need to go to larger lures or bait as you would in lake fishing for lunker fish.

Two years ago on our "Old Man River Float Trips" in September we boated twenty-nine muskies and twenty-seven were caught on brown, one-eighth ounce Ugly Bugs tipped with a night crawler. They were caught while we were fishing for smallmouth bass. I took eleven that year on small Ugly Bugs using eight pound test line and the largest was twenty-seven and a half pounds. You just don't need large lures or large bait for trophy fishing in rivers.

Are rivers going to produce any of Minnesota's new state record fish?

Gapen: Yes. Many of the new state record fish will come from rivers. I had the world record spotted redtail gar for one year. It was fifteen pounds. A year later it was broken by a young fellow who caught one that was sixteen pounds even. I caught mine near Hastings on the Mississippi River and this new record was caught on the Mississippi near Wabasha.

And last year I caught the world record short nose redhorse which was six pounds. This year it was broken by a seven-plus-pound fish.

I'm a great believer in promoting fishing for rough species. In Europe the carp is the main sport fish. Pound for pound a carp will fight harder than anything else, and the carp has more protein than most sport fish. In England they have carp clubs like we have bass fishing clubs in this country.

I went a long way to answer your question, but to be specific, the Lower Mississippi River in Minnesota has the potential to produce some new state record fish.

Somebody told me that your favorite eating fish isn't the walleye. That's very un-Minnesotan-like you know.

Gapen: You can't eat trout and walleyes for more than two weeks without getting sick of them, but you can eat perch every day. Also, the tail sections of the northern pike are very good and you can eat them every day of the year without getting sick of them. I guess I have to admit that my favorite fish to eat is the perch.

Do you ice fish?

Gapen: No! I hate it with a passion.

Do you ever fish at night.

Gapen: I don't do it! I don't like it! And the few times that I've tried it on a river, it wasn't very good. The fish shut down after sundown on rivers.

What does fishing do for you?

Gapen: I fish to relax. To get away from people and the telephone. I can't stand to go to Lake Mille Lacs on opening weekend. If there's another boat on the lake, I want to leave.

I tell people I could catch half as many fish on a river and enjoy it twice as much as lake fishing simply because rivers have a mystical quality to them. It's what might be around the next corner, and even if you're not catching fish, you know there's another ripple, another pool, and so on.

Comment on "catch and release".

Gapen: "Catch and release" is a way of making us appreciate the sport. It's our pay back. Besides the best eating smallmouth and walleyes are the two pounders, so release the big ones.

What are your thoughts about acid rain?

Gapen: It's a sad part of our society. I think it's overdramatized, but, I think, it has to be overdramatized.

Actually, forest fires put as much acidity in the lakes as anything else does. But I really don't know that much about acid rain, and I don't think anybody really knows that much about it at this point in time. A long way down the line I hope that fishing doesn't suffer too much from it.

What types of people do you and don't you like to fish with?

Gapen: I'm always accused of fishing with good looking ladies. And that's because it's true. I'd rather fish with a lovely lady than an ugly old man any day of the week. But there's more to it than that.

I like to fish with gals and children simply because they don't care who I am. I don't have to prove anything to them. They aren't saying, "Ha, ha Gapen I've got one more fish than you."

I dislike fishing with people who make a competition out of it. I'm not out there to compete. I'm out there to enjoy the surroundings and the sport. I detest people who make it a big contest.

I've fished with my good friend Dave Conn for twenty years and we never compete. I'm just as thrilled when he catches the biggest fish of the trip, as he is for me when I catch the biggest fish.

I find that women and children don't have that crazy macho competitiveness that many men seem to have about the sport of fishing. And women and children are happy even when they don't catch a large fish.

This seems like the appropriate time to ask you about tournament fishing.

Gapen: Once we start challenging each other when we go fishing and we're in it for the money, I think that we've lost the whole purpose of the sport. I dislike competition. If you and I get in a boat and I put you in the front, I'd much prefer to see you catch fish. I've caught enough fish in my life that I don't need to prove anything to myself anymore. I don't need to see how many walleyes I can catch off of a reef or how big a one is down there. I much rather see the delight my passenger gets out of catching fish.

What are some of the major mistakes fishermen make when fishing a river?

Gapen: So many people see a boil [surface disturbance] on the water in eight feet of water, for instance, with a current of four miles an hour, and they cast at the boil thinking there's a fish holding on a rock right below the boil. There's not a damn thing below that boil. It's sixteen feet upriver.

That is, in eight feet of water with a four mile an hour current, it takes sixteen feet for that boil to come to the surface. So when you are casting, you've got to cast thirty-two feet upriver from the boil and draw your line down to that rock or whatever the structure is. Lead structure in running water like you'd lead a duck when you're duck hunting.

If the water is four feet deep, cut the distance in half, and so on. Leading structure is very important.

When you are working a flat properly, you take every boil and you figure out where the structure is that is causing the boil and cast the appropriate distance above the boil bringing your lure down by it or across it. If you cast downstream and retrieve upstream, you will very seldom hook a fish. Also, when casting crosscurrent, you've got to allow for line drift—the pull of the current. Plus it's hard to cast toward shore and bring your lure to the cover or structure properly because of drift. So cast upstream and bring your lure downstream, or cast upstream and bring your lure downstream at an angle which is much easier, plus it imitates natural bait much better.

Another mistake fishermen make is expecting too much. They expect to go out and load the boat when in reality even those of us who fish for a living, don't often do that either. The mistake they make is they don't enjoy the over-all picture. They don't enjoy fishing for all the other things that it encompasses besides catching fish.

We have promoted the take in fishing too hard. We haven't promoted the over-all benefits. So we've got a tremendous amount of unhappy and disgruntled fishermen because they don't catch five to six pound walleyes every time they go out.

Comment on the future of river fishing.

Gapen: I grew up on the Nipigon River and watched it become inundated with powerdams. The world's record brook trout came from the Nipigon River eight miles from our resort. I've watched modern man dam the only Nipigon River in the world. They ruined something that God had put there and it will never come again.

My fight to preserve running water probably came from that experience. The most frustrating thing in life is to fight politicians. And the apathy of man. Unless it directly affects him, he does not come forth; he can't see beyond his nose it seems.

They talk about flooding on rivers in this country, and they've increased double fold the property damage, etc. I say good; we deserve it. And the chances of the Upper Mississippi being preserved properly is past.

I hope the towns of Minneapolis and Saint Paul end up with twenty feet of water running down Hennepin Avenue and West Seventh Street because we deserve it. The Mississippi is a tremendous resource, and now, at least, some people refer to it as the beautiful Mississippi as opposed to the dirty Mississippi. From Saint Cloud to Minneapolis is one of the best smallmouth fisheries in the world. Lots of them over five pounds. You can float a stretch from Monticello to Elk River and in one day catch a hundred smallmouth bass weighing up to four pounds. We've got good walleyes in that area, too.

The Blue River in Indiana is nothing but a creek, but down there they treasure it. They're so proud of it. My God! We've got twenty-seven thousand miles of rivers in Minnesota and we are treating our river like trash.

Be more specific.

Gapen: Housing ruins a river. That first one hundred feet of vegetation is so important. They've raped the banks of plants and grass right to the river's edge. I've seen guys on the steep banks put a rope on a lawn mower so they can mow the grass right down to the river. It's a habit. They came to the river to get away from suburbia, and then they recreate suburbia here. They cut everything down. It looks like an Orrin Thompson park. If they don't protect the upper corridor of the Mississippi, the northerns suburbs, particularly the Coon Rapids area, will someday really get hit by flooding. They've got to protect that upper corridor since there is no way to dam it.

Why?

Gapen: If you dammed it, you'd flood half the state of Minnesota.

By protecting it I mean they've got to stop defoliating and stop building on the banks. What's the difference if you build your house back a hundred and fifty feet from the bank instead of fifty feet from it. But man's greed will probably win out. It's the insanity of man!

What's special about Minnesota river fishing?

Gapen: We've got twenty-seven thousand miles of navigable and fishable rivers in this state, some of which may only see four or five anglers a year.

Any final comments?

Gapen: Rivers are adventure; they're soothing to the soul.

Chapter 10

CAPTAIN DAVE COOLEY ON LAKE SUPERIOR FISHING

What does Dave Cooley do for a living? This isn't actually going to be a test, but follow along and use fisherman's logic to see if you can ascertain the answer.

Fact: At one time Dave Cooley was a Naval helicopter crewman who operated sonar in an anti-submarine unit. Fact: Dave Cooley attended Northern Michigan University for four years and received a bachelor's degree in marketing. Fact: Dave Cooley once operated his own construction company. Fact: For a few years Dave Cooley successfully sold insurance, tax shelters, and annuities. Fact: Dave Cooley is often referred to as Captain Dave Cooley. Fact: (And for those of you who aren't really good at riddles, this next clue is a biggie.) Dave Cooley loves to fish.

Now comes the hard part where I test your deductive skills and your fisherman's logic. What does Dave Cooley do for a living?

"I heard you sir! That's right! He's a charter boat operator on Lake Superior. That's absolutely right! You must be a savvy fisherman to have figured that out so quickly."

Well anyway, that's logic according to Dave Cooley since Cooley's law states: "If you are fishing every free moment you have, why not try to make a living at it."

And that's what Captain Dave Cooley did. He took his own advice! Purchasing a twenty-eight foot twin engine Chris Craft boat, he began taking charters out on Lake Superior in search of trout and salmon.

During the course of this interview, Dave spoke of the Rockland, Michigan winters of his youth when he thought he would die from the anticipation of waiting for spring when once again the walleye season would open. When he thought he couldn't stand it any longer, his father would announce that it was time to head down to the Ontonagon River and bring home some of those lunker walleyes. Actually, they weren't world class lunkers, but they did weigh in at three to eight pounds; considering they didn't own a boat and were limited to fishing from shore, these were respectable size fish.

However, when Dave was fourteen, he and his father built a wooden boat. It wasn't much by today's standards, but it did take them to fishing spots they were previously unable to fish. Now that Dave had access to a boat he expanded his fishing horizons and began to pursue bass as well as walleyes.

Dave then progressed from walleye and bass fishing to northern fishing, a skill he learned from his uncle Melvin. His uncle wasn't an authority on northern fishing, but he would have certainly qualified as a local expert. However, it wasn't as much the fishing knowledge that Dave gained from his uncle as it was the enthusiasm his uncle showed for fishing that influenced Dave.

As any serious Rockland, Michigan fisherman did, Dave and a friend purchased a boat and set out to fish the "Big Lake"—Lake Superior. Rockland's proximity to Lake Superior and the lake's reputation for big trout made it a challenge they couldn't avoid.

It was 1963 when they first launched that old boat on Lake Superior. And it was the fishing they did from that unseaworthy craft that began a love affair for Dave with the "Big Lake". Today that love has blossomed into Sport Trolling, Inc. which is Dave's charter boat company.

After high school, Dave attended Northern Michigan University, and then he joined the Navy where he became a sonar operator on a helicopter in an anti-submarine warfare unit. Although Dave never had the occasion to detect an enemy sub, he did learn the principles of operating sonar which is an asset to him in understanding how to best use locators, graphs, and video display units used in today's fishing techniques.

Upon completion of his tour of duty in the Navy, Dave returned to Northern Michigan University in Marquette, Michigan where he earned his bachelor's degree in marketing.

Since Dave had worked as a heavy equipment operator while he was attending college it was an easy transition to start his own excavating company. Business went well, but that was just before hard economic times hit the Upper Peninsula of Michigan. So Dave sold his excavating company and went on the road selling electronic and construction supplies.

Even though he was on the road much of the time he arranged his schedule so that only on rare occasions did he miss a weekend's fishing on Lake Superior or Lake Michigan. "Fishing has always been a priority in my life," Dave said. "No matter where I was or what I was doing, I would take time to fish."

Now well into his late twenties, Dave still felt something was missing in his life, and he thought a change in scenery might help. He moved to North Carolina where he began selling insurance, tax shelters, and annuities. Although he found North Carolina pleasant, he soon realized that it wasn't the missing ingredient he'd been looking for so he moved back to Minnesota and settled in Eden Prairie.

While in North Carolina he did have the opportunity to do some ocean fishing for gray trout and sharks.

Of course, I couldn't resist asking him how large was the largest shark he'd caught. He replied, "An eight footer." "An eight footer!" I said, "I'll need the details of that catch."

He began. "After I got the shark up to the boat, I told my fishing partner that I wanted to keep it. Well, he thought I was crazy. He didn't like sharks so he wouldn't allow me to bring it aboard his boat. After I killed the shark, we tied it by its tail and dragged it to shore. When we got to shore, we loaded it in the back of my pickup truck and I brought it home.

"When I got home, I hung the shark in a tree on my front lawn just like you would hang a deer. My God! In a matter of minutes there was a traffic jam in front of my house. People stopped and asked if they could have a piece of the shark; so I'd cut a big slab off and give it to them.

"Well, I like eating shark meat, but the good tasting ones are the two to three footers. That old eight footer tasted pretty tough."

Presently, Dave and Mary Cooley make their home in Knife River, Minnesota, a small town on the shores of Lake Superior about fifteen miles up the North Shore from Duluth. Mary commutes to Superior, Wisconsin where she works as a chiropractor, and Dave operates his charter boat business which is a polite way of saying he goes fishing a lot.

Although Dave is mindful of the fact that he will never become rich from operating his charter boat business, he strikes me as a contented and happy man. A man who finally seems to be doing what he was born to do.

Dave's boat, the Skeeter Lynn, is fully-equipped for fishing. It's twenty-eight feet long with twin engines which makes for a smooth and comfortable ride even in rough water. He is licensed for up to six fishermen, and his schedule is flexible.

For more information write to: Captain Dave Cooley, Sport Trolling, Inc., Box 96, Knife River, Minnesota 55609 or phone 218-834-3296.

TROUT AND SALMON BEHAVIOR ON LAKE SUPERIOR

How many different types of salmon are there in Lake Superior?

Cooley: Atlantic, coho, chinook, and pink. They have planted some Atlantics, but the chinook is the one they are mainly planting nowadays.

Why?

Cooley: It's too hard and expensive to get the spawn of some species of salmon. In fact, the Atlantic salmon program has never been that successful so they aren't putting that much effort or money into the Atlantics, although they are still planting some.

What types of trout are found in Lake Superior?

Cooley: Brown, lake trout, splake, and several strains of rainbow. But don't forget Lake Superior has many other species of fish besides trout and salmon. Northerns and walleyes are caught regularly down near the Saint Louis River.

How does the schooling behavior of trout and salmon affect your fishing for them?

Cooley: They all school. If you catch one, you should catch more in that same area. Or a certain temperature zone, that is. I've got spots I've fished in the fall where I've caught good limits almost every day for a three week period. Those are definitely schooled fish. I had one spot that was less than a quarter of a mile long where I took good fish for a couple of weeks in a row, and if I went a little too far past this point, I wouldn't get any. Obviously it was a real tight school of trout.

After a few days of coming in loaded up with big fish, other boats started showing up on this spot, and they started catching them, too. At this time, other fishermen were also catching trout in several other spots, but they were catching small ones. Those fish they were catching were schooled too, but they were schools of smaller fish.

Too bad for them! Just kidding. Anyway do you think that trout and salmon usually school by size?

Cooley: I really don't know. Sometimes you'll catch all small ones and other times you'll catch all big ones. But usually when you're catching fish, they will vary in size, so I really don't think that trout and salmon always school by size.

I find it interesting that the chinook salmon dies after it spawns. Seems a high price to pay for sex.

Cooley: Yeah! The Atlantic lives to spawn again, but, as far as I know, that's the only salmon species in this lake that does.

Also, the chinooks come back to the same streams they were born in to spawn; so it is easy for the D.N.R. to collect their eggs and then eventually plant them back into the lake.

They catch the chinooks and strip the eggs and sperm from them and mix it right there on shore. Then they take it back to their hatcheries for it to develop and hatch.

Which is the largest of the salmon species?

Cooley: The chinook is and the cohos and Atlantics run smaller. The biggest Atlantic that I've ever caught on Lake Superior was eight and a half pounds. Although Atlantics can reach the twelve to fourteen pound size, there aren't very many of them caught.

In the spring I catch a lot of cohos, but actually I haven't caught that many Atlantics. Most of the salmon we catch on my charter boat are cohos and chinooks.

Also, the hatchery resources are tied up much longer when they are raising Atlantic salmon. Chinooks are ready for release back into the lake much, much sooner. Since they tie up the hatchery resources for a shorter period of time there is an incentive for the D.N.R. to promote the taking of chinooks. Besides that, they are the biggest salmon in Lake Superior; consequently, most fishermen prefer to catch chinooks.

Which is the biggest species of trout?

Cooley: The laker. Steelhead also can run very large. Now Lake Michigan has huge brown trout, but in Lake Superior most of the charter boats don't spend much time fishing for browns. Most of my charter fishing is for lake trout, steelhead, and chinooks.

What are some of the behavioral differences in trout and salmon?

Cooley: Let's talk about the different tactics used in fishing for the various species. When you are fishing for salmon, you usually have to troll faster than you would for trout. For lake trout the best speed is about a mile to a mile and a half an hour and up to three miles an hour for salmon.

How about steelhead?

Cooley: Faster than lakers. And, of course, it depends on the time of the year you are fishing. In the spring, for instance, you are not going to troll as fast as you would in the summertime. A slower presentation is a given in the spring no matter what species of fish you are fishing for on any body of water.

What motivates a fish to strike a lure?

Cooley: I think trout and salmon will strike a lure because of aggression as well as hunger. I've caught many fish that were hooked in the tail or side instead of the mouth. These fish are just coming up and slapping at the lure, and that's aggression. In fact, the biggest fish I thought we had last summer turned out to be only a five and a half pound laker. My customer was fighting and fighting that fish. I actually stopped the boat and pulled up all of the other lines. When we finally landed it, after a tremendous fight, it turned out to be only a small lake trout that was hooked in the tail. He was being dragged backwards in the water, and the fight he was able to put up was just unbelievable.

Then there are other times when they are hitting so lightly that you have to add a stinger hook on your lure to catch them. They're just not aggressive at all.

Why are fish sometimes really active and catchable and other times they are very negative and uncatchable?

Cooley: A change in weather or atmospheric pressure perhaps. After a storm, for example, it usually takes a few days before the fish are real active again. But right before a storm you can have a bang-up day.

Sometimes you can catch fish and you'll find that their stomachs are empty, and other times you'll find that they are full of forage, but they hit your lure anyway. I've had as many as a dozen smelt come out of a fish; that fish couldn't have been hungry. What triggered him to hit (on a full stomach) had to be something in the presentation of the lure; so trial and error is always important, especially when you are not catching fish.

Some of the other contributors to this book feel that fish have cycles where they gorge themselves and other times when they really don't eat much at all.

Cooley: I agree with that. But I don't think anybody fully understands what triggers those feeding and non-feeding cycles.

You'd think since fish are cold-blooded they would have to eat almost constantly in the summertime.

Cooley: You would think that, but there are times when they don't seem to be interested in food even during the hottest weather of the summer. But in the winter you can still catch lots of nice trout through the ice. Although in the winter they seem to bite a little lighter, they still bite fairly regularly.

Comment on water temperature preferences for trout and salmon.

Cooley: They definitely have a water temperature preference, but at times they will go out of that preferred temperature zone to feed. For example, lake trout like the water temperature to be forty-eight to fifty-two degrees, and salmon like fifty-two to fifty-six degree water, and steelhead prefer it even warmer (fifty-six to sixty degrees). In the spring, however, I just look for the warmest water I can find.

Use these preferred temperature zones as a good place to start fishing, not as an absolute. Actually, an easy way to start is to drop your bomb down with an electronic temperature gauge on it until you find what depth that preferred temperature is at. Then start fishing there.

Sometimes, even though you can pinpoint the fish on your graph and run lures right through that depth, no matter what you do, they won't touch 'em.

Give me an example.

Cooley: Say you've got a temperature break in eighty feet of water. A thermocline. There's a thermocline at eighty feet, that is. Below it is colder water, and above it is warmer water. Also, there will be a band of water in between. If you're fishing for salmon, since you know they prefer fifty-two to fifty-six degree water, you look for the band of water in that temperature range. That temperature range is a good place to start looking for fish.

I run one lure at the top of that temperature band which is the fifty-six degree water, and I run one lure at the bottom of that temperature band in the fifty-two degree water. Also, run at least one lure right in the middle of the temperature band.

If you are not catching fish after working this preferred temperature band, then start fishing above it or below it since the active fish might move out of that band of water to feed.

I run four downriggers, and I usually use one rig to experiment with. I vary the depth, presentation, and color on the experimental rig just for my own education. Of course, if we're really catching fish at a certain depth, I will run all four riggers at that depth.

How important is a trout or salmon's ability to smell and taste?

Cooley: A fish's ability to taste isn't all that important to fishermen when trolling. By the time they taste the lure, they are probably hooked anyway.

As for their sense of smell, that's very important. I've tried several fish scent products and found that Dr. Juice seems to work pretty well for trout and salmon.

But most of the time I still prefer to use a natural scent. When I'm handling lures, I like to have the smell of a fish on my hands. Just rub a piece of cut sucker in your hands before you handle your lures and you'll have all the scent you'll need.

Because scent is very important I don't like other people handling my lures when we're fishing. You never know what odors they might have on their hands.

Do fish use their sense of smell to find food?

Cooley: They see a lure going through the water and the scent is that little added incentive for them to strike. It probably triggers something in their brain that suggests that your lure is food. After you've got their attention with your lure, it helps trigger them to strike.

Also, scent helps mask any odors that your lures might pick up from your hands, etc. I always wash my hands with an unscented soap before I go fishing. And keep your lures clean. Don't leave them laying around where they will pick up foul odors.

Do trout and salmon chase schools of forage fish?

Cooley: Sure they do. Both trout and salmon will follow schools of forage. Sometimes they will also follow your lure for a good distance before they strike it. If you do something to change the direction or speed of your lure quickly, like turning to the right or left, they will then strike it. Sometimes when they are following your lure and you suddenly turn causing your inside lure to slow down and your outside lure to speed up, that can trigger them into striking.

Never pop your lures loose from the downriggers and then reel them in fast. Just pop them loose and let the speed of the boat bring them to the surface before you reel them in. By doing this you can often trigger a strike.

Does it necessarily follow that if your boat is moving at, say, two miles an hour, that your lure is moving at two miles an hour also?

Cooley: Absolutely not. Because you don't know how the currents down below are affecting the speed of your lure. A company called B-C Electronics has a device that will tell you how fast your lure is moving through the water.

What's that device called?

Cooley: A Pro-Combinator. It's a lure speed indicator which also tells you the water temperature at the depth you're fishing. It attaches to your downrigger.

Many times when you are fishing an area, you will catch fish trolling in one direction, but you won't catch them trolling in the other direction. There's a reason for that: down below there might be a current that is causing your lure not to work properly or work at all. If the current is pushing on your lure from behind at a speed faster than your boat is moving, the lure will probably just be hanging there limp. Or you might have a current working against your lure which can cause it to just spin in circles. In the "Big Lake" current is always a factor.

I'd like you to be more specific on how current can affect lures.

Cooley: Well, for example, if you are trolling at one mile an hour and your lure is working against a three mile an hour current, the lure is probably just spinning in circles not working properly at all. On the other hand, if you're trolling at one mile an hour and your lure has a three mile an hour current hitting it from behind, your lure is probably just hanging limp.

How does the fisherman who doesn't have an electronic lure speed indicator deal with this factor, or is he just at the mercy of the currents?

Cooley: If you notice that your downrigger bombs are running farther back (at a greater angle from your boat) than normal, you know that there is a current working against them. Of course, the speed at which you are trolling will affect the angle of your bombs, too.

Watch the angle of the downrigger cables and adjust your speed accordingly. You just keep experimenting until you find the right speed at that depth.

Although the electronic devices take a lot of the guess work out of it, you'll always have to determine what the best speed is on a given day.

Back to forage fish. Can their presence help you locate trout or salmon?

Cooley: In the spring trout and salmon are mainly feeding on smelt which is why Rapalas, Rebels, and other fish-bodied type lures are very productive. And often in the spring, the trout and salmon movements are determined by the smelt movements.

Comment on movements and migrations of trout and salmon.

Cooley: Salmon are great migrators. They make a big clockwise swing up the coast of Lake Superior as the year goes on. No one really has pinpointed their exact movements; we only know in general terms where they go. That's why the Michigan D.N.R. is clipping the fins on the salmon that they are stocking. By doing this they hope to determine where those fish go.

When the currents warm the water on the south shore of Lake Superior at Duluth, for instance, the salmon will begin to migrate up the North

Shore. In the month of August I'll be chartering out of Grand Marais because that's where the salmon should be by then. Two years ago in August the salmon fishing was great in the Grand Marais area, but last year it was poor. We can't predict with exact accuracy where they'll be at a given point in time, but usually we can guess pretty well. You take your chances. No one knows exactly why salmon are such great migrators, but it's a good bet that they're just following the temperature patterns in the lake.

Lake trout will move from location to location, but it's more of a movement than a migration. They don't really migrate.

Comment on the greatest fishing myth of all—fish don't bite during "dog days".

Cooley: I've caught fish under almost every possible condition you could imagine on Lake Superior. I've caught them at noon, in the middle of the night, when the sun was bright, when it's cloudy, and so on, and so on. Possibly some of those myths hold true for shallow water lakes, but not with Lake Superior.

Do trout and salmon respond differently to lures from Lake Superior to Lake Michigan?

Cooley: Somewhat. For example, some of the lures that produce well on Lake Michigan don't work as well on Lake Superior. In fact, I've tried using the bigger J-plugs that I use on Lake Michigan and they don't work very well on Lake Superior. In general, you will need to use a little bit smaller lure on Lake Superior.

Give me an example.

Cooley: For salmon in the month of August on Lake Michigan I'll run J-plugs, but on Lake Superior during August I find that spoons work much better.

Do trout prefer different size lures than salmon?

Cooley: You really don't need to compare lure sizes for trout and slamon since you will use different lures for trout than you would for salmon. The size of the lure you are using depends on the time of the year that you are fishing. I use larger lures as the season progresses all the way to ice-over. Late in the fall I'm using the largest lures that I've used all season, and that's for both trout and salmon.

Do you think that a trout or salmon's memory is developed enough so that they can become lure wary?

Cooley: Sometimes a lure stops producing, but I don't think it's because the fish remember seeing that lure. To say that fish have memory would be to say that they have the ability to learn. I don't think that they have that ability.

Where do trout and salmon spawn?

Cooley: All salmon spawn in rivers, as do brown trout and steelhead trout. Lake trout spawn on reefs out in the lake.

Is there anything that you would like to add regarding the behavior of trout and salmon?

Cooley: Generally, if I'm looking for salmon in the spring, I'm looking for the warmer water or any temperature break in the water. It doesn't have to be in their preferred temperature zone. Of course, water temperature is an important variable anytime you are fishing, but in the spring, for instance, it could be a temperature break of thirty-seven to forty-three degrees.

LOCATING TROUT AND SALMON ON LAKE SUPERIOR

Let's begin this section by talking about structure.

Cooley: You always like to fish structure. Structure is as important in Lake Superior fishing as it is in any type of fishing.

Actually, I love to fish points. If I'm fishing a rocky point, I'll come into that point and try to follow it with my graph.

Do you troll parallel to it?

Cooley: Sometimes I do. But you can fish right over the top, too. I know it's coming and as soon as I see it (on my graph), I'm cranking up the downriggers because sometimes you'll have a rock that comes straight up twenty feet or more.

Although salmon are migratory fish, they still relate to structure. Mouths of rivers are a good place to look for salmon. They might be a mile out in the lake, but they are actually relating to that river mouth.

When salmon migrate, do you think that they move from a particular piece of structure to another piece of structure?

Cooley: Not exactly. I think the salmon is interested in structure because bait fish relate to structure. So the salmon are coming onto structure just to get a meal. Lake trout relate more to structure the way a walleye or bass does, but salmon do not. They relate more to the bait fish that are relating to structure.

Remember, at times, structure can be the key in locating trout and salmon in Lake Superior and Lake Michigan. In fact, in Lake Michigan there are reefs where salmon hang on the top or just off of the edge. They might be twenty feet above the structure or they might move off of it, but they will come back.

Is pH a variable in locating trout or salmon?

Cooley: I haven't really spent a lot of time studying it on Lake Superior.

Comment on the salmons' preferred water temperature with location in mind.

Cooley: The salmon species prefer the fifty-two to fifty-six degree water temperatures.

That's if that temperature is available?

Cooley: That's a good place to start fishing. And at certain times of the year none of the water is that warm.

In the spring, for instance, you might find thirty-eight degree water and then suddenly you hit some forty-three degree water, well, for salmon, that's where you would want to fish.

But I found that even in early spring the lake trout will often be on the bottom regardless of water temperature. Lake trout are a bottom origin fish, but you will catch some on the temperature breaks, too.

Let's go through the same thing with lake trout using their preferred water temperature in locating them.

Cooley: Lake trout prefer forty-eight to fifty-two degree water which means you'll usually find them in deeper water than salmon. They're considered a bottom fish. And brown trout and steelheads like it somewhat warmer: fifty-six to sixty degrees.

If I can find those preferred temperature zones, I will definitely fish them. However, the preferred temperature zone you may be looking for in Lake Superior can vary with the season.

Does the direction of the wind affect fishing?

Cooley: If I could choose which direction I wanted the wind to be coming from, it wouldn't be the east.

Why?

Cooley: I guess maybe I'm superstitious. You know the old saying: If the wind is from the east, fish bite least. I know that's never been proven, but given my choice, I wouldn't pick an east wind.

Besides that, a northeast wind on Lake Superior on the Minnesota shoreline is a very dangerous wind. If you have a good northeaster blowing, sometimes you can't get on the lake for three or four days.

Why is a northeast wind so dangerous?

Cooley: It blows right down the coast and has a lot of time to build in strength. That is, when the wind is coming over the water instead of overland, it is more likely that it will create larger waves. Huge waves sometimes.

Comment on the barometric pressure's affect on fishing.

Cooley: I've got to produce fish whether the barometer is rising or falling. If the barometer fell, I wouldn't cancel any of my charters.

Comment on how the sky conditions affect trout and salmon behavior.

Cooley: I think most fishermen prefer the darker days for fishing. I know I do. And on cloudy days I switch to a little darker lures. The general rule is: On light days use light lures and on dark days use dark lures. That won't always be true though.

Is water clarity an important aspect in locating trout or salmon?

Cooley: Yes. After a storm, I like to fish a mud line.

What exactly is a mud line?

Cooley: Mud lines are at the mouths of rivers where the dirty water is running into the lake. They're easy to see; so they're easy to fish.

How do you fish mud lines?

Cooley: I like to zigzag through them.

Why is a mud line a good place to fish?

Cooley: Two reasons: First, there is always a temperature break on a mud line; second, there is usually forage or feed for fish along these mud lines.

Water clarity on Lake Superior depends on which way the wind is blowing. If it's blowing into a bay, the bay will be dirty. If it's blowing out of the bay, you might be able to see thirty feet deep or more. In the Duluth area it's much more a factor than up where I usually fish. Also, a rain will bring dirty water into the lake from the streams creating mud lines.

Comment on the thermocline as a locational variable.

Cooley: To locate the thermocline, drop a temperature probe down into the water and where you get a temperature change of five or six degrees within a few feet you've located the thermocline. It's an area of the lake where the lake's water temperature is sharply stratified. And sometimes your graph will print a thermocline if it's a real radical change in water temperature. But the thermocline doesn't really develop in Lake Superior until late, late June or early July since the lake is so cold. On Lake Michigan, since it's shallower and warmer, you can find thermoclines much earlier in the season than you can on Lake Superior.

The depth of thermocline can change from day to day in the same area of the lake. And sometimes you can be fishing a thermocline one day and the next day that thermocline is gone. The lake's currents and the wind or a storm affect the thermocline's depth and whether or not you have one in a given part of the lake. For example, if the wind was blowing into the area you were fishing, it could force the thermocline to go deeper. And if the wind was blowing away from you, it might create a situation where it's all cold water and the thermocline is nonexistent.

What do you do when you're having a hard time locating active fish?

Cooley: I try different depths. I stagger my lines anywhere from zero to one hundred and seventy feet deep. I cover different depths looking for them, and I will change my lures and lure speed frequently until I hook one. Then when I've hooked a fish, I'll mark it [Dave marks it on his Loran C. How this unit works is discussed in the Equipment and Tackle section of this chapter.] and make several more passes through the same area noting the speed and the lure that caught the fish.

Of course, when you fish almost every day like I do, you usually start fishing where you caught fish yesterday, and that often works. But if they're not there, you have to start looking—changing depths, trolling speed, and lures until you find the combination that works.

Do you ever have those periods in trout and salmon fishing where it seems every fish you catch is large to very large?

Cooley: Yep! Last year I had a good stretch of about three weeks on one little spot where we caught trout from six to twelve pounds. During this time everybody else was catching fish too, but they were catching mostly small ones. (Two to three pound lakers.) I was lucky enough to have located a school of bigger fish. And eighty percent of the time during this three week period we came in limited out in the morning and afternoon both. Of course, then a lot of other boats began to follow me. I guess I'm too honest on the radio.

How much of that talk you hear on the marine radios about fishing is the truth?

Cooley: You get so you recognize the voices or the boat when they identify themselves, and after a while, you know who tells the truth and who doesn't. Some guys have codes they use when they are talking on the radio. And, of course, if you're talking to another boat, and he doesn't respond or suddenly he stops talking to you, you can bet he's too busy to talk since he's catching fish. During fishing contests some guys will get together and decide on a specific channel (a working channel) to use so it's harder for other contestants to listen in because they don't know which one it is.

If somebody asks me what I'm doing to catch fish and where I'm catching them, I almost always tell them.

If you're a beginner, ask the charter boat captains where and how they're catching fish. They will usually tell you what you need to know.

Does it bother the charter boat captains when people follow them all over the lake?

Cooley: Not as long as you don't crowd right in on them. I've had people come right in on me so close they hook my high lines which does make me mad. Now on Lake Michigan where there's a lot more boat traffic having somebody follow you can be a pain. In fact, over there you can't even run board lines because somebody will cut them off. You have to keep everything tight to the boat.

Is night fishing for trout and salmon productive?

Cooley: Fishing is good at night. I used to do a lot of it. Real early in the morning right after daybreak is excellent for salmon fishing.

How about early morning lake trout fishing?

Cooley: Generally, what I like to do is fish salmon in the early morning hours and then a little later in the day fish deep water for lake trout. That usually works pretty well.

What is the best method of locating fish if you haven't been on the water for a week or more?

Cooley: When you haven't been out for a while, you might have to do a lot of running before you locate productive water, especially in the spring. But there are general seasonal locational patterns that you can look for.

In the summer I generally know where the lake trout are going to be. But the bottom line is: you decide what species of fish you are looking for, then look for them based on seasonal locational patterns.

Let's go through a typical season from ice-out to ice-over with location in mind.

Cooley: In the spring just after ice-out you'll be looking for the warmest water you can find (surface temperature). And in the spring it's going to be the top forty feet of water that will be the warmest.

Later on in the year about late June you should start looking for thermoclines. In Lake Michigan these seasonal changes take place earlier since Lake Michigan is shallower and warmer than Lake Superior.

Then in the fall if you're fishing for salmon, you'll be fishing in the mouths of rivers and in close to shore running high and fast. Also, in the fall the lake trout start moving in on the shallow reefs looking for a place to spawn. But on October 1st the lake trout season is closed since the D.N.R. wants the lake trout to be able to spawn without being disturbed by fishermen.

How much do you depend on charts for locating fish?

Cooley: I use charts of Lake Superior quite often but not for locating fish. Usually I use charts when I'm going long distances.

When I'm fishing all day in the fog, for instance, I use my compass, depth finder, and watch to determine where I am. Of course, if you have a Loran C, it takes all the guesswork out of it. That unit can put you within three or four feet of where you want to be no matter what the conditions are.

What are the most common mistakes that fishermen make in trying to locate trout and salmon?

Cooley: The biggest mistake fishermen make is driving out on the lake, dropping some lures in the water, and then sitting back popping open a can of beer and listening to a ball game or something like that. They aren't experimenting or paying attention to their fishing. Good fishermen use everything they've got to their advantage.

I'm not saying there's anything wrong with going out on the lake just to have a good time regardless of whether you catch fish or not. That's fine for some people, but if you're not paying attention to details like whether or not you're using complementary lures, your trolling speed, water temperature, depth, and so on, you're probably not going to catch very many fish.

I'm glad you mentioned complementary lures; I didn't have that on my list of questions.

Cooley: Well, lures are designed to work at a certain speed. If you are using one lure that is designed to run at a slow speed and the other three that you are running are designed to run at high speeds, they are not complementing each other very well.

You can't use two fast running lures with two slow running lures since at slow speeds the two fast running lures will be just hanging there not doing what they were designed to do and vice versa.

And since trolling speed is the most important aspect of presentation the concept of using complementary lures is very important.

PRESENTATION FOR TROUT AND SALMON ON LAKE SUPERIOR

Do you ever use live bait?

Cooley: I use a piece of cut sucker minnow on my herring dodger and fly, especially if I'm fishing for lake trout. Just cut a piece off of a three inch sucker. I like to use the tail sections.

What affect does that have?

Cooley: It's used for scent. If you're out on my boat, you'll never see me eating food or handling anything that will put an odor on my hands other than what we discussed earlier about crushing up a sucker minnow in my hands for scent. I'm a great believer in scent being a factor in successful fishing.

In fact, once I had taken a charter out in the morning and we came in with a limit. That afternoon I was out with another charter and after fishing for two hours, we didn't have a strike. It was driving me crazy. I kept wondering what I was doing differently than I had that morning. I was doing everything the same.

Then I remembered, while I was in port waiting for my afternoon charter, I had checked my transmission fluid. Well, after remembering that, I immediately washed my hands and pulled up all of the lines and rerigged them. As soon as I put the clean lures in the water, we began catching fish. All it took to ruin my fishing was transmission residue on my hands.

Now that's not absolute proof of anything, but it certainly suggests that bad odors can spoil your fishing.

You've said that you cut sucker minnows for bait; why don't you use the whole sucker?

Cooley: I feel, if you cut the bait you will get more scent. A stronger scent, that is. Another thing is that if you use too large of a piece of live bait, fish will often hit your lure short and rip the minnow off and, as a result, you'll miss the fish.

Comment on trolling.

Cooley: There are hundreds of aspects to fishing Lake Superior for trout and salmon, but with regards to presentation, in my opinion, your trolling speed is the most important. They won't touch a lure if you are going too fast or too slow. That lure has to be down there at the right depth, and it has to be going the right speed.

As a rule, you'll be trolling faster for salmon and steelhead and slow for lake trout. Lake trout just respond to a slower moving lure better than steelhead and salmon do.

Is there a good method to estimate how fast your lure is moving through the water without an electronic trolling speed indicator?

Cooley: Before the trolling speed indicators were available I would tie a lure right next to my boat and just watch it to see if it was working properly. Now that helps, but it's not foolproof because of the currents down below. It should give you some idea of what your lure is doing down a ways if there aren't any real radical currents below you. And watch the angle of your downrigger cables, which we talked about earlier.

Another nice thing about have a lure tied to the side of your boat is that when you switch directions you'll be able to tell how much you'll have to speed up or slow down to keep that lure working properly.

Also, the distance between the lure and the downrigger bomb will affect how your lure will run. A herring dodger will run differently in the water if it's three feet behind the bomb, than it will if it's twelve feet behind the bomb. That is, the action of the lure will be faster and tighter the closer it is to the bomb. Frequently I will vary my trolling speed when I'm looking for fish until I find the speed that is best at that time.

Be more specific.

Cooley: In general, you should be trolling about a mile to a mile and a half an hour for lake trout and up to three miles an hour for salmon.

If you're fishing for salmon, you use different rigging than you would use for lake trout. So if you're rigged with herring dodgers and flies for lake trout, you can't very well run a spoon for salmon with that rigging.

But if you hope to pick up stray salmon or steelhead when you are fishing for lake trout, you can use high lines off to the side of your boat rigged with spoons that are designed for slow speeds. Sometimes I use a pencil weight so they will run about five feet deep. And with this presentation you will occasionally catch that stray steelhead or salmon while you're concentrating on lake trout.

What spoons work best for this technique?

Cooley: Light spoons like Suttons or Flutter spoons work well, but sometimes it is good to give them more of a bend so they work better at slower speeds. Or a Lightning lure; they've been a real good lure for me.

How long are the outrigger poles that you use for this method?

Cooley: I've got sixteen footers on my boat, and they seem to work well. The reason I like sixteen footers is that it keeps the lines out and away from the line I'm using for lake trout.

How far back are you running these lures for the straggler steelhead and salmon?

Cooley: Between a hundred and fifty and two hundred feet. But at the same time the lake trout lures are running maybe one hundred and sixty-five feet below the surface.

What function does a downrigger perform?

Cooley: Basically one function: It allows you to control the depth that your lure is running. And if you're just beginning to get involved in trout and salmon fishing and you don't want to spend the money for downriggers, you can buy or make diving planes which at times will work well, too. They're just not as convenient.

Of course, with downriggers you're not guessing as to how deep your lure is running as you are with diving planes. Downriggers have a gauge that tells you how much cable you've let out which is an indication of how deep your lures are running. By indication I mean, it records how much cable is out, that's how deep your bomb would be if you were dead in the water [not moving]. But you have to allow for drag angle when you are trolling: you let out one hundred and thirty feet of cable, but your bomb might be running at one hundred and fifteen feet because of the drag created by currents and the speed at which you are trolling. Therefore, if you wanted to fish at the one hundred and twenty foot depth, you would have to let out one hundred and thirty to one hundred and thirty-five feet of cable.

What size bombs do you use on your downriggers?

Cooley: I use heavier than most. Most fishermen use eight to ten pounders, but I prefer fifteen pounders because they hang straighter in the water and release more easily and they seem to be easier to control. Also with a heavy ball you can get your lure back to the depth that you want to fish much faster since it is heavier, and they also prevent having as many tangles.

You went by me there; how do heavier bombs prevent line tangles?

Cooley: The straighter your bomb hangs the few tangles you'll have.

How do outriggers differ from downriggers?

Cooley: An outrigger is designed to run off of the side of your boat rather than right behind it like downriggers. Its main function is to keep lines away from the lines that you have running right behind your boat. I run sixteen foot outriggers with high lines (surface type lines). I've also run Dipsy Divers on outriggers.

What do you do when you get lines tangled when you're out with your charters (customers)?

Cooley: I just cut all of the lines and retie as fast as I can. I certainly don't bother trying to untangle 'em.

How often do you put fresh line on your reels?

Cooley: Often! You don't ever want to chance losing a big fish because you didn't have good line on. And a couple of times a day I will cut the first thirty feet or so of line off because it gets frayed and becomes very weak from working in the releases.

Do you modify your lures?

Cooley: Oh yes! I do all the time. When you take them out of the package, you assume two lures of the same size, same color, same design, etc. will work the same. But they don't. Invariably you will catch more fish on one of those two supposedly identical lures. So I'm always bending on them trying to improve the way they work.

Once when my boy was little, he got into some of my lures, one of which was my favorite lure. He was sitting on the sidewalk beating on this lure with a hammer. When he had finished with that lure, it was a mess.

What kind of lure was it?

Cooley: It was a little copper colored Cleo which I used for casting off of breakwalls in the spring and fall.

Then about six months later, I noticed I still had that beat-up old Cleo in my tackle box, so I decided I should find out if it would still work. I tied it on and was dragging it along the side of a breakwall and it looked like it still had good action. I cast it out and caught a fish. As it turned out, in the next three years before I lost that lure, I caught more fish with it than any other lure I'd ever used for casting.

You can imagine what that lure looked like after it had been pounded on with a hammer, but I almost cried when I lost it.

You can buy two identical lures, and one of them may produce well, and the other one won't produce very well at all. I guess that's why I'm always bending on the ones that don't produce hoping I'll change that lure in some way for the better.

What about Rapala type lures; you can't do much to them, can you?

Cooley: You can't bend 'em or pound on 'em if that's what you mean. But you can add color to them.

Actually, have you ever met a fisherman who didn't think he could improve on his tackle?

What can one do to modify a spoon?

Cooley: You can put a little bit bigger bend in them which will make them run a little bit more erratically. But there are no set rules. Just keep bending them until they run the way you want them to run.

Are you one of those fishermen who's always sharpening his hooks?

Cooley: Absolutely. I even sharpen them while we're out fishing. If I hit the bottom, when I bring the lure in, I will check to make sure the hooks aren't bent and they are still sharp. In fact, I carry a little hook sharpening stone in my pocket every time I go fishing. There's no excuse for having dull hooks. Even after you've caught a fish, you should check to see if the hook is still sharp.

How do you set the drag on your reels when you are trolling?

Cooley: That's really important especially for charter fishermen since many of their customers aren't experienced fishermen. And since they aren't experienced at handling fishing equipment, I prefer to set the drag a little big light. And I have to admit that I've lost a lot of fish because I had set my drag too tightly. You get a little overanxious and the line will snap quite easily.

A good reel with an easy to use drag adjustment can be tightened down while you are fighting a fish. I use the 209 Penn reels which are good reels except the drag adjustment is a little too sensitive.

How does your presentation change when night fishing?

Cooley: I prefer darker colored lures at night. I've heard that some guys have good luck on fluorescent colored lures at night, but I really haven't ever done that well with them.

Of course, if I'm out there and nothing is working, I'm liable to try anything which applies to my daytime fishing, too.

When you're rigging your lures, do you tie them on with swivels?

Cooley: I always use swivels. With the Rapala type lures I tie the lure directly to the line and then use a swivel farther up on the line. If you have a swivel on the nose of a Rapala, it doesn't work right. The action isn't right. And, by all means, buy the good ball bearing swivels rather than the cheap ones. The ball bearing swivels work better, and they don't break when you've got a trophy fish on.

What are some of the basic lures that a beginner should have in his tackle box?

Cooley: For salmon fishing in the spring you should have a good selection of minnow imitation lures like the Rapalas or Rebels. Later on in the year (toward the end of June) I usually use a spoon type lure for both trout and salmon all the way up to ice-over.

How about J-Plugs?

Cooley: I don't use J-Plugs very often in Lake Superior like I do on Lake Michigan. I've caught fish on J-Plugs in Lake Superior, but not consistently. But the best lure one year might not be the best the next year. It changes from year to year.

Do you troll more slowly in the fall than you would in the summer?

Cooley: No. I know that most of the walleye fishermen, for instance, will slow down their presentation in the fall, but for trout and salmon on Lake Superior I don't slow down in the fall. Generally, the ideal trolling speed will be a little faster as the season progresses until late June or early July, and then it levels off. But that's only a general rule; don't be afraid to experiment.

Explain that "bouncing the bottom" technique that you used for lake trout.

Cooley: When I first began using that technique back in 1966 or '67, we used wire line with a two pound weight with some monofilament line and a lure behind it. We'd drop it down on the bottom. You'd pick it up and then drop it back down and wait until the weight hit the bottom again. It was all attached to a stiff pole, and we'd lift it up and drop it. It was a lot of work, but it caught fish. Today we're basically doing the same thing but with much better equipment.

There are a couple of ways of "bouncing the bottom"; the easiest being shifting your motor in and out of gear. You put it in gear and go a little ways and then shift it into neutral. When the downrigger bomb hits bottom, your rods will straighten out. When they straighten out, shift your motor back into gear and do it over again. That's called "bouncing the bottom".

But the method of "bouncing the bottom" that I like to use is different. I use a graph in conjunction with my downriggers. I know where the bottom is because I dropped the downrigger ball down to where it hits the bottom. Then I crank it up three-quarters of a crank, and that's where I fish. Then I watch the graph, and if it gets deeper or shallower, I adjust my downriggers accordingly.

The main aspect of presentation for lake trout is fishing near the bottom. Very near the bottom! (Sometimes you'll find lake trout suspended, but that's usually toward the end of summer, very close to fall.) Lake trout are bottom orientated fish.

Now a lot of fishermen don't like bottom bouncing since you can lose a lot of rigging doing it. When you get hooked, you can lose downrigger cables, lures, and bombs, and that can be expensive.

Bombs are expensive, but not as expensive as downrigger cables, releases, and lures put together. So when I'm "bouncing the bottom", I don't hook my bombs directly to the cables. I tie a piece of fifty pound monofilament line between them so when I do get hooked good, the monofilament line will break and all I will lose is the bomb. It's much cheaper to lose a bomb rather than a cable and a lure. In fact, if you get the bomb hooked really good, when you've hooked the bomb directly to the cable, it can snap the cable way up near the downrigger, and then you will lose all of your gear.

Another trick that you can use is to run longer cables on each downrigger so you have enough cable that you don't run out before you're able to stop the boat if you get hooked. That is, if you are fishing in one hundred and sixty feet of water and your cable is only two hundred feet long, you don't have much time to stop when you get hooked.

"Bouncing the bottom" can often be the difference between coming in with a few fish or a cooler full.

We've discussed trolling speed, scent, and so on. How about color?

Cooley: Color is an important aspect of presentation. But the color that fills your cooler today might not work very well tomorrow. You can be using the exact same spoon as another person and he's catching fish and you're not because your spoon is a little different color.

So what's the solution; carry thousands of different colored lures?

Cooley: I always carry colored tape with me so I can change the colors of my lures quickly. It's just more convenient to carry a selection of colored tape than it is to carry hundreds of different colored lures.

And, as I mentioned before, I always start with the general rule that on dark days use dark lures and on light days use light lures. But, as far as color goes, that's only a good place to start. In the fall, for example, gold is an excellent color and many times copper is good. Greens are also often very good, and there are days when they'll only hit fluorescent.

These colors you've mentioned, do they apply to spoons as well as minnow imitations?

Cooley: Sure! And flies, too.

If I hear on my marine radio that somebody's catching them on blue Rapalas, for instance, and I don't have a blue Rapala, should I try a blue spoon or some other blue colored lure?

Cooley: Yeah. I would. Blue might be the ticket.

Are you saying that color is more important than the type of lure that I might choose?

Cooley: I would say that color is often as important as your choice of lure type, and on occasion it can be more important. But, of course, color and lure choice won't help you unless you are paying attention to the other aspects of presentation such as trolling speed, depth, and so on.

How does your color choice change from season to season?

Cooley: Early in the spring, silver and fluorescents can be a good choice. Then toward the end of June, greens and fluorescents are good choices. As fall approaches, gold and copper are usually a better color.

Do those color choices apply to both trout and salmon?

Cooley: I guess the best answer for both trout and salmon is that you have to keep experimenting since a color that produces for you today might not work at all tomorrow. I always start with a pretty good complement of colors until I find the one that works best.

I try to have one line in the water that I'm experimenting with—a different color or lure type altogether. Sometimes just having dots on a spoon seems to make a difference.

How heavy of line do you use on your charter trips?

Cooley: Twenty pound test. I've tried using lighter lines, but when you've got people who aren't used to landing big fish yanking on those rods, they'll too often break the fish off if the line is too light.

But I also carry an extra set of rods with light line for people who really want to battle a fish. I leave the choice up to my customers. If they want to take on a big trout or salmon with eight pound test line, I let them go at it.

Do you feel you get more strikes when you're using lighter line?

Cooley: Yes. But not because heavier line is more visible to fish. I feel, it's because lures work better on twelve pound test line than they do on twenty pound test line, for instance. The heavier the line, the more it will impede your lure from its maximum action. And the lighter the lure is, the more obvious this becomes.

List the most important aspects of presentation.

Cooley: Trolling speed is number one, then temperature, color, the types of lures you are using, and how far back you are running your lures from the downrigger balls. Usually I run my lures about twelve to twenty feet behind my downriggers, but sometimes the fish will hit them better if they are closer to the downrigger balls. In the spring when I'm fishing shallower water, I might run the lures thirty to forty feet behind the balls to keep them away from the boat which is less likely to spook fish in shallow water.

If I'm experimenting to see what the best distance to run the lures behind the bomb is, I will run one five to six feet back and another thirty-five feet back and the other two somewhere in between. If I find that one rig is consistently working better than the others, I will of course switch all of my lures to the length that is working best.

Is there anything that you want to add regarding trolling speed?

Cooley: You can't say too much about trolling speed since it's so important. But, in general, just keep adjusting your trolling speed until you find out what speed will work best.

How about depth?

Cooley: Depth is mostly a seasonal variable especially with lake trout. Salmon, on the other hand, will stay relatively shallow throughout the year. Also, depth patterns can change from year to year.

Is there anything that you want to add regarding color?

Cooley: Color is somewhat seasonal, but, for the most part, it's a daily variable that you should always be experimenting with.

Comment on boat control.

Cooley: On charters I always have a first mate aboard to help run the boat while we're fishing. It's too much for one person to do alone.

I prefer making subtle changes in course. That way if you are continually catching fish on the outside line (when you are turning) instead of the other lines, you know that you're trolling too slow. That is, if fish are hitting on the outside line when you are turning, you know that the outside lure is traveling faster than the others, so adjust your trolling speed accordingly.

Fish seem to respond to lures on their change in direction or change in depth or change in speed, and when you are turning, all of those variables are changing somewhat. The fish might be following that lure and when that lures doe something a little bit different, instantly, it will provoke the fish into striking.

Very seldom will you see my boat going in a straight line when I'm fishing. Maybe people think I'm crazy or drunk, but I think it improves my fishing a lot.

Is the sound a lure makes running through the water important?

Cooley: Sound must be important because there are days when rattle spoons will out-produce others. But more specific than sound, is vibration. I'm sure it's the vibration a lure makes that initially attracts fish.

How important is the texture of a lure?

Cooley: Not so much when you are trolling. In fact, the texture of a lure is of very little importance in trolling. By the time they feel the texture in their mouth they're already hooked.

Earlier we discussed the concept of using complementary lures. I think we should spend more time on that.

Cooley: When you are trolling, you can't just take, for instance, a Sutton and a Loco and, maybe, a Flat Fish and run them at the same time. They're made to run efficiently at different speeds.

You've got to classify lures into at least three categories: slow, medium, and fast running. When you're trolling slowly, you'll have to use only slow running lures, and so on. If you use a fast running lure at a medium or slow trolling speed, it will just be dragging behind the boat with little or no action on it at all. And slow running lures at medium or fast speeds will just be spinning around.

Give me an example of some slow running lures.

Cooley: If you're running slow for lake trout, you're probably going to want to run Herring Dodgers and flies with light Sutton spoons, or some lighter Fin spoons. Lightweight lures are generally considered slow running lures.

What are some spoons that are designed to run at medium speeds?

Cooley: Heavier spoons like Cleos, Doctors, and Rattle spoons. And Daredevles, too. J-plugs, Rapalas, and Rebels, which are plugs, are designed to run at fast trolling speeds.

Just get all of your lures working together: Complementary lures; and don't mix 'em.

Is there any best method of landing a trout or salmon?

Cooley: You have to be really careful in landing a big fish. That's why I do all of the netting of my charters. We usually don't stop trolling when we've got a fish on; if you just bump the fish with the landing net, there's a good chance you'll lose him.

I drop the net down in front of the fish and scoop him up quickly. Don't leave the net hanging in the water for a long time before you intend to net the fish. Some fishermen like to net fish from behind, but that method doesn't seem to work as well for me. Besides that, if the fish goes into the net head first, he's much less likely to get out. And if you've got a boat like mine that's high off of the water, you'll need a net with a very long handle.

With salmon you never know where they are going to run after you've hooked them. One time I was fishing with my brother and the line released and was straight under the boat. For a moment we thought it had got caught in the prop. Then all of a sudden a salmon surfaced about seventy-five feet in front of the boat. Then he swam all the way around the boat and tangled every line we had out. We finally landed him, but he sure messed up our rigs. He was only a twenty-two pounder, but he sure did run hard. It was great!

Recap the important aspects of presentation.

Cooley: Trolling speed, water temperature, color of lures, type of lures, the length of line from the downrigger balls to the lures, and using complementary lures are the main factors to remember in presentation. Write those down on a piece of paper and put it in your pocket when you go fishing.

WEATHER AND BIOLOGICAL FACTORS AFFECTING TROUT AND SALMON ON LAKE SUPERIOR

What affect do the moon's phases have on trout and salmon fishing?

Cooley: Of course there are guys who swear by the moon phase theory, but in my business I have to fish and produce fish most every day regardless of what phase the moon is in.

Do you like to fish in cloudy weather like many fishermen like to do?

Cooley: I always like to fish in cloudy weather. And I like to hunt in cloudy weather, too. I've caught fish on sunny days, rainy days, cloudy days, and anything in between, but I think fishing is somewhat better on cloudy days.

Is the sun's angle a factor that affects fishing?

Cooley: I never really thought about that. Usually you're supposed to catch more fish early in the morning and later in the evening, but I've had many days where I really didn't get into good fishing until one o'clock in the afternoon. Then I might have been doing something wrong up to that point.

I worry about the factors that I have some control over, not the ones that are impossible to change.

I know you like to fish before a rain. Comment on that.

Cooley: It seems right before a rain I'll do really well. Then while it's raining fishing seems to slow down until it stops raining. Then it will pick up again.

How does lightning affect trout and salmon fishing?

Cooley: Sometimes while it's lightning the fishing can be real good. But if the lightning is the cloud to ground type, I'm off the lake as fast as I can get off. If the lightning is the cloud to cloud type, I will continue fishing.

One day last summer I had a charter out and we were really catching a lot of big fish. We were starting to fill our second cooler with salmon as a storm was approaching. With this storm came lightning which was streaking down—straight down at the water and ground. Well, good fishing or not, I got off of the lake very quickly. No fish is worth getting killed for, and, besides that, I'm responsible for a lot of people's safety.

How about the old cold front condition?

Cooley: If a low pressure condition exists, you can bet a storm is coming, and that's usually a good time to fish.

But there are cold fronts that will shut down fishing for a couple of days before things return to normal.

How does fog affect fishing?

Cooley: Fog doesn't hurt fishing at all. The only factor it plays in my fishing is that in fog it can be a little more dangerous out on the lake.

I've caught a lot of fish in the fog. In fact, I've spent entire weekends fishing in the fog and done pretty well. You go out in the fog and come back in the fog and never see land in between.

Sometimes when you are out fishing in the fog, suddenly you'll get to a place where there's a little clearing and another boat will bob past. It gives you an eerie feeling.

One time I was way out on the lake and suddenly a small bird crash landed right on the dash of my boat. He sat there puffing for a few minutes and then went to sleep. Apparently, he had been out there flying around looking for some place to land and rest. I watched him for about forty-five minutes then he woke up and flew away.

A couple of years ago a huge swarm of bees landed on a boat in Lake Superior. They were all over the boat. I was listening to the people on my marine radio, and, needless to say, they were getting pretty excited about those bees. After awhile, the bees flew away without bothering anyone. They must have been out there flying around, maybe caught in an air current, and got tired and decided to land on that boat to rest.

I always enjoy a story like that as long as it's not my boat they're landing on.

Cooley: Me, too!

EQUIPMENT AND TACKLE FOR TROUT AND SALMON FISHING ON LAKE SUPERIOR

Since we covered it before, comment briefly on light -vs- heavy tackle.

Cooley: I use fairly heavy tackle and line when I'm charter fishing since most of my customers are beginners and would lose too many fish on light line. But for fun fishing, I prefer lighter line. The eight to twelve pound test. It's more fun, and I feel that lures work better on lighter line.

How do you go about choosing a rod?

Cooley: You should get a rod that complements the reel you're going to be using. Or the other way around. For trolling you need six to eight foot rods that are flexible. A medium action rod will work well unless you're out there trying to do the ultralight thing, which I like to do.

How about reels?

Cooley: You should use a good quality level wind reel with a large line capacity.

What types and brands of lures do you like?

Cooley: Probably the best way to determine a good lure selection is to go to a reputable bait and tackle store and explain to them the type of fishing you're planning to do. They should be able to help you pick out the lures you need for your particular situation and the hot ones for that particular time of the year.

Another good bet is to subscribe to a good magazine that specializes in trout and salmon fishing such as the Great Lakes Fishermen. It will help you keep up-to-date on all of the latest information on Great Lakes fishing.

Do you do any field testing for equipment or tackle companies?

Cooley: I field test for several companies. Basically it entails using their lures throughout the year under varying conditions and then at the end of the season reporting on the success or failure rate of those lures. I've run across some exceptional lures doing this.

What brand of graph do you use?

Cooley: I've tried many different kinds of graphs, but I'm quite happy with the Si-Tex I'm using now. Out on the big lake you need a graph or a video so you can see what's going on underneath you. Also, it's nice to be able to keep track of your downriggers which you can do with a graph. If you set your transducers up right, you can see your downriggers on the screen.

When you purchase a graph, buy one that is waterproof and has the cartridge type paper since they are much easier to load. Also, you'll want one that runs on low kilohertz which means it will pick up fish a little better. Its signal goes down and back slower. Low frequency transducers will give you a better picture on your graph with a wider cone angle.

Comment on temperature gauges.

Cooley: There's a lot of them on the market and most of them are pretty good units. I really like the B-C Electronics Pro-Combinator which tells you the water temperature at the depth you are fishing and the speed at which your lure is moving through the water. It's a beautiful unit. The sending unit is attached to the downriggers.

Do you use remote control steering on your boat?

Cooley: No. The mate takes care of that.

What other electronic equipment do you use on your boat?

Cooley: I have a locator with a digital readout on it which is handy in some instances. Also, I have a surface temperature gauge.

What is a Loran C?

Cooley: Most of the charter boats are now using Loran C units. It tells you exactly where you are within a couple of feet.

It runs off of radio beams that are either shore or satellite based. It lets you determine your position at any given time according to longitude or latitude.

If I punch my range and bearing in at the Knife River, for instance, when I want to go back there, the unit will tell me which direction to go, how far I have to go, and at the speed I'm traveling, how long it will take me to get there.

Will it direct you back to a fishing spot you were on yesterday, for example?

Cooley: Yeah. Or last week, too! If you punch the information into the unit, it will stay there until you need it.

What brand do you use?

Cooley: I use a Si-Tex 797 model. But there are many models with varying degrees of sophistication so each person will have to determine which unit would best serve his particular needs.

Also, many boats use radios that can home-in on other fishermen. When they hear you talking on your radio and telling someone else that you're catching fish, their radios have direction finders that will enable them to find out where you are fishing.

What are the best downriggers?

Cooley: There are several good brands. Pick the one with the features you need.

What brands do you use?

Cooley: I use the Penn manuals simply because I can run them with one hand. I might switch to electric downriggers, but they're somewhat slower than manuals, and I use very heavy bombs which the electrics sometimes have difficulty picking up.

Penn, Cannon, Big Jon, Walker, Proos, and Riviera are all good downriggers. There's a downrigger for everybody, so it comes down to your own preference and pocket book.

How heavy is the cable that you use on your bombs?

Cooley: One hundred and fifty pound test.

What shape downrigger bombs do you prefer?

Cooley: The ones I'm running right now are made by a guy in Duluth. They're a ball shape with a fin on them and they track really well.

Is there anything in general that you want to add about equipment and tackle?

Cooley: I buy products that are efficient to use. But the bottom line is you should buy what you prefer and what you can affort to buy.

And, daily, check your line for frays. Also make sure you're not getting foul odors on your tackle, always have spare downrigger cables on board, and sharpen your hooks frequently.

What about radios?

Cooley: I just use a marine band radio. A good marine radio is a must on the "Big Lake" not only for weather information, but you can get an idea from other fishermen about where to fish and what they're biting on. And with a marine radio you can call the Coast Guard if you have an emergency.

MISCELLANEOUS INFORMATION ABOUT TROUT AND SALMON FISHING ON LAKE SUPERIOR

How does one acquire a Coast Guard license for chartering on the Great Lakes?

Cooley: First of all you must document over three thousand hours of experience on the body of water that you want to be licensed for. Then you must pass an intensive and in-depth test administered by the U.S. Coast Guard. It's a tough test. They make sure that licensed charter boat captains know what they're doing since they are responsible for people's safety. The license has to be renewed every five years and you have to take a physical.

Does the Coast Guard inspect your boat?

Cooley: My boat is not required to be inspected by the Coast Guard, but I do have the Coast Guard Auxiliary inspect it anyway. Every year.

Charter boats are required to have more safety equipment on them than pleasure boats. For example, you must have type I life vests which is the type of life vest which will keep your head out of the water if you are unconscious. Also, you have to carry flares and fire fighting equipment, etc.

Have you ever cancelled a trip because of weather?

Cooley: Oh yes! If I can't go out on the water and be safe, I won't go out. Last year I cancelled several charters because of bad weather. It's pretty hard to fish when it's that rough anyway.

What is included in your charter package?

Cooley: I furnish everything needed as far as fishing goes. People usually bring a lunch, warm clothing, and their own beverages. And I permit the moderate use of alcohol.

How much does it cost to charter your boat?

Cooley: I usually run two five hour charters a day, but I'm flexible. I charge $175.00 for five hours and since I can take up to six people it costs each fisherman $29.00 a piece. And some groups charter my boat for the whole day. We leave the dock at seven in the morning and don't return until five or six in the evening. If a group of fishermen want to fish longer than five hours, I charge them $35.00 an hour for each hour beyond the five hours.

What are the psychological aspects of fishing for you?

Cooley: I feel really great when I'm able to take people out and have them catch a mess of fish. I'm on top of the world. But there are, of course, those days that really humble you. I've had days when I've fished all morning and all afternoon and only caught a couple of fish. Once in awhile you can try everything you know and still have poor fishing. The best feeling I have is when I come in with a limit of fish for all of my customers.

Are there any myths about fishing that you would like to dispel?

Cooley: A lot of times people say the fish just aren't biting. But if you get your trolling speed right, the depth is right, the color right, and so on, you can still go out there and catch fish. It usually just depends on who you're talking to.

Just remember what worked yesterday might not work today. Maybe today you have to change your speed or the color of your lures, etc. I never stay on shore just because someone said the fish aren't biting.

A professional should be able to go out and consistently catch fish, and I pride myself on being able to do that.

Is all of your chartering on Lake Superior?

Cooley: Right. Although I do have a license to chart on all of the inland lakes, I just charter on Lake Superior.

Comment on Lake Superior fishing.

Cooley: People are just starting to realize they don't have to drive eight to ten hours to Lake Michigan to have good trout and salmon fishing. A few years back when Lake Superior had the lamprey problem, it was like the dead sea. But now the lamprey problem is about ninety percent eliminated, so Lake Superior is once again a great lake to fish.

Occasionally, you will catch a fish with a lamprey on him. But when you start to bring the fish up, the lamprey will usually drop off. In fact, you will rarely see one. I've only caught one. I netted the fish before the lamprey dropped off.

Are lamprey just a large blood sucker?

Cooley: Sort of. They have a round, suction type mouth with teeth, and they hang on the side of the fish and suck the blood out of the fish.

Why are the trout and salmon in Lake Michigan larger than the ones in

Lake Superior?

Cooley: Lake Superior has much colder water so it has a shorter growing season for fish. And Lake Michigan has better forage for the trout and salmon. But the fish in Lake Superior don't have anywhere near as much pollution in them as the fish do in Lake Michigan.

Comment on "catch and release" in Lake Superior fishing.

Cooley: There's a lot of interest in "catch and release", but if you are fishing for lake trout, for instance, in one hundred and sixty-five feet of water, by the time you land that fish he will have the bends and probably die anyway. Their air bladder breaks. If you throw them back, in a few minutes they will float to the surface belly up.

"Catch and release" is fine, but lake trout and salmon are some of the best eating fish there are so it's nice to take some home to eat, too.

What would you recommend for beginners who want to learn how to fish the Great Lakes?

Cooley: There are a lot a seminars all over the state which is a good place to start. Or go out fishing with someone that fishes Lake Superior. But if you really want to learn fast, it's probably best to charter a boat. Charter two or three different boats since everybody fishes a little differently.

I like to go out with other charter captains because I always learn something from them. And I hope they, too, learn something from me. It's fun to see how they handle their boat and what techniques they use to catch fish.

Another aspect of Great Lakes fishing is that there is a tremendous amount of equipment that you will have to become familiar with. Chartering a few different boats is probably the best way to determine which equipment you'll want to buy for your boat.

Comment on acid rain.

Cooley: I don't know too much about it, but I don't think it's affecting the type of fishing that I do on Lake Superior. But I have heard that many of the smaller lakes in northern Minnesota have been affected quite badly already. The more industrialized we become the more we are going to have to deal with new and more pollutants.

Lake Superior is a pretty clean lake, and I would hope they find the answers to the acid rain problem soon.

How much of fishing is luck?

Cooley: Luck is always involved. Why does some guy who's on his first fishing trip catch the big one. But in the long run to consistently catch fish you have to have a lot of knowledge about fishing. Knowledge is probably ninety percent of it in the long run.

What is your range of fishing success on a charter?

Cooley: Usually we come in with a good cooler of fish. My job is to get out there and locate fish and help people catch them. But success to me is when we return to port and my customers are happy, even if they didn't catch the state record trout or salmon.

Is Lake Superior going to produce any state record fish in the near future?

Cooley: I hope so, but I'm not betting on it. There are big fish in the lake, but they're so few and far between. There has to be more cooperation between the various user groups before the lake will be able to consistently produce large fish.

Do you like to fish in tournaments?

Cooley: There's something about a fishing tournament that really gets the adrenalin in my system goin'. Of course, most of them are on the weekends, and that's my busiest time of the week so I miss most of them.

How much money can you win in a tournament on Lake Superior?

Cooley: Lake Superior doesn't have too many big money tournaments, but on Lake Michigan they have some really big ones—first prize is up to ten grand.

Over the years I've done pretty well fishing tournaments. Last year I placed second and fifth in the two tournaments that I was able to enter.

How big were the largest fish that you have taken on Lake Superior? The trout and salmon species specifically.

Cooley: The largest Atlantic salmon that I've caught on Lake Superior was eight and a half pounds. As for chinook salmon, it was about twenty-two pounds. Lake trout eighteen pounds and my largest steelhead was twelve and a half pounds.

How does the size of trout and salmon vary from Lake Superior to Lake Michigan?

Cooley: A lot. If the average of all the trout and salmon in Lake Superior were seven to ten pounds, the average for those two species in Lake Michigan would probably be eighteen to twenty-two pounds.

The average fish in Lake Superior is much smaller, but on Lake Superior there is much less boat traffic and Superior is much cleaner. These differences make up for any size differences in my opinion. Besides that, I feel a whole lot better about eating fish from Lake Superior since they have much, much less pollutants in them. But I do still enjoy fishing on Lake Michigan; these days, I get over there about twice a year.

Are there any areas of Lake Superior that produce bigger fish than other areas of the lake?

Cooley: Yeah. Out around Isle Royale on the reefs there are very large fish. They're native fish.

Do you recommend using larger lures if you're trying to catch a large fish?

Cooley: In general that will help. Of course, sometimes you'll catch some very small fish on very large lures.

One time when I was trolling with a big Doctor Spoon, I noticed that something didn't look right. When I reeled in the lure, there was a little lake trout on the lure that wasn't more than an inch longer than the spoon. In fact, he wasn't even big enough to release the line from the downrigger cable.

What were some of the hurdles you had to overcome in becoming a charter boat captain?

Cooley: I always loved fishing and especially fishing the Great Lakes so the decision to start running a charter boat was an easy one. I guess the hardest part is accumulating the required hours on the lake before the Coast Guard will let you test to become certified. Of course passing the test isn't easy either. You can't just walk in off of the street and become a licensed charter boat captain. They only license you for certain parts of the lake, too.

Why is that?

Cooley: They want you to know the area that you are licensed for. Some charter boat captains, for instance, are only licensed for western Lake Superior. Other guys might be licensed for the Sturgeon Bay area of Lake Michigan only.

What areas does your license include?

Cooley: I'm licensed for all of the Great Lakes because I've spent enough time on those bodies of water. Now if I wanted to charter on the ocean, I would first have to get a job on an ocean-going boat, and then I would have to log the required amount of time on that portion of the ocean that I wanted a license for before I could even take a test for that license.

What's special about Minnesota fishing?

Cooley: All the good lakes. We've got good fishing for so many species of fish. There's something about being able to fish in clean lakes, and in Minnesota you can always find a place to fish where it's peaceful and quiet.

The reason I live in Minnesota is that my main interests in life are fishing, hunting, and trapping. I've hunted in Montana and I've fished on the ocean and many places in between, but Minnesota is my preference.

I like living up north; I like living where it's rugged. I am willing to do with a little less so I can live the way I want to live.

And fishermen are the nicest people in the world. You can walk up to them on a dock—a stranger—and start talking to them, and you might even end up going out fishing together. That's the way fishermen are.

Chapter 11

PAUL HEDLUND
ON STREAM FISHING

Stream fishing is perhaps the only style of sport fishing that today resembles the styles of sport fishing that were practiced two to three hundred years ago. Its history is well documented. In fact, "The Compleat Angler" which was written by Izaak Walton in 1653 is still being read by stream fishing enthusiasts, perhaps suggesting whatever old Izaak had to say is still relevant to today's stream fishermen. (Most of the stream fishing done in this country until the mid-eighteen hundreds was done for food rather than sport. Conversely, in England and Ireland stream fishing was considered a sport for gentlemen as far back as the seventeenth century.)

If there exists a hierarchy of purist in the fishing world today, the stream fisherman would be the purest of the pure. No electronic gadgetry for these guys. But since the underlying theme of this book is: "All good fishermen are versatile fishermen" it became necessary to find an expert stream fisherman who hadn't carried the concept of purity too far. That is, he had to be more than a one method fisherman.

To find the individual that would be best suited to be the interviewee for this chapter I called on my friend John Daily who is the Fish Production Superior for the D.N.R. (Department of Natural Resources for the State of Minnesota.) He suggested I contact Paul Hedlund who worked for the Minerals Division of the D.N.R.

After spending a few moments explaining to Paul what I hoped to accomplish in this book, I went right for the proverbial jugular vein. "I'm curious as to what type of stream fishing you prefer," I asked, "that is, do you consider yourself a purist?"

Paul responded by saying, "In many ways I'm a purist when it comes to fishing, but if I'm not catching fish on flies, I will switch to spinners or live bait." Then he added, "Many fellows will come home empty-handed only because they were too stubborn to try something other than flies." Well, before I left Paul's office, I was satisfied I had found an expert stream fisherman who was a versatile stream fisherman and could speak knowledgeably about various methods of stream fishing from experience.

Paul Hedlund is an expert stream fisherman, but it was refreshing to learn that he is also accomplished in other areas. He has made his living as an engineer and after a career change several years ago, he has become a graphic artist for the Department of Natural Resources. His love for the out-of-doors goes beyond his fishing. He is also an artist whose paintings of wildlife, landscapes, and seascapes have been featured in more than fifty shows throughout Minnesota and Wisconsin.

Paul was born and raised in Duluth, Minnesota where he became interested in fishing when he was fourteen years old. Later, when he was in high school, he became interested in trout fishing and purchased his first fly rod. It was a telescopic, steel fly rod which was, to say the least, very heavy and bulky. At this time, most of his fishing was on the French and Lester Rivers for trout; he did occasionally fish for walleyes and northerns, too.

After a three year hitch in the Air Force, Paul returned to Duluth where he attended college, working part-time for the Duluth Sports Shop. Initially, he began as a salesman, but when he learned to tie flies as well as the pros did, he began tying flies commercially for the shop. The flies that Paul produced in the shop were sold to North Shore fishermen and fishermen who fished the Brule River which is nationallly famous for brown and steelhead trout.

His part-time job at the Duluth Sport Shop also gave Paul the opportunity to give instructions in the art of fly fishing since the shop offered a guiding-teaching service to its customers. The customers would come in the shop and purchase flies and other necessary equipment for fly fishing and if they desired instructions in the use of that equipment and tackle, Paul would take them to a nearby river and instruct them in the basics of fly fishing.

Then Paul moved to Saint Paul, Minnesota where he completed his education at the University of Minnesota, receiving his degree in engineering. To earn money while attending the University, he tied flies commercially for the Prescott Spinner Company. Literally, thousands of them.

He continued fishing and eventually joined the Saint Paul Fly Tying Club. He spent three years as the club's secretary and taught classes in fly tying. Paul enjoyed his seven years in the club, especially the fishing trips which weren't regarded as fishing contests—they were social events and learning experiences.

It was in his early years in the club that Paul met Rod Naumann who became his trout fishing mentor. Together they fished many of Minnesota's and Wisconsin's streams and rivers. According to Paul, Rod was an expert in "reading water" and taught him a lot about fishing. In the beginning, Paul found himself being out-fished ten to one. It took time, but Paul gradually caught up. "Rod was very secretive and wouldn't tell me all of his favorite spots," Paul said. "He would say, 'It's all good water; you take your pick'." Paul continued, "Trout fishermen are usually friendly and helpful, but they are also very secretive and won't ever divulge their best spots. They will tell you how to fish, but not where to fish."

Although Paul finds stream fishing a good way of getting plenty of exercise and a good place to be when he needs to get away from the crowds, it also has its dangers. Besides occasionally having to avoid a rattlesnake, he once almost had a head-on collision with a cow. In a stream!

It was a hot July afternoon, and Paul was fishing near a grazing herd of cows when suddenly he heard a crashing sound. An instant later a full grown cow landed in the stream next to him. She had hurdled the fence next to the stream in an apparent attempt to get some relief from several hornet stings she had just received. Needless to say, Paul's concentration was somewhat interrupted.

Paul's unusual 'encounters of the animal kind' didn't end with the flying cow. On another occasion when he was night fishing on the Kinnickinnic River in Wisconsin, he began getting the feeling that someone or something was watching him. Soon the feeling of being observed passed and he regained his concentration. The area that he was fishing had heavy running water which blocked out most of the evening's sounds, and he was casting to a rise where he knew there was a large trout.

Then once again he had that eerie feeling that someone or something was watching him, and that someone or something was about to touch him. As he was pulling back his fly line, he looked over his shoulder and saw a pair of large green eyes only five feet away looking right at him. The mysterious feeling suddenly had substance—a pair of green eyes. Just as he looked at this creature, it let out a neigh, but Paul didn't realize it was a horse until after he returned to earth from an estimated standing vertical jump of three feet. In fact, Paul claims his hair actually stood straight up from fright. Soon the horse left and Paul resumed his fishing, but he never did catch that large trout he saw rise.

Beyond the challenges that fishing provides, Paul finds aesthetic value in having spent a day on the stream. Being out where you can hear and see birds and other wildlife is good therapy in a far too busy world.

STREAM TROUT BEHAVIOR

What are the various types of trout an angler could expect to catch in Minnesota's streams?

Hedlund: Brook, brown, and rainbow trout. The rainbow trout is native to Minnesota, and we also have various strains of rainbows such as the Donaldson trout which was developed out west and is a very fast growing breed of rainbow trout. The browns we catch here in Minnesota came from Germany and are often called the German brown trout.

Are there any differences in the variety of trout that are stocked in lakes as opposed to rivers?

Hedlund: No. A certain percentage of hatchery fish are designated for lakes and others for streams, but they are the same fish. The D.N.R. doesn't stock one variety of rainbow trout in lakes and another variety in streams. Any differences that may occur, occur after they are stocked.

Such as?

Hedlund: They may take on a different coloration, and trout will grow faster in lakes than they will in streams.

Do stream trout school?

Hedlund: Rainbows and brookies do to some degree, but browns do not. Browns will usually run in pairs.

Male/female pairs?

Hedlund: Not always. But if you catch one, another one will replace the one that you caught. The same spot, that is.

Immediately?

Hedlund: Perhaps not immediately, but soon. What is good cover for one trout, is good cover for another trout.

Is there a hierarchy of spots in a stream for trout?

Hedlund: Oh yes!

If you catch a two pounder, for instance, will the fish that replaces the one you caught in that spot be larger, smaller, or of similar size?

Hedlund: Usually it will be one of similar size. Not a bigger or a smaller one. If a fifteen incher is taken off of a spot, the one that replaces it will not be an eight incher or, for that matter, a two footer.

Back to the hierarchy of spots for trout. Is it actually a pecking order, so to speak?

Hedlund: That's right. The smaller trout know where they belong in the stream, and the larger trout know where their domain is also. The larger trout obviously take the better feeding spots—the easiest pickings as far as food is concerned.

Which type of stream trout is the most aggressive?

Hedlund: I have found that the average brook trout (ten to twelve inches) is very aggressive which means they are much easier to catch. In fact, it is not uncommon to take ten to twelve brook trout out of a single beaver pond. Now with browns in that same beaver pond, you would probably never do that. You would not catch ten to twelve consecutively, that is.

After you have caught two or three browns, they become more wary than brookies do. You might catch a few browns in a given pool and then return later and catch a few more, but you won't be able to catch ten in a row. Browns are the most wary trout.

Do different varieties of trout mix or school together?

Hedlund: Browns and brooks will mix with each other, but rainbows usually do not mix with the others. When you are catching rainbows, you will usually catch nothing but rainbows. Although browns and brooks don't usually mix, you can sometimes catch some of each from the same area.

Rainbows almost never occupy the same stretch of water that browns and brookies do. I think it's because the rainbow trout is migratory in nature so their needs are different from the browns and brooks. Having different needs is perhaps why they don't school together.

Is it true that if the water temperature reaches eighty degrees, it will kill trout?

Hedlund: Although each of the trout varieties has a somewhat different ability to tolerate extremes in water temperature, generally speaking, eighty degree water will kill them.

So that eliminates most of the lakes in Minnesota as potential trout lakes?

Hedlund: That's true. A great percentage of Minnesota lakes have water that is too warm for trout. They would most likely die in the summertime.

When do stream trout spawn?

Hedlund: Brook trout spawn in the spring, rainbows spawn in the fall, and brown trout (in streams) generally spawn sometime during the month of September. Rainbows can be found spawning all the way into October.

How does spawning affect fishing?

Hedlund: Salmon and steelhead trout fishing on the North Shore streams is much better during spawning. Other than spawning season, you would have to go out on Lake Superior in a boat in order to catch them. And during spawning season, anything that you can do to imitate or duplicate the actual spawn will help you catch fish.

Are stream trout territorial?

Hedlund: Yes. Browns especially. The large browns will even kick northerns out of an area in a stream or river. In fact, smaller browns will not mix with larger browns either.

Trout occupy what is called a holding station, and the smaller ones won't come into the larger ones area and attempt to feed. The larger browns will protect that area by patrolling up and down it and drive out anything that isn't one of them, including the smaller browns. And when you find schooling browns, they will be made up of relatively the same size fish.

Do you have any idea what triggers feeding and non-feeding moods in trout?

Hedlund: I'm not sure, and I don't think anyone knows. Maybe it's a combination of factors—temperature and barometric pressure possibly.

I find it very interesting that there are occasions when I have been fishing in a stream with a friend who is a half a mile down from me, and when he starts to catch trout, I also start to catch them.

That's interesting.

Hedlund: Yes. I think so, too. And when it slows down for him, it slows down for me. To me, that indicates that trout feed pretty much on the same timetable. Trout also have feeding periods, say between nine and ten o'clock at night, and then the next period might be at two o'clock in the morning. This feeding schedule will vary, a little to a lot, from night to night and from day to day. No one, or at least no one I know of, has been able to explain that phenomenon very well.

Do trout bite a lure out of hunger or can you trick them into striking out of anger or aggression?

Hedlund: I think the only reason trout, especially those in streams, strike a lure is because they think it's something to eat. I don't think you could get a stream trout to strike a lure out of anger like a northern pike. Either a trout is feeding or he is not. It's one or the other. If a trout is not in the feeding mood, any presentation you use will not generate a strike. Sometimes you can actually see the trout and put a lure right in front of him, but he is not going to take it if he is not in the feeding mood.

Frequently, when you approach a stream, you can look down from a bridge, for example, and if you can see trout swimming around, they are probably in the feeding mood. This means they are probably catchable. If you see them stacked up like cord wood, and can count them, they are, more than likely, not catchable. At least, they are not catchable right at that moment.

Many times I have let my lure drift right in front of these fish, and they don't even move toward it, much less strike it.

How significant is the trout's ability to smell and taste?

Hedlund: I'm certain a trout can smell and taste bait. In fact, I sometimes take a fly and rub mud on it to remove the gloss and scent from the fibers. I feel this makes flies look more natural. Also, I rub mud on my leaders to remove the gloss from the leader making it more camouflaged. The mud makes them look more natural, and it can remove much of the unnatural scent.

Do all trout migrate?

Hedlund: No. Most of the streams that I fish are not lake run streams which have a concentration of fish moving up them. They are usually just streams that are stocked by the D.N.R. or have naturally reproduced trout in them.

Is a trout's memory developed enough so that he can become lure wary?

Hedlund: I would say that if you caught a trout on a certain lure last week, he's not going to remember it this week. If you were consistently catching trout in a certain area of a stream on a Mepps Spinner, you are probably doing something right, and the next time you fish that area, chances are you will do just as well using that same spinner.

Would that notion hold true for flies since they are seasonal lures?

Hedlund: Sure! In the spring of the year, for instance, there are certain species of bugs that appear on the stream. And for the most part, every year it's the same species. A trout has what is called a feeding station. He does not dash about the stream feeding at random locations. He stays in a small area and therefore doesn't burn up a lot of energy feeding. He holes up and then swims out when some food sources comes by. But it has to be the right food source. The right fly must be used because trout are very selective in feeding, especially when the water is low.

Why are they more selective during low water conditions?

Hedlund: Trout become more selective when the water is low due to better visibility of stream insects. Also, when the water is high, it is usually cloudy. Cloudy water cuts down on their ability to see, especially shadows.

Is there any difference in the fighting ability of brooks, browns, and rainbows? Pound for pound, that is.

Hedlund: I'm amazed at the strength of a large rainbow. (Two to three pounds.) They are like a coiled spring, and they are extremely strong since it's in their nature to be constantly on the move. Any fish that is constantly on the move the way a rainbow is has got to have more muscular power than a fish that stays in one place most of the time and ambushes its prey.

What is the best time of day to fish for stream trout? If there is a best time?

Hedlund: I used to make an effort to get up very early in the morning (daybreak) since I believed the myth that the early morning hours were the best time of day to fish. But in later years, I have found that better and longer fishing occurs during the evening hours right into the night and right through to daybreak. I fish all night on occasions; that is, in Wisconsin where it is legal to fish streams after eleven p.m.

Of course, when night fishing, you should fish only waters that are known to you, and you don't walk a stream at night either since it would be too dangerous. You fish pools, beaver dams, and areas like that. Although I take a flashlight with me when I'm night fishing, I still only fish areas that I have studied during daylight hours.

Fishing at night is done by feel. Night fish are bolder so you don't have to be quite as careful in your approach. You also don't have problems with shadows either. As a result of the darkness, the fish are on the prowl, and you will catch more brown trout since they are very heavy night feeders.

But there is no specific time at night when they are most likely to feed. It could be eleven to twelve at night or three to four in the morning. There is a brief period of time, about a half an hour just before the sun comes up when there is a lot of activity on the stream, which can indicate excellent fishing.

I should mention that in Minnesota, it is illegal to fish between the hours of eleven p.m. and one hour before sunrise in Minnesota streams.

What is the best time of year to fish for trout in lakes?

Hedlund: October has been my best month for lake fishing. Also, the Saint Croix River is very good in October.

In the fall, some of the trout species in lakes will spawn, and then they are very vulnerable because during the daytime they will come up into the shallows. Sometimes they are so aggressive in the fall you can see their dorsal fin sticking out of the water.

You wanted to say something; go ahead.

Hedlund: Yes. Trout fishing slows down in the summertime (mid-July to the end of August) because as the streams and pools warm up, the fish will go deeper. And since the water level is dropping in the summertime, the streams will become clearer which means you have to be much more cautious in your approach. In fact, in July and August you can go to your favorite springtime spots and not catch a trout. Rain will help since it will make the stream cloudy, usually causing food to wash in.

Do you prefer to fish for one species of stream trout over another species?

Hedlund: Yes, I prefer to fish for brown trout. They are larger than the brooks and easier to find than the rainbows. Browns will hole up in a pocket, and they are more concentrated.

Is there anything that you would like to add regarding the stream trouts' behavior?

Hedlund: If there are many tributaries coming into a stream, it's a good clue that the stream will be a good stream to fish.

LOCATING STREAM TROUT

What are the main aspects of locating stream trout?

Hedlund: The main ingredients in stream fishing are: Fish only known productive areas; be cautious in your approach; use the proper presentation; and be patient.

Fish only known productive areas. How does that apply to the beginner or if you are fishing new water?

Hedlund: For a beginner, you have to assume someone has told him about an area that might be productive. For the veteran, he would be fishing areas where he has caught trout before. What I'm suggesting is that you should concentrate on areas of the stream where you have had success before.

When I fish a stream that is new to me, a stream that I have never fished before or a stream that I haven't been told where the best areas are, I pick a starting point, perhaps a bridge. I usually walk downstream on the bank and study the stream well before I begin to fish it. I don't even take my rod and reel with me. I usually walk from a half to three-quarters of a mile just to get the feel of it before I do any fishing. As I'm walking, I pick out the spots that will likely hold trout.

Such as?

Hedlund: I look for current breaks, eddies, undercut banks, and obstructions in the water such as logs or other hard to get places, that would offer protection for the trout.

Will trout hole-up in ponds like other species of fish will?

Hedlund: Oh yes! They'll go up feeder creeks and hold in areas behind beaver dams, for instance. When you find trout in beaver ponds, usually they will be brook trout. During the nighttime, the brook trout will go down the feeder creeks to where they enter the main stream and stay there to feed.

Do they feed in the ponds?

Hedlund: They will, indeed, feed in the ponds, and you can catch them there during the daytime. It's during the evening hours when they tend to leave the ponds to go to the main body of water right where the feeder creek enters it. Then they will swim back up to the ponds during the daytime.

I'd like your comments on "reading a stream".

Hedlund: "Reading a stream" is an aspect of stream fishing that usually applies to a new or uncharted section of a stream that you have not previously fished. There are productive and nonproductive areas of any stream, and, obviously, you want to put your hours of fishing to productive use.

Look for bends holding tree stumps or clumps of bushes. These areas provide shade and protection from predators and will hold trout. Also, any near shore cover allows trout to feed and then hide when danger arises. Obstacles embedded in a stream such as fence posts, timbers, and fallen branches all offer excellent cover. Undercut banks usually seen on bends of streams often hold large trout.

Lastly, any pool should be carefully reviewed for main current flow. The main current in any pool or the fastest flow section also holds feeding trout. Most food is washed down this fast flow area and the trout know it. Usually the downstream side of a feeder stream and near the bank holds the most trout. Both brooks and browns.

In short, look for obstacles, over-hanging tree foliage, undercut banks, and pools. These are choice areas in almost any stream for holding both large and small trout. Do not waste too much time in any one area if trout are not seen or strikes do not occur.

You can probably expect zero results the first time and even the second time that you are fishing a new area of a stream because you don't know what insects are common to the area, and you don't know the lay of the stream. In other words, you haven't had enough time to study it. You should think of it as an experiment and don't be disappointed if you get skunked the first few times on a stream that is new to you.

What are some locational clues for locating lunker stream trout?

Hedlund: There are clues for locating larger or trophy size trout. And since large trout usually feed in the early evening hours at dusk, that would be a good time to be at that trout's feeding station to catch him. [Feeding station is a place in the stream where an individual trout feeds. This is not the same location as his home area.] It is important after you have located a large trout, that you remember exactly where that location is.

Please elaborate on that.

Hedlund: You see him. You have visually located him in the water. Now you can certainly try to catch him in his home area, but when he is in his home area, he's probably in a negative feeding mood. Since he will continue feeding in the same area [his feeding station], it is much easier to catch him when he is at his feeding station. He will be there when he is actively seeking food.

How do you know that a certain fish lives in one location and then moves to another specific location to feed? How do you know it's the same fish?

Hedlund: By observation. He will swim to his home area and return to his feeding station when he is in the mood to feed.

Is there a general rule as to how far apart a trout's feeding station and his home area will be?

Hedlund: It could be anywhere from a hundred feet to several blocks and sometimes a bit farther. Of course, it could be less than a hundred yards, too.

What kind of behavior is typical of a trout who is actively using his feeding station for feeding?

Hedlund: He'll make his presence known. He might break the water or you may see his dorsal fin sticking out of the water. If you watch closely, you'll know he is there.

Frequently, you will see hundreds of bait fish scurrying near the surface of the water, and then you can be sure that there is a large fish feeding nearby.

What kind of minnows?

Hedlund: Small minnows. Black nose dace minnows, shiners, etc. are common in Minnesota streams. If you see these minnows breaking the surface, that's where you drop your lure or bait hoping the trout will mistake your offering for one of the minnows in that school.

Is there anything in your presentation that will make your offering more ap-

pealing to the trout?

Hedlund: Make it look as natural as possible and don't disturb the area. Throw it where you see the bait fish, and let the stream's current do the work of making it look natural. Often the less you do, the better your presentation will be. Make it as natural as possible; if he's in the area, there is a good chance he will strike your lure.

Comment on beaver dams.

Hedlund: Beaver dams are nothing unique. You usually wade them unless they are too deep. Fish stumps or whatever other obstacles might be in the pool behind the beaver dam. It is very easy fishing, and you should stay in one spot as a rule.

Let's discuss bends and eddies.

Hedlund: Bends are good areas to find trout, if at least one side of the bend has an undercut bank or a deep pocket or a rock, or all three. If it is just a bend in the stream without any other structure, it probably won't attract trout.

How about eddies?

Hedlund: Eddies are choice spots for holding trout since food coming down the stream is tumbled and slowed down by the circular motion of the water making that food source easy prey. Eddies also tend to stir up the stream's bottom which reveals more food for the trout. Most pools, especially big pools, will have an eddy in front of them.

Define an eddy.

Hedlund: It is a place in the stream where an obstruction in the stream diverts the normal flow of water, causing the water to briefly reverse its direction. It might be a rock or a log, for example.

Are feeder streams important locational clues for trout?

Hedlund: If I know that there are brooks, browns, and rainbows in a stream, but I know very little else about that stream except the lay of the land, I will first be looking for small feeder streams that come into the main stream. That's the point where the brookies will generally hang out in the daytime. Brookies will lie in the holding water which empties into the main stream. Other areas would be ponds, beaver dams, and any water that has backed up or been dammed up off of the main stream.

Another clue is that brookies prefer cold water, and brown trout can withstand much warmer water. The rainbows preference for water temperature is somewhere in between.

Are many trout lost to winter kill?

Hedlund: There is always a certain amount of loss to predators like the kingfisher, other birds, and hawks.

The trout that survive the winter are holed up in the deeper water in the stream. I suppose that many of them must die from the lack of oxygen if they are trapped in shallow ponds.

Are there any general areas in a stream that will usually hold certain species of trout?

Hedlund: Yes there are. The brown trout is notorious for staying in the pools; they just seem to concentrate in deeper holes. Usually rainbows are found in the faster water, wing dams, etc. Also, remember the rainbows are usually instinctively wandering fish. Brookies prefer water that has debris in it. They seem to pick spots that are inaccessible to the fisherman. If you can get at brookies, they are easy to catch. In fact, if you could measure the trouts' intelligence, the brookies would be third on the list.

Does the coloration of a trout suggest anything to the angler?

Hedlund: With brook, brown, and rainbow trout you can tell where they have been living by the shade of their color. If they are real dark in color, they have probably been living in a heavily shaded pool or an area with a lot of cover. On the other hand, the lighter colored a trout is, the most likely he has been living in open water with little or no cover. They don't take on a dark coloration if they have been living in relatively open water.

Comment on fishing streams with a lot of cover.

Hedlund: Streams or areas of a stream that have a lot of cover tend to be cooler so they will often be better streams or areas to fish. The heaviest cover in a stream will hold the most trout, and bigger trout, too. Trout always seek out protective cover and the heavier, the better. Of course, they might not be very easy to fish for when they are in heavy cover.

PRESENTATION FOR STREAM TROUT

Comment on presentation.

Hedlund: Proper presentation is an absolute must to become a successful trout angler. Proper presentation starts before you make your first cast: you have to be very quiet, eliminate shadows if at all possible, and, in general, keep the noise level down to a minimum.

Something else you will need to consider is vibrations. When you are walking along a stream bank, you create vibrations. You should walk in the stream since there will be much less vibration carried upstream from the noise you generate in the stream as opposed to the noises you generate on the bank.

What if the water is too deep?

Hedlund: Well, that often is the case. When walking along the stream, try to stay at least six or seven feet from the bank of the stream. If the stream is a series of deep pools, you will have to walk on the bank. Stay back several feet from the edge of the stream.

When I get to a spot that I'm going to fish, I approach it on my knees and then fish it from the kneeling position rather than standing up. Many times you must wait long periods of time for the trout to begin feeding.

When you wait, I assume you mean you are continually fishing waiting for a strike?

Hedlund: That's right. The fish are there. It's just a matter of time before they are going to feed, and that's what you have to wait out. Worst of all, there is no method to determine when they are going to feed. If they were feeding yesterday at ten o'clock in the morning, there is no guarantee that they will feed at ten o'clock in the morning today. You fish continually until they are ready to feed.

Usually, if they are feeding in the area that you are fishing, they are also feeding upstream and downstream as well. They all seem to know when it's feeding time.

Many fishermen feel that with the proper presentation they can entice or anger a fish into striking, even if he is in a negative mood. Are you saying that with stream trout, that can't be done?

Hedlund: That's correct. Perhaps northerns, walleyes, bass, etc. can be enticed into biting when they are not in the mood to feed, but if stream trout aren't in the feeding mood, you rarely will be able to entice them into biting. If your presentation is perfect, you may occasionally be able to get them to strike even if they're not in a feeding mood. The larger stream trout only feed every two days or so, but they are more likely to strike out of aggression than the smaller ones. Larger trout can refrain from feeding after a feeding binge for at least two days or more.

Let's go through a typical season of insect hatches from the opener to the close of the stream fishing season.

Hedlund: One of the first flies to hatch would be the stonefly. They are about an inch long and have two tails.

When does the stonefly hatch occur?

Hedlund: In May. You know that they are going to hatch every year in May; it's just a matter of which day or week.

How do you apply this knowledge to fishing?

Hedlund: First of all, you know that there are stoneflies in the stream since you have taken trout that have stoneflies in their stomachs. You've examined the trout's stomach content so you know that they are there. When they are hatching, the trout anticipate the hatch. You should be trying to imitate the stonefly the best way you can in order to make a trout strike your lure. With your presentation, you are creating the illusion of an insect hatch. In this situation, it's a stonefly hatch.

You mean you are trying to make your presentation look like insect eggs are hatching on the water's surface?

Hedlund: Yes and no. The proper way to present a stonefly is on the bottom of the stream which means you may have to use a little weight to get your fly down on the bottom. It's a sunken patterns. Mayflies are also presented on the bottom. There are other flies which hatch on the surface, and for those imitations you would try to create the illusion of a surface hatch. Don't forget to let the stream's current do the work of making your presentation look natural.

Also, you can use a little screen to sift the muck on the stream's bottom to determine what insects are currently present in the stream. Then use those imitations too for bait.

Do all species of insects hatch every year?

Hedlund: No. Some of the mayflies will only hatch every three years or so. They may be down in the silt on the bottom of the stream for three years before they hatch. And when they are down there, a trout, using his nose, can actually dig them out. When the unhatched mayflies float out of the silt, the trout will eat them.

Then in June, what kind of insect hatches should we look for?

Hedlund: In early June, the sedge fly hatch will occur. The sedge fly is a tan colored fly. When you see them, or other flies, for that matter, you should try to use an artificial fly that most closely resembles them.

You watch for trout to rise and cast ahead of the rise. Then let your lure drift down to where the trout rose. If your presentation is natural enough, the trout will probably take it. If there is something suspicious about your lure or presentation, he will not take it. You will perhaps have to switch to a different variation of that fly.

How do they vary?

Hedlund: In color and size.

In July are you still using the sedge fly lure?

Hedlund: Yes, but there are also others. At this time of the year, there is a hatch of flies called the green drake which are a very large mayfly. At this time, the dun fly is hatching, too.

What do dun flies look like?

Hedlund: They are a sort of smokey-blue color. A very small fly.

What flies hatch in August?

Hedlund: There are several. The brown drake, grasshoppers, and some beetles and ants. This is not the June beetle which, of course, hatch in June. Also, in the later part of July and early August crickets and grasshoppers will hatch, and they predominate on the streams in Minnesota. When imitating crickets and grasshoppers, you must use a surface lure that floats.

Then in September when the water temperature drops, the trout tend to lie at deeper depths in the stream and avoid surface feeding.

Are you saying that as we get into September, insects aren't a significant part of the trout's diet?

Hedlund: Right. Insects are not as plentiful, so trout seek other likely morsels.

What type of lures would you be using after the insect hatches are over?

Hedlund: Spinners, minnow imitations, and live bait. Other than the North Shore streams, most of the streams in Minnesota are closed for the season by the end of September.

The D.N.R. has some experimental lakes that are open for fishing all year around. Grindstone Lake is one of them.

Stream and river fishermen tend to stress the importance of fishing upstream or upriver. Why?

Hedlund: Although I have fished downstream on occasion, usually your presentation will look much more natural if you fish upstream or across the stream's current.

Also, fish face upstream because of their anatomical make-up. Since they usually don't swim backwards, it is unlikely that you would find a fish waiting for food facing downstream with the current pushing at his back side. And another reason they face upstream is that the stream's current brings food downstream. A fish facing downstream would be like a center fielder on a baseball team facing away from the hitter. He wouldn't very likely catch any balls.

Because of their facing upstream, it limits their ability to see the angler if the angler is fishing from behind the fish.

Earlier you mentioned that if a trout missed a food source when the stream's current carried it by him, he would sometimes swim downstream after it. Would that apply to lures, too?

Hedlund: They will turn and watch a lure for quite a while. If your lure and presentation look natural enough to them, they may swim downstream a very short distance and pick it up. That's not saying they will generally chase after food downstream.

Also, trout are very slow eaters. If they are feeding on a night crawler, they will pick it up by its head and go back to their feeding station, and it will take them up to five minutes to eat that night crawler. They eat in very little bites. If there is another trout in that same area, the trout with the food will run away with the food and eat it elsewhere.

Is the feeding zone defined as the zone they occupy when they are waiting for food to come downstream to them?

Hedlund: Yes. When they see food coming downstream, they will swim out and grab it and then return to their feeding station.

Since they are such slow eaters when do you set the hook when you are fishing with live bait?

Hedlund: There is no general rule to cover that. Usually, it is best to wait a bit before you set the hook.

Comment on trout "rising" in the water.

Hedlund: Splashy surface rises are an indication that trout are feeding on the surface, and you can usually assume that means insect hatches are occurring. Watch for surface hatches when trout are rising.

Explain what a surface hatch is.

Hedlund: What I mean by surface hatches is, you can actually see the insects hatching on the surface of the stream.

Now rising trout should not be confused with trout boiling in the water. When trout are boiling, they are coming up near the surface but not actually breaking the surface of the water. [Boiling—the water momentarily bubbles up as though it were boiling water.] And when you see boils and no insects are present, the trout are most likely feeding on rising nymphs. The nymphs are rising up off of the bottom of the stream, and the trout are feeding on them before they get to the surface. Now this can give the impression that a trout is feeding on the surface (rising), but he is not. He is subsurface feeding.

I understand the distinction that you are making, but why is it important to the angler to know whether they are surface or subsurface feeding?

Hedlund: When trout are subsurface feeding and you attempt to catch them with surface flies, for example, the trout will refuse to strike them. When they are subsurface feeding, you will need to use a small nymph pattern or a spinner might work, too.

How does your presentation change from dirty to clean water?

Hedlund: Presentation in dirty or cloudy water requires much less finesse than it does in clear water. It is also much to the anglers advantage to fish in dirty or cloudy water since it is harder for the fish to see you, so it will be less likely that you will spook him. However, don't forget that the fish can still hear vibrations from the angler if he is careless in his approach.

Also, shorter casts can be used in dirty water since you can get much closer to the fish without spooking them. Your shadow will not be as visible to the fish in dirty water.

How long would you spend fishing an area if you are not catching fish?

Hedlund: Don't spend too much time fishing, even usually productive areas, when the trout are not in a feeding mood. Try new areas when this happens and return to the usually productive areas later.

How soon would you return?

Hedlund: That's going to vary. But chances are if they aren't in a feeding mood in the known productive area that you are fishing, they are probably not in a feeding mood in other areas of the stream. There is always a chance that you might catch an unwary trout elsewhere. It's worth a try.

Comment on presentation with live bait.

Hedlund: When you are using live bait, you should cast upstream or upstream and across stream. Allow the bait to drift downstream with the current. A live bait presentation can be the most natural of all presentations, after all, you're using the real thing.

When you are casting across a stream, what would be the maximum angle you could cast?

Hedlund: About a forty-five degree angle. Then about the time the current has carried your line downstream to where it is perpendicular to you, you will have to begin to feed line out so the current can continue to carry your lure or bait downstream in a natural manner. If you don't feed line while your lure or bait is being carried downstream, it will look unnatural. This should be done in pools as well as when you are fishing the riffles. [Riffles are the shallow, flat areas of a stream filled with little rocks.] Let the line continue drifting downstream with the current until it's at about a forty-five degree angle downstream from you. That's about as far as you will be able to effectively present a lure or bait without losing the natural effect.

With this method you have described of casting across stream, it seems to me that at times during this presentation there would be a great deal of slack in your line?

Hedlund: There will be some slack. Of course, you don't want too much slack because with too big of a bow in your line you will lose control of your presentation. It's like most other presentations, to do them properly, it takes a great deal of practice.

You haven't said much about presentation when fishing a pool or other still water off of a stream?

Hedlund: If you are fishing a pool, sometimes it is better to make your cast and then prop your rod and wait for the trout to pick up your bait. With this method you will avoid accidentally shaking your rod and alerting the trout that there is something unnatural about your presentation. And when your rod is propped, watch for the strike on your line since you will see it there long before you will notice your rod tip bending.

Do you use fly casting equipment when it's windy?

Hedlund: Sometimes. But when it's very windy, it is much easier to use spinning gear with minispoons or spinners with treble hooks on them than it is to constantly have to fight the wind with fly-casting gear. Even for the best fly fisherman, it can be very difficult to cast with a fly rod when it's very windy. If you are unable to cast accurately, you might as well switch to spinning gear.

Also, when hatches fail to materialize or live bait won't work, you should try spinners and spoons.

Do spinners and spoons sometimes out-produce live bait?

Hedlund: Sometimes they will.

If you are using a fly that is not in season or doesn't exist in the stream that you are fishing, how much less of a chance do you have of catching a trout?

Hedlund: It would take a lot more luck to catch a trout if you are using an inappropriate fly. Of course, if you use an inappropriate fly often enough, you might catch fish on it, but you won't catch as many as you would using an appropriate fly.

Another aspect is that you shouldn't use a fly that you do not have confidence in. Sometimes beginners will use flies that another trout fisherman has recommended, but if the beginner isn't catching fish on it, stop using it. The other fisherman might be presenting that fly differently; therefore, he's catching fish on it and the beginner is not. If you can't find out what he is doing differently in his presentation, use something that works for you.

Although I'm willing to give a new lure a try, I am not willing to spend much time if it doesn't produce fish for me. Frequently, new lures just end up being a big waste of time.

Comment on shadows.

Hedlund: Shadows are very, very important to consider when fishing for trout in a stream. On bright days they tend to spook the trout. Of course, the brighter the day, the more cautious you have to be in your approach. Trout avoid shadows; that is, moving shadows. They will hide in the shadow of a log, for instance.

I guess a rule of thumb would be: Always consider your shadow when you are determining how best to approach a spot that you are going to fish, especially on bright days. And on bright days you should attempt to position yourself so your shadow is behind you. But, obviously, that isn't always possible.

Are long casts ever necessary in stream fishing?

Hedlund: No. If you've made your entry into the stream carefully, you can take just as many trout on short casts as long casts.

Is there anything that you would like to add regarding presentation?

Hedlund: Never stick to one method of retrieving a lure. Try various speeds and depths until you have determined what the trout will hit. It's up to the fisherman to figure out what presentation the trout wants and don't be afraid to experiment.

Earlier I stated that a trout would not strike a lure out of anger or aggression. I was referring to trout in general and not large trout. A large trout will strike a lure if you can make him angry enough. Just run the lure past him several times, and he may well strike it. I have found that large trout are really quite aggressive and bold. Although they are smart and cautious, they are also very bold at times.

When you are referring to large stream trout, how large do you mean?

Hedlund: Two pounds and up. Two to five pounds; in that range.

Any further comments on "matching the hatch"?

Hedlund: There are tables available that you can purchase in sporting goods stores that tell you what hatches occur and when they occur. Buy one that is specifically for Minnesota and Wisconsin since all Minnesota stream fishermen will, sooner or later, fish in Wisconsin, too. These tables will give you approximate dates as to when the various hatches will occur.

Some hatches occur in certain parts of the state and not other parts. Mayflies will vary in size from the giant green drake to the very, very small mayflies, all the way down to a size eighteen hook.

One mistake that many stream fishermen make is that they don't fish deep water properly. You must fish it from the top to the bottom until you find what is working on that particular day.

WEATHER AND BIOLOGICAL FACTORS AFFECTING STREAM TROUT

Comment on the weather's affect on stream fishing.

Hedlund: Unfortunately, the angler has little control over the changing weather patterns. When starting to fish, the weather conditions may be ideal, then suddenly they can change, affecting the trouts' feeding pattern and ruining your fishing.

Do cold front conditions adversely affect stream fishing the way they can with lake fishing?

Hedlund: When the weather begins to get bad, trout will move to a comfortable holding area. When severe weather moves in, trout are not interested in feeding, which means they will be very difficult, if not impossible, to catch. Gradual changes in weather, whether it's becoming warmer or colder, will have little affect on the feeding patterns of stream trout. I find the weather's affect on stream fishing is much less than it is on a lake.

How does rain affect stream fishing?

Hedlund: A soft rain can stimulate trout to feed and often is a very good time to fish. But a heavy rain storm is not a good time to fish since during heavy driving rain storms trout will quit feeding. Also, during a heavy rain that is accompanied by lightning, it can be a very dangerous time to fish.

How about prior to a storm?

Hedlund: That often is a very good time to fish.

Is there any relationship between moon phases and one's being able to catch stream trout?

Hedlund: There could be. There is definitely a relationship between moon phases and fish activity. I know guides on the Saint Croix River that rely on moon phases in their scheduling of fishing trips. And we know that the oceans tides are affected by the moon, so I think the moon does have an affect on streams and lakes which would affect the fish in them. But what that affect is, no one seems to know.

Comment on rising and falling barometric pressure.

Hedlund: I much prefer to fish when the barometric pressure is rising, and

I tend not to fish when the barometric pressure is falling sharply. Again no one really knows why or how barometric pressure affects fish, but it does.

But what is known is that the barometric pressure does have an affect on a fish's ability to breathe.

It does?

Hedlund: Yes. It changes the pressure in the water, and fish will seek out the most comfortable depth for breathing.

Changes it which way?

Hedlund: A falling barometer will make it more difficult for fish to breathe since it will increase the pressure in the water.

So a falling barometer would cause them to do what?

Hedlund: It would cause them to move to a more comfortable depth. And that depth will be the depth at which they can breathe comfortably.

After they have found that comfortable depth, they will again soon become interested in feeding at which time they can be caught.

Does a shift in the wind's direction affect stream trout?

Hedlund: Yes. A shift in the wind direction will affect their feeding schedule which may or may not be good for fishing. It can shut them down or suddenly turn them on to feed. And the quicker the wind changes directions, the greater the affect on the trout will be.

Does the change in the wind's direction have a greater or lesser affect on fish in a stream than it does on fish in a lake?

Hedlund: It seems to have a much greater affect on fish in a lake. But it might be that it is just more noticeable in lake fishing.

Comment on sky conditions.

Hedlund: A very cloudy and overcast day is preferable to a clear, sunny day since shadows are nonexistent on overcast days. Generally, when it is very sunny, I prefer not to fish.

Do you prefer to fish rising or falling water levels?

Hedlund: High water levels are usually easier and more productive to fish because during high water conditions a trout will roam more and be more active in general. When the water level is low, trout tend to hide in the small, little pockets near logs, brush, etc., and you have to approach them much more carefully.

I prefer to fish rising water after a heavy rain because at this time the water becomes cloudy which makes the angler less visible to the trout. In cloudy water, the trout will not see the lure as soon as he would in clear water, so he will have less time to decide whether to take a lure or not. He's easier to trick. Further, high water washes new food into the stream which seems to stimulate trout to go on feed.

Actually, even cloudy water that has been caused by cows crossing a stream is better to fish than clear water.

Often I've read stories about the exceptional eyesight that trout have. Is there any truth to those stories, or have they been exaggerated to make the trout seem more difficult to catch, etc.?

Hedlund: Many of those stories are exaggerations. In fact, trout, much like other fish, have monocular vision which means as it lies in the stream facing upstream, it may spot something coming downstream, but it will only see it with one eye. It will then have to turn its body ninety degrees so it can see this object coming downstream with both eyes. And when he can see it with both eyes, he can determine what the object is by its shape and size. Actually, their vision is such that it has blind spots.

They do not have Superman-like vision. And the rainbow, brook, and brown do not have equal vision either. Offhand, I can't remember which can see better than the other, but their ability to see is somewhat different.

EQUIPMENT AND TACKLE FOR STREAM TROUT FISHING

Since trout fishing equipment can be very expensive, let's begin by discussing how much one should spend to get good equipment.

Hedlund: You certainly don't need to purchase the most expensive equipment that is available for trout fishing. Purchase equipment that appeals to you and is comfortable to use.

When selecting reels, always stick to name brands because it is much easier to get replacement parts and service when you need them.

Name some good ones.

Hedlund: Mitchell, Garcia, Johnson, Shakespeare, Pflueger, Hardy, and Daiwa are all good quality reels.

What do you look for when you are purchasing a rod?

Hedlund: I choose one that is comfortable to handle. Action, weight, and length are important considerations, too. I prefer a six and a half to a seven foot spinning rod with a fast action. I have found that with the fast action rods you can do more with the lure. They are just better for casting.

How about fly rods?

Hedlund: Again, with fly rods, I prefer the fact action type over the buggy whip slow action rods. Even with fly line on a fly rod, the fast action rods are easier to cast accurately and you get more distance quickly.

What type of fly line do you use?

Hedlund: I like the double taper fly line since it is easier to cast. With double taper, not only can you cast more accurately, you can cast farther, too. That is, farther with less effort.

Do you ever use level line?

Hedlund: No. Although it's cheaper, it's mainly a beginner's line.

How about three taper fly line?

Hedlund: Three taper line is the best, especially in the wind.

What brand of fly line do you use?

Hedlund: I like Courtland. Scientific Anglers line which is put out by the 3M Company is excellent line, also.

I forgot to ask you about the length of the fly rods you use.

Hedlund: I have several fly rods. They range in length from six and a half feet to nine feet.

What are their various applications?

Hedlund: Shorter rods tend to be better for panfish. The one I have weighs only two and a half ounces. Then I use a seven foot three inch fly rod that weighs three and a quarter ounces for light trout fishing. Also I have a heavier seven and a half foot rod that I use for bass fishing. One of my favorites is an old three piece bamboo rod. I also have a nine footer which is a real old-timer that was manufactured by South Bend.

Can you cast farther with a longer rod?

Hedlund: They say you can, but I tend to disagree. The longer the rod, the longer the cast to a point. But, I feel, a nine footer is beyond the point of diminishing returns. A shorter rod with a fast taper is actually better for casting and casting farther. In fact, you can cast equally as far with less effort with a seven and a half footer with a fast action as you can with a nine footer.

And if you are in the stream four to five hours at a time, those long, heavy rods tend to be very, very wearing on you. Generally, you want to use the lightest equipment possible to do the job.

Do you use the automatic fly reels?

Hedlund: No. I prefer the manual single action type. I use a Pflueger Medalist with interchangeable spools to accommodate different line sizes.

What are the different types of fly line?

Hedlund: Fast sinking, slow sinking, and floating line. The sinking lines have weight built into them which causes them to sink in the water; they are used for deeper streams.

I should stress that it is important to carry the different types of line with you when you are fishing, especially when you are fishing several miles upstream. Conditions might not be what you expected or they may have changed. You don't want to hike back to camp for a different line. Also, the sinking lines are easier to cast because of the weight that is built into them.

How much money should I spend on a pair of waders?

Hedlund: You can spend a lot of money on waders; the cheapest ones are about forty dollars. It doesn't pay to buy the cheap ones. Buy the lightest ones you can find. Furthermore, heavy waders don't necessarily keep you warmer than the light ones anyway; they just weigh you down and tire you out much faster when you are walking. Spend a little more money and get the insulated ones with impregnated cloth uppers. Nylon waders aren't too bad, and they don't tear or snag as easily, but they can become very heavy.

Besides flies what type of lures do you use?

Hedlund: I like the French spinner type, and I use the zero size in gold and silver only. It's also important that some part of the spinner has a little red on it. I'm not sure why that's true, but maybe the color red simulates salmon eggs.

What are the brands of French type spinners that you prefer?

Hedlund: Abu-Reflex is a good one, and I also like the Swedish made Veltic as well as Prescott.

Comment on spoons.

Hedlund: I like the little copper, gold, and silver colored Daredevles and Cleos that are about an inch long with a treble hook. And on dark days fluorescent green can be very good. Fluorescent orange can be good sometimes, but, I found that over the long haul, gold or silver and the gold and silver combination seems to work best.

I understand that you used to do production tying of lures.

Hedlund: Yes I did. When I went to the University of Minnesota, I tied lures for the Prescott Spinner Company. That was production tying. I would tie a specific pattern then it would go to an assembly plant where it would be assembled into a spinner or some other rig and then packaged for sale. Over the years I have probably tied in excess of sixty thousand flies for production and for my personal use.

Is the quality of production tied lures very good?

Hedlund: The ones I tied were of pretty high quality. You have everything pre-cut and ready to go. Uniformity is the most important aspect when tying for production so they will all look alike with no variations.

When trout fishermen look at a half a dozen flies and if they're not uniform, I doubt that they would buy them since they've determined the size and style they like. They don't want any variation.

Comment on leaders for fly-fishing.

Hedlund: I use a seven, eight, or nine foot leader. These leaders are tapered all the way down. You can purchase the manufactured knotless leaders or make your own. I make my own and I might begin with eight pound test line and the tippet might be as light as a pound and a half test line. You tie them in sections with blood knots.

An example would be starting with eight pound line and then tying it to five and a half pound line which is tied to three pound line which is tied to a pound and a half test line for the tippet. You might have as many as five to six sections of line in a leader with a total length of ten feet. Of course the leader line weight will vary depending on what type of fishing you are doing. Follow standard length leader charts to get the correct individual leader lengths.

Give me an example of what fly you would use to "match the hatch".

Hedlund: If I see a hatch of blue dunflies on the water, which is a very, very small fly of bluish-grey color, I will select an artificial fly that resembles or duplicates it.

What size hook would that be tied on?

Hedlund: A fourteen, sixteen, or an eighteen. [The higher the number, the smaller the hook.] "Matching the hatch" is simply using an artificial fly that most closely resembles the insects that are hatching on the water at that time. Matching it in color and size.

Is there anything that you would like to add regarding equipment and tackle?

Hedlund: You might like to know that spinners account for a large percentage of the lunker trout that are taken. It's probably because you can fish them fast or slow, and you can work them from the top to bottom which makes them a very versatile lure.

Remember, the most expensive equipment is no guarantee of catching fish.

MISCELLANEOUS INFORMATION ABOUT STREAM TROUT FISHING

What has been your most successful day on a Minnesota stream?

Hedlund: A few years ago I was on a trip which was the best trip I've had in Minnesota. We were fishing the north fork of the Whitewater, and it had been stocked the winter before with browns. It was the end of April on opening day, and we had very little trouble taking many nice trout. They ran from eleven to fourteen inches.

Have you ever been skunked?

Hedlund: Sure I have. I've gone fishing when I thought it would be good, and I've been absolutely skunked. I'm sure that's happened to every fisherman at one time or another. I've experienced the very good and the very poor times when it comes to trout fishing. I have the confidence that I know where the trout are; it's just a matter of being there when they feed. If I'm there when they are feeding, I will manage to get a few.

I don't waste much time fishing unproductive spots, and that seems to work better. Any stream is that way. Some areas look great and there's nothing. Other areas look marginal and there might be lots of trout there.

You just have to investigate a stream very thoroughly.

Name some of your favorite streams in Minnesota.

Hedlund: On the Whitewater there is the middle branch, south fork, and the north fork. Also in southeastern Minnesota there is the Beaver Creek which has good trout. The stream that I know and like the best is the north fork of the Whitewater. It is the smaller of three parts of the Whitewater, but it has some of the bigger trout in it.

How big?

Hedlund: The largest one that I have taken out of there was about a three and a half pound brown trout. I have never taken a rainbow trout out of the north fork, but there are rainbows in other areas of the Whitewater, particularly the middle branch.

I know you like the Saint Croix River.

Hedlund: Yes I do. I've fished the Saint Croix for about ten years now and it's usually pretty good. I fish it anywhere from a mile above Hudson, Wisconsin to a mile below the Kinnickinnic which is about a twelve mile stretch of water. I like the Snake and Rum Rivers since almost one hundred percent of the gamefish I take in these two rivers fall to flies.

Also, up near Duluth you have the fast flowing streams like the French, the Sucker, and the Gooseberry which are good trout streams, but I prefer streams like the Baptism since it has slower moving water which makes it easier to fish.

The Straight River at Park Rapids is also an excellent brown trout stream.

The Trade, Willow, and Clam, which are in Wisconsin, are within an hour of the Twin Cities.

What are some of the differences in fishing fast and slow moving water?

Hedlund: Streams like the Whitewater tend to be on the shallow side with slow running water, and they are easier to fish since you can walk for miles in them. Although the Whitewater is a shallow stream, it does have some deep holes, too. The North Shore streams that have fast running water tend to gouge out deep holes which makes them harder to fish because it's more difficult to wade. I like fishing those streams; it's just access to the holes that is difficult and treacherous.

Earlier you said that your best day in Minnesota was on the Whitewater and you caught ten fish from eleven to fourteen inches. What did you catch them on?

Hedlund: Almost everything. I used flies, spinners, and live bait as I recall.
But if I was out to catch a limit of fish, I wouldn't start out using flies. I would begin with spinners or live bait.

Comment on some of the largest trout that you have caught in Minnesota.

Hedlund: The largest brown that I have caught in a stream was a three and a half pounder. My largest rainbow was a seventeen inch three pound six ouncer which I caught in a metro lake while I was wading. Actually, the largest trout that I have ever taken in Minnesota, other than a steelhead, was a five and three-quarter pounder which I caught through the ice in thirty feet of water using a marshmallow on an icefly in Courthouse Lake at Chaska. It was a rainbow. And several years ago I caught a seven and a half pound steelhead on the Knife River near Duluth.

Have you ever had the "monster" on and lost him?

Hedlund: Yes. I once had a brown trout on in the Clam River in Wisconsin that probably would have gone ten pounds, but I lost him. He broke my rod when he raced downstream on a bend in the river and it was over my head at that point.

Are maps of streams helpful?

Hedlund: Most maps that I've seen of streams are not specific enough. They show the basic bends in the streams, but they don't show the smaller bends and things like that. So you more or less have to construct your own map.

What is the most common mistake that stream fishermen make?

Hedlund: Probably the biggest mistake stream fishermen make is stirring up the stream too much. They are just too noisy. They approach the stream wrong—with no caution or common sense.

The best advice I could give is that when you are approaching a certain area that you intend to fish, particularly a pool, wait five to ten minutes after entering that area before you begin to fish.

Many fly fishermen do not master more than one or two types of casts. That is much too limiting. Depending on the situation, you may need to know at least six or seven different types of casts.

Comment on "catch and release".

Hedlund: Trout fishermen in Minnesota usually keep the fish that they catch. Out in the western states the "catch and release" concept is gaining in popularity. Also, there are quite a number of fishermen in Wisconsin that catch and release fish. Most Minnesota stream fishermen have to drive a good distance to where they are going to fish so, I suppose, that is one of the reasons that they are more likely to take home the fish that they catch.

Why are you a successful fisherman?

Hedlund: Like anything else, one becomes successful by spending a lot of time angling. I get out as often as I can, and I've been doing it for years.

Each stream is a little bit different so you have to be versatile in your methods of stream fishing. If you are fly fishing, for instance, you have to study a stream for awhile to determine what insects predominate. Studying a stream and knowing where to look for fish is more than half the battle.

Where will the next state record trout come from?

Hedlund: I don't think there are any streams in Minnesota that will break any of the state records for trout. Possibly if a state record rainbow is caught, it could come from one of the North Shore streams. Brook trout in our streams are of the smaller variety and cannot grow to trophy size.

I should mention that the Straight River near Park Rapids has produced some browns in the seven to nine pound range. But as for trophy trout in Minnesota waters, they will probably come from a lake, perhaps Grindstone Lake.

How much luck is involved in fishing?

Hedlund: Luck is only involved with certain aspects of fishing. For example, knowing when, where, and how to present your lure and knowing how to handle a fish is done with experience. There's no luck involved when you have had a fish on for a half an hour and you're still able to land him. It's savvy!

Is there anything special about Minnesota stream fishing?

Hedlund: Minnesota and Wisconsin have very good stream fishing. In fact, many of the streams that I fish are in Wisconsin, most of which are within an hour of the Twin Cities.

I think it's foolish to drive several hundred miles for a day's fishing when you can obtain a survey report from the D.N.R. which will indicate the stocking of trout in your area.